T0152855

1st edition named one of *The Progressive* magazin.
of 2011"

"Can anarchism actually work? Yes, as a matter of fact. There is no better example than that of the Common Ground Collective's remarkable accomplishments within the most oppressed communities in and around post-Katrina New Orleans. scott crow's lucid first-hand account is a story that simply must be told. This book should be read as widely as possible."
—Ward Churchill, author of *Acts of Rebellion*

"The real story of the storm, the story of the majority, is of heroic acts of solidarity from the outset and the volunteers who came later. It's about generosity, courage, and the prefiguration of a better society. This book is a key document in that real and remarkable story"
—Rebecca Solnit, author of *A Paradise Built in Hell: The Extraordinary Communities That Arise in Disaster*

"The story of the Common Ground Collective is that of one of the greatest triumphs of democratic self-organization in American history. Their spectacular success in the wake of the devastation of Katrina made clear for all the world to see that in even in the midst of catastrophe, command structures are not only unnecessary but actually stand in the way of getting things done."
—David Graeber anthropologist, author of *Debt: The First 5,000 Years*

"Anarchist and veteran organizer and an aficionado of civil disobedience, Mr. Crow comes across as more amiable than combative."
—*New York Times*

"Honestly this book would make an exciting movie. It's got everything—suspense, action, drama, good guys, villains. A real page-turner! But more important is the message—what ordinary people were able to achieve through working together without leaders telling people what to do. This is a book for every activist and anyone who wants to know more about how private efforts can work effectively."
—Sharon Presley, professor, author, and coeditor of *Exquisite Rebel: Essays of Voltairine de Cleyre*

"Ultimately, *Black Flags and Windmills* is about envisioning a better world and trusting ourselves to believe that our dreams actually contain the paths to make it happen, not as voters, not as consumers, but as participants in a spontaneous, horizontal democracy that looks different everywhere but meets the needs of the people where they are."

—*The Indypendent*

"This revised and expanded edition weaves scott crow's frontline experiences with a much-needed discussion of movement building. For decades he has approached his political organizing with humility, resilience, and honesty, and he continues to do so in *Black Flags & Windmills*. In many ways this work is about dealing with trauma—socially, politically, personally—and responding with courage."

—Will Potter, author of *Green Is the New Red: An Insider's*
Account of a Social Movement Under Siege

"There is a sense of no return that pervades this deep and intense work. In passionate and effusive prose, crow describes the nature of Hurricane Katrina's impact as well as organizing efforts to support communities of color and poor people. But crow lends an equal amount of time to exploring the logistical aspects of organizing, and how they relate to anarchism. Radical in its self-critique and anarchist praxis, *Black Flags and Windmills* has become a classic in the genre of non-fiction, and an important tool for folks today working in the context of rising catastrophe."

—*EarthFirst! Journal*

"It is a brilliant, detailed and humble book written with total frankness and at the same time a revolutionary poet's passion. It makes the reader feel that we too, with our emergency heart as our guide, can do anything, we only need to begin."

—Marina Sitrin, author of *Everyday Revolutions:*
Horizontalism and Autuonomy in Argentina

"One of my favorite books and a classic of contemporary anarchism. *Black Flags and Windmills* is a superb piece of work by any standards. The revised edition gives us even more insight into how mutual aid communities are being formed and sustained. It deserves the widest possible readership."

—Andrej Grubačić, professor in the Anthropology and Social
Change Program at California Institute of Integral Studies, and
author of *Don't Mourn, Balkanize: Essays after Yugoslavia*

"The story scott crow tells is one of desperation and of hope. It shows us something of what people are capable of, even in the worst of circumstances. And it reminds us that we can count on each other, better than we can rely on the institutions of power."

—Kristian Williams, author of *Our Enemies in Blue: Police and Power in America*

"Common Ground reflected the anarchist philosophies—both thought, action and proof—that we don't need the state to get things done."

—*Death and Taxes Magazine*

"*Black Flags and Windmills* combines hands-on information about what it really takes to change this world, one big mess at a time, and a seeker's vision of a better world."

—*Ragblog*

"As someone who's followed the Arab Spring and Occupy movements very closely, I find Crow's account of organizing the Common Ground Collective extremely relevant to the problems the movement faces today."

—Kevin Carson, Center for a Stateless Society

"*Black Flags and Windmills* is an incredible book about a group of dedicated men and women who, faced with challenges from all sides of the United States government, built an oasis in a desert."

—*Razorcake*

"A frenetic account of how grassroots power, block-to-block outreach and radically visionary approaches to sustainability can rattle the ruling class and transform people is positively searing."

—Ernesto Aguilar, cofounder of People of Color Organize

"Crow's testimony following in the aftermath of Hurricane Katrina further indicts a flawed political and economic system that was bankrupt long before Hurricane Katrina. The reader will find within the pages a life built on principals that have propelled crow to fight injustice in a story well told!"

—Robert Hillary King, former Black Panther, former U.S. political prisoner, and author of *From the Bottom of the Heap*

"*Black Flags* is less a cohesive story (or even set of stories) than a record of part of a conversation. crow took the format—papers bound together with glue and a cover—and made it his own."

—*The Anvil*

"This book is an example that should be studied by activists of all stripes, to learn the lessons of wisdom inside. This is Anarchism-in-Action in a real world setting, and it is an example of mutual aid at its best."

—Lorenzo Kom'boa Ervin, former Black Panther and political prisoner, author of *Anarchism and the Black Revolution*

"Playful, irreverent, and deadly serious, *Black Flags and Windmills* is . . . a moving testimony of love, solidarity, betrayal, and the collective struggle for the freedom that so many of us yearn for."

—David Naguib Pellow, author of *Resisting Global Toxics: Transnational Movements for Environmental Justice*

"This is an excellent manual on community organizing. It's a beautifully written raw story that does not try to downplay the difficulties, betrayals, and mistakes that are inevitable in authentic collective work."

—Roxanne Dunbar-Ortiz, author of *Outlaw Woman: A Memoir of the War Years, 1960–1975*

" . . . crow is a puppetmaster involved in direct action."

—FBI (Joint Terrorism Task Force internal memo)

"*Black Flags and Windmills* introduced me to countless contemporary free-thinkers and rule breakers whose very lives are emblematic of what is means to be liberated."

—Diana Welch, coauthor of *The Kids Are All Right*

Black Flags and Windmills
Hope, Anarchy, and the
Common Ground Collective

Second Edition

scott crow

Black Flags and Windmills: Hope, Anarchy and the Common Ground Collective Second Edition
By scott crow

This work is licensed under a Creative Commons Attribution-ShareAlike 3.0 Unported License
2014

This edition © 2014 PM Press

Published by:
PM Press
PO Box 23912
Oakland, CA 94623
www.pmpress.org

Cover Graphics: John Yates / www.stealworks.com
Cover photos: Ann Harkness / www.annharkness.com
Inside photo credits: Liz Highleyman, Todd Sanchioni, Jackie Sumell, Jake Applebaum, David Ampersand
Interior design by briandesign

ISBN: 978-1-60486-453-3
Library of Congress Control Number: 2013956930

10 9 8 7 6 5 4 3 2

Printed in the USA.

*This book is dedicated to everyone whose emergency
hearts refuse to give up hope, who fight oppression
and want to create futures where we are all free
that we are only beginning to imagine.*

Contents

"Even before the thoughts occurred . . ."

"Like concrete . . ."

"Dream the future . . ."

Glossary

For quick reference in the context of this book, I want to point out that these words are part of the jargon of radicals and anarchists.

Accountability
Affinity groups
Alternative/Anti-Globalization movement
Black Bloc
Civil society
Consensus decision-making
Guidelines
Leadership
Privilege
The State

There are exhaustive definitions, sometimes volumes, written on these words. I encourage readers to seek out multiple definitions of each term to understand how they are used.

These terms are defined on pages 76–77:

Autonomy
Cooperation *or* Mutual Aid
Direct Action
Horizontality
Liberation

Civil society is a term I adopted from *Zapatismo*. I use it here to refer to individuals, organizations, and even institutions as opposed to the state apparatus or even the multinational corporations that use force to reinforce their power. Civil society is you and I and everyone else who associates without coercion.

Leadership (for lack of a better term) represents for me guidance by individuals or groups within communities. This guidance is based in the recognition that there are power relations even within horizontal organizing, based on social, cultural, experiential, or political factors. Individuals or groups in guidance roles may have more power (or be perceived to have more power). The practice of leadership seeks to subvert the familiar figure of the authoritarian leader who delegates tasks, makes unilateral decisions, and takes actions without discussion or accountability to those involved. The practice of leadership seeks to create and reinforce power-sharing rather than power over others.

Marginalized or **Neglected Communities**
I use these terms instead of, or sometimes interchangeably with, typical sociopolitical language (like working-class, queer, poor, etc.) that have been used to qualify people or communities pushed to the margins in civil society. Traditional political language takes many of the complex relationships within civil society that make up people and communities, making them one-dimensional. This leaves out the complex humanity of those involved. People and communities are often marginalized for more than one reason. These phrases address the fact that there are multiple issues at stake, instead of running a laundry list to illustrate the marginalization or neglect.

Power
I use the term "power" in three ways:

1. **power (with a little 'p')**: power that is exercised directly by individuals and communities, as part of civil society, working to make changes in the world. It is what grassroots democracy is based on. This kind of power is derived from recognizing that we do have the abilities, creativity, and strength to make the world better. It is the collective power of everyone, from the middle class to the marginalized.

2. **Power (with a capital 'P')**: concentrations of authority and privilege in economic, political, or cultural institutions that exercise undue influence on the world. In this sense, Power is identical with the state, multinational corporations, or the rich, who are unaccountable to and derisive of civil

society. It operates through bureaucracies, executive boards, the military, and transnational corporations and corporate media of all forms. It is exercised through brute force, neglect, and manipulation or corruption of economies, for example. It results in control over resources as well as social and cultural norms.

3. I sometimes use the phrase **those who assume to have Power**. It is my way of recognizing that such forms of Power do not have legitimate claims of authority over civil society. It is also a reminder not to automatically give legitimacy to those institutions or people who don't deserve it. My underlying philosophy is that once we see past this illegitimacy, we begin to recognize that we have the collective capacities to directly make changes and influence the world ourselves rather than appealing to these coercive hierarchies and bureaucracies that claim this Power over us.

People and Organizations

Association of Community Organizations for Reform Now (ACORN): U.S. community-based organization that advocated for low- and moderate-income families from the 1970s until 2010.

Reggie: Reginald Bell, Algiers resident who helped with many tasks and outreach in the early weeks of Common Ground.

Black Panther Party (BPP, Panthers, or the Party): Influential revolutionary black political organization that existed from the 1960s to the '80s in cities across the U.S. They instituted programs that advocated for community control, empowerment, and self-defense within black communities. Their models of organization influenced numerous other revolutionary groups.

Pastor Brown: Headed St. Mary's Baptist in Algiers. Collaborated with Common Ground in the early months after Katrina on many initiatives.

Continental Direct Action Network (CDAN): Network of anarchist affinity groups, collectives, and organizations formed to coordinate direct action at mass mobilizations across the U.S. in the early 2000s.

Dirty South Earth First!: Militant anarchist, direct-action environmental organization that operated in Texas from 2002 to 2004.

People's Hurricane Relief Fund (PHRF): Coalition of mostly New Orleans people of color-led political and grassroots organizations from New Orleans. Founded in 2005 after Katrina. It began with about twenty groups and eventually grew to over a hundred local and national organizations. It later split into two organizations and ceased to exist in 2008.

United Houma Nation: First Nations tribe residing within six parishes along the southeastern coast of Louisiana.

Veterans For Peace (VFP): National organization of military veterans. The group works to promote alternatives to war.

Zapatistas (EZLN): The Zapatista National Liberation Army, an indigenous rights organization in Chiapas, Mexico, which came to the forefront in 1994 and still struggles for rights today.

In the Right Place, at the Right Time

John P. Clark

There are very few books with a message as urgent as the one conveyed by scott crow in *Black Flags and Windmills*. It's a message about how to live in a state of emergency, or as, scott states it, how to act with "an emergency heart." It's a story of being there, for the community.

In one sense, the "state of emergency" is the normal condition of a human being in constant need of the responsiveness of other human beings. In another sense, it is the *extreme* condition in which persons in crisis, communities in crisis, and a world in crisis increasingly find themselves. This book gives testimony to our desperate need to learn how to care for, and not to abandon, all those who live in the midst of such crisis.

The state of emergency has been a major preoccupation of recent social thought. There has been extensive analysis of the ways in which reactionary ideology manipulates fear and insecurity to justify a state of emergency, or "state of exception" that expands domination and control, and crushes dissent and resistance. Fear of the terrorist, the foreigner, the other, and the unknown is invoked to give legitimacy to an authoritarian state of emergency and to a regime of repressive control.

But there is another, much more authentic state of emergency that arises when people and communities face an existential crisis, whether from natural disaster or from the artificial disasters imposed by systems of domination, exploitation, and oppression. It is a state of emergency that can lead to the emergence of extraordinary acts of love, dedication, and creativity, to the emergence of an emergency heart.

We live in a world in which we do not have to go far or wait long to encounter such emergencies. It is a world facing catastrophic climate change, a world entering the sixth great mass extinction of life on earth, a world facing unprecedented technological domination and spiritual desolation, a self-contradictory world of abundance in which billions face economic exploitation, imposed scarcity, and absolute poverty. The condition of such a world is increasingly a universalized state of emergency.

This book speaks to such a world with a message of hope. It tells a real-world story of hope, the story of the emergence of free, cooperative community based on mutual aid and solidarity in the midst of devastation. For this reason, it is essential reading for anyone interested in the possibilities for liberatory social transformation in communities facing crisis.

The core of this story is scott's account of the history of the Common Ground Collective in post-Katrina New Orleans. Common Ground is, as scott points out, the largest anarchist-influenced organization to appear in recent U.S. history. Its importance goes far beyond the good work that it did in New Orleans. In fact, its greatest importance lies in what it has continued to do, and is doing now, in the hearts, minds, spirits, and lives of those who participated in its work, and in the far-reaching effects it will certainly have in the future.

As scott's account demonstrates, Common Ground has been an important part of an organically growing ethos, a transformative community, a communal subject of social transformation and liberation that has been developing for some time. Its roots go far back in history and have been seen recently in the global justice movement, in the peace and antiwar movements, and in a growing antiauthoritarian culture that has manifested itself in such projects as Food Not Bombs, infoshops, prisoner support and prison abolition movements, Really Really Free Markets, diverse cooperative and mutual aid projects, and a multitude of affinity groups and intentional communities. Recently, we have seen this culture manifest itself in Common Ground, in elements of the Occupy movement, and in subtle moments of refusal and reaffirmation that may not yet have a name.

The Occupy Movement at its best seemed like a miracle. It was as if, in hundreds of places at the same time, cooperative, egalitarian, participatory practice appeared out of nowhere. But as you read scott's story, you find out that such miracles have deep roots. You can discover some of these roots in his life and in the lives of others, roots that led him and them to Common Ground. And found in the story of Common Ground itself are some of the roots that later helped grow the Occupy Movement. Such stories are all stories of miracles and of the roots of those miracles in earlier miracles.

The personal story recounted here shows the power of a radical ethos of solidarity and justice, and the importance of subtle processes of the formation of a selfhood beyond the dominating, appropriating, all-consuming ego. Thus he tells us of his early experience in a "free multiracial preschool" run by the Black Panthers and a child-centered Montessori School, of his early exposure to courageous eco-activism, and of his confrontation with violence and injustice, and also solidarity and justice, in their most concrete, experiential forms. He tells us of a life in which music, the aesthetic dimension, and the liberated imagination play a central role. He shows us the importance of a loving parent and others in the community who value the flourishing of the child.

He shows us how the encounter with elders of the movement, like the Wobblies and Black Panthers who influenced him so deeply, can offer inspiration and a connection with the heroic age of working-class and community solidarity. When scott writes and speaks about such predecessors, you see his great humility that comes out of respect and reverence for those who have gone before, enduring great sacrifices and making great contributions. He speaks not as a mere individual but as one who carries on a legacy.

We learn from his eloquently told story, as we learn from so many such shared stories, that the transformative moment of dedicating our lives to the liberation of humanity and the earth is the product of many small but powerful transformative moments. We learn that our task must be to create a culture of liberation and solidarity in which the conditions are present for the appearance of more such moments in the lives of many people, and scott's story shows us how Common Ground helps us with this task.

I was in Dharamsala, India, working with a Tibetan refugee organization when the Katrina disaster hit. As I watched the images of devastation, I had one overriding question (after the immediate one of how to get back): Who will do the real work needed in New Orleans, and who will come to lead not by leading but by serving? I wondered about various groups and movements of the Left I had worked with: the Greens and radical ecologists, the religious Left and spiritual radicals, and the anarchists, among others. I was not at all confident that it would be the anarchists who would step forward. But it was. Not that there were no greens and environmentalists, pagans and Quakers, etc. who did good work at the most difficult of times. But it was, above all, the anarchists who came in great numbers. And, above all, they came to Common Ground.

In telling the story of Common Ground, scott stresses the importance of its famous motto: "Solidarity Not Charity." This concept is significant in that it puts values like solidarity, mutual aid, cooperation at the center of concern. It was always much more than a mere slogan, for Common Ground was in practice the site for a revival of a deep sense of solidarity and love of the people, values that typified the popular culture of classical radical movements, but which have been far less central to the outlook of the American left in recent history.

One of the most inspiring things about Common Ground was hearing volunteer after volunteer express love and respect for local communities and for the people of the neighborhood. *Black Flags and Windmills* tells a story about the radical aspirations that Common Ground volunteers brought to New Orleans, but it is above all an account of their dedication to working (often from dawn to dusk and beyond) for the survival and regeneration of threatened communities. If you read Common Ground's "Guidelines of Respect," you will see that although the practice may not have been perfect, the group's ideals were impeccable. We see a recognition that the true community of solidarity aspires to be a community of infinite respect and recognition, of boundless compassion.

The Common Ground experience helps guide us toward a different model of revolution from the dominant (patriarchal, masculinist) one that is familiar on the Left. It helps teach us that we need to see revolution not as the heroic Act or Event, but as an ongoing practice of care, compassion, and nurturing—for one another, for the land, for the earth. We begin to realize that the most radical form of revolution is the process of social, spiritual, and ecological regeneration. (Significantly, the anarchist Magonist movement in the Mexican Revolution called its publication *Regeneración*.)

The burning practical question is how to create specific structures and forms of activity that effectively put such ideals into real-world practice, here and now. Informing scott's insights in this area is the experience of his involvement with worker co-ops, economic entities that engage directly in the immediate practice of cooperation and mutual aid. This is an area in which Common Ground cofounder Malik Rahim has also worked, and this background was reflected in the organization's activities.

Such cooperative activism responds to the need to move beyond a necessary, but necessarily reactive, politics of resistance, toward a more active and affirmative politics of cultural creativity. We begin to actualize the society of solidarity and free cooperation. Martin Buber wrote in *Paths in Utopia* about four kinds of cooperatives: the producer cooperative; the consumer cooperative; the housing cooperative, and, finally, what he calls "the full cooperative," one that combines all of the previous ones into a cooperative community, and which must be our ultimate ideal.

Whether or not we all choose immediately take this step to the cooperative intentional community, we all need to begin living as soon as possible in communities that in significant ways incorporate all of these dimensions of cooperation. And as scott shows, Common Ground acted in a prefigurative manner in this area by promoting worker cooperatives, striving to create cooperative housing, and combining elements of cooperative work, consumption, and living in its centers. It thereby made a concrete contribution to the project of "building the new society within the shell of the old," and thousands of volunteers carry with them the lessons of their participation in this project.

Despite Common Ground's admirable goals and impressive achievements, scott does not try to deny that the collective also had serious weaknesses and made many mistakes. He mentions fundamental problems such as having "no clear processes on how to start or stop projects, or how to get support for them, or where we were trying to go with any given project." He cites the problem of "patriarchy and power dynamics within the organization," which he does not limit entirely to the adept wrecking activities of budding government agent Brandon Darby. He notes failures in dealing with volunteers with disruptive personal agendas that left a legacy of damage and bad feelings.

Yet, in spite of all such debilitating shortcomings and contradictions, Common Ground achieved miraculous results, due to the intelligence, skill, dedication, and idealism of thousands of volunteers and community members working together. We need to learn from the errors of Common Ground, but above all we need to be inspired and given transformative hope by the seemingly impossible things that were achieved in this extraordinary undertaking by ordinary people.

Considering some of the other groups active in the recovery effort, scott is aware of their weaknesses and strengths. He is wise and generous enough to stress what is most important about their work, not simply what was wrong with them—a wisdom that, sadly, many critics of Common Ground have not exhibited. Their weaknesses should never be minimized, but the positive lessons must never be neglected or forgotten. We need to avoid the temptation to dwell obsessively and morbidly on the past, and instead focus on using our best judgment and most far-reaching vision to put both positive and negative lessons of the past into a creative practice of personal and social transformation, never losing sight of the possibilities that exist here and now.

In his reflections on the history of Common Ground, scott refers to "a crack in history" that occurred in Post-Katrina New Orleans, a theme common to many of the personal stories of volunteers and survivors in Francesco DiSantis's moving and illuminating collection *Post-Katrina Portraits*. For scott, this "crack" was the appearance of "a transition from hopelessness to hope." Amid the work of Common Ground, one could see hope emerging not only for a particular community devastated by storm and flood, neglect and repression, but for a whole society that is devastated by domination, exploitation, and nihilistic egoism.

The "crack in history" that we discover in scott's story is part of a developing break with the monolithic History imposed on the world by Empire. Common Ground is part of an enduring, age-old counter-history, the history that writes itself against History. "Against Leviathan," as Fredy Perlman phrased it. In it, we get a taste of what a future historical epoch of freedom and solidarity might be like. We catch glimpses of "the End of Pre-history," the point at which we transform ourselves from mere objects of history into its subjects, or rather its co-subjects with the earth itself.

The story of Common Ground, in both its successes and shortcomings, helps us to see better what conditions need to be created in order for such cracks in history to occur more often, and for these cracks to widen and open up larger spaces of liberation. It supplies us with additional empirical data concerning the institutional, ideological, imaginary, and practical preconditions for a world of communal freedom and solidarity. It helps us discover what we might call "the grounds of the common."

As Leonard Cohen said, "There is a crack in everything. That's how the light gets in." The system crack appears when all those little cracks in things (including us) converge. This often requires crisis, trauma, or catastrophe. At such times, we are finally willing to face death and destruction and in the midst of desolation allow our ego boundaries and defenses to crumble. We find common ground in our broken hearts. Our common brokenness allows us to open ourselves up to one another. This is precisely the story that scott tells. A story of quixotic impossibilities become possible and real.

For this to happen, we need to learn to live in emergency time, the kind of time that was called *kairos* in Greek. This term meant, in oratory, the perfect time to make a certain statement, in medicine, the crucial time for a life or death decision, in spirituality, the "fullness of time" at which one might receive an epiphany or revelation. It is also the time of poetry, of the creative imagination, including the social imagination. It is the time of inspiration, the time at which one becomes capable of receiving a great gift, and acting creatively.

In telling the story of Common Ground, scott tells the story, to state it simply, of people being in the right place at the right time, and doing the right thing. This work was a great gift, as is scott's book.

Foreword
Kathleen Cleaver

The embattled Black Panther Robert Hillary King, whose decades of solitary confinement in Angola Prison had sparked a protest movement in Louisiana, moved to Austin after the Katrina evacuation from New Orleans. I was visiting Austin back in 2009, around the time of the presidential inauguration, when King introduced me to his neighbor scott crow. He and his partner Ann Harkness had shot a documentary about the incredible case, *Angola 3: Black Panthers and the Last Slave Plantation*, which they promised to show me. I had supported political prisoner cases for decades and learned from Geronimo ji Jaga about the Angola 3 case back while I was working on the habeas petition that won his release in 1997. Those days few people had heard about these prisoners languishing in punitive solitary confinement back on the Angola plantation prison, and I'd only met a handful of devoted Angola 3 supporters before visiting Austin.

Once King won his freedom, he had continued to campaign to free the other two Black Panthers still behind bars in Angola. We had met several times earlier at political forums, or social gatherings. I considered his friends scott and Ann welcome supporters of a human rights struggle I'd waged for generations—the scattered committees for black political prisoners tend to be small, underfunded missions of love, with few victories.

That was before his FBI files became public. The FBI's post-9/11 mantra of "never again overlooking terrorists hiding in plain sight" apparently led to this unlikely counterterrorism target, a neighborhood activist who worked at a recycling center and ran a thrift shop on the east side of town, one of those areas developers regard as "in transition." According to the May 28, 2011, *New York Times* front-page story, the FBI had spent years engaged in surveillance of this "Texas anarchist," handing in reports with terms like "hippie" and "nonviolent direct action." The word "counterterrorism" to me evokes a surreal world of Guantanamo Bay and Abu Ghraib prison torture, or arrests of potential bombers crossing our borders, so the idea of government agents following and spying on scott crow surprised me at first.

His book tells a story of courage and friendship, scott's friendship for King that spins across the post-Katrina deluge of New Orleans, a place he wrote where "everything disappeared under water, leaving thousands to fend for themselves." What deep motivation drives anyone to travel by boat across an unfamiliar flooded city looking for a friend under life-threatening circumstances? There was no FEMA, no Red Cross, no protection from armed vigilantes except what community people organized themselves.

Something Geronimo ji Jaga once said to scott stuck with him: *revolutionaries are motivated by great love for a better world*. That gave scott his notion of "emergency heart" love. He understood this powerful "emergency heart" love being the core of the revolutionary movements that inspired him: the Black Panthers, the Zapatistas, and the anarchists fighting in the Spanish Civil War, on whom he molded his values and drew his consciousness. These movements drew together advocates of a different world, a better world, women and men ready to fight and die for that better world. It was this emergency love that fueled his courage to continue to look for his friend left behind in the New Orleans flood. His journey led to the creation of the Common Ground Collective that first week after Katrina at the home of Malik Rahim, a veteran of Vietnam and the battles of the New Orleans Black Panther Party.

The New Orleans community on the west bank of the Mississippi where Malik Rahim was raised was known as "old Algiers," a place of close families with old stories of resistance reaching back to the earliest slave landings, the earliest maroon settlements. These families had stood off slave masters, Klansmen, and other predatory racists; these were hard working, peace-loving, Christian black people who stood their ground, demanded respect for their families, and protected their homes. Years before the Katrina catastrophe, I'd met Malik's mother, Lu Bertha Guyton, at her Algiers Point home.

Geronimo took me to meet Mrs. Guyton during one of his first summers back in Louisiana after twenty-seven years of California prisons. She was tall, had a smooth voice, and seemed a centered, strong woman of faith, the kind of person who anchors a family, a community, a movement. Her sons who became close to him back in the California prisons were a bond between them. One was still incarcerated in California, Malik was back home, and the other one had moved away. Framed Bible verses were hanging on the walls of her hallway, and we relaxed in her kitchen, where she insisted on feeding us—something warm and delicious, poured over rice. Years later, it was from this same family home, surrounded by wealthy white landowners in Algiers Point, and fully in her spirit that Malik sent out the call to start Common Ground, the SOS for his community.

The very first response came from scott crow, I learned. Volunteers continued to arrive, drawn to establish emergency services needed in an isolated community left to die. Solidarity Not Charity became the mission of the Common Ground Collective; the rapid influx of people, supplies, equipment, support, Internet, and media coverage propelled its growth. They faced armed vigilantes who—enjoying the collaboration of the city police—patrolled the streets, shooting potential looters and unarmed black people with impunity. Malik Rahim himself saw nineteen black people killed, and local authorities—black and white—refused to listen to his accounts. In scott's view, "our stance and practice of armed self-defense protected us from being 'dropped in the street.'" He wrote that the police and military personal "wanted to shut us down as if we were insurgents in some foreign war."

The bloody past of the toxic war to restore white supremacy after the collapse of the Confederacy still nourishes violence in Louisiana—right there in Algiers where Common Ground had hundreds camping on their grounds. scott crow became a "race traitor" to the local white land-owners, derided as a "Yankee" even though he was born and raised in Texas. Somehow a contingent of Young Patriots and Black Panthers had been involved with an early school scott attended. Somehow he escaped the typical racist indoctrination given working-class boys living on the out-skirts of Dallas. As an adult, he turned away from his successful furniture business and devoted his energy to environmental concerns. Becoming active with Amnesty International introduced scott to political prisoners, and later, after moving to Austin, his work with Anti-Racist Action taught him about confronting white supremacists from an anarchist framework. His political orientation grew more radical and his thinking was revolu-tionized during a time of enhanced government monitoring to sustain the politics of the "War on Terror." He learned that, like thousands of other radicalized citizens, his ideas or associates or actions were being scruti-nized by the FBI. That's the response government agencies generate when the protected racial and class hierarchies of the United States face funda-mental challenges. My closest friends, comrades, and even my children have been on the FBI radar screen as well.

Read his book—sometimes it's a journal, parts may be a memoir of growing up with a single mother, and other times you'll have an organizing manual wrapped in an adventure story. Learn the path scott found to unearth hidden truths of America's radical traditions, and what empowered him to reach out with an emergency heart love to show solidarity with those in jeopardy.

Power to the people!

Kathleen Cleaver
Atlanta
June 2011

Even before the thoughts occurred . . .

Picture moments in dreams, nightmares—or terrors, really— where many waking realities were not as they were before in the Gulf Coast Region in the early years of this new century, but as they became within hours, within days, within weeks.

Those realities began to unfurl themselves in tattered forms under dark heavy clouds on those long hot days and longer sleepless nights in the late summer that held on in 2005. Like our worst dreams, they moved slowly and wouldn't end.

While the waters rained down, the tides rose from below and structures—real and imagined—collapsed from years of forgetting and of neglect. They allowed tides and governments to wash away families, wash away communities, wash away lives and all their expectations for something better— something other than the realities they were forced into.

While in other places—emotionally and physically— others struggled in shifting moments, in waking dreams and nightmares of helplessness and fear, in disbelief and paralysis, that ultimately led from stupor to actions that couldn't have been imagined just hours or days before.

Then as the storm waters receded and governments continued to fail—don't they always fail? Watermarks and time were to show compassion, determination and resistance to forgetting and to neglect in sharp contrast to some of the worst in all of us that emerged on the toxic and degraded landscapes of what was once New Orleans in the Gulf Coast Region of the United States in the early years of the new century.

Even before the thoughts occurred . . .

Waking up from Oblivion

There is a crime here beyond denunciation. There is a sorrow here that weeping cannot symbolize. There is a failure here that topples all our success.

—John Steinbeck, *The Grapes of Wrath*

Think about waking up one day and finding that everything you count on in your life is gone. All the basic amenities that you expect in a *first world* nation have disappeared: no clean water, no housing, no food, no communication, no jobs, and no transportation. Nothing. For most of us, this is simply unimaginable. Most disasters around us are relatively isolated events. If your house burns down, you can still go to your neighbor's for shelter. If a tornado destroys your town, then you and your neighbors can get help in the next town. But what happens when the next house, the next town, and the next city, for hundreds of miles in all directions, are also gone? When the very fabric of all the communities around you has been destroyed?

That is what happened in the Gulf Coast region in the fall of 2005 due to Hurricane Katrina and the failure of the levees in New Orleans.

We must never forget these facts that made Hurricane Katrina a travesty: That climate change is creating unprecedented storms in size and intensity. Katrina was one of them. That ongoing ecological destruction in the name of profits has been perpetuated for more than a hundred years, including the destruction of wetlands and other natural barriers along the coastlines, allowing hurricanes to move further inland than ever before, in order to open up access to Gulf oil and commercial shipping routes. Next, it was that levees were built substandard by corruption and greed when contractors and some politicians knew they would never hold. And, finally, that the government response at all levels left thousands of people to die who had no means to evacuate due to health, age, and lack of funds, transportation, or connections. Individuals and families were trapped in their homes, on the streets, on their rooftops, and in their attics. Power reacted with brute force and criminalization of the people. It was criminal neglect. This was the latest in a long history of largely invisible disasters of neglect in these communities. To me, the levees became a symbol of the way that the corruption and arrogance of governments disregards the most vulnerable people.

After the storm, the government had lost control. Everything disappeared underwater, leaving thousands to die or fend for themselves. In the bleak early days, there were no services, and little emergency aid was being rendered due to law enforcement's preoccupation with maintaining order. On one hand, it was chaos, with confused and desperate people trying to get out to safety. On the other hand, it was true anarchy: people with nothing, waiting for no one to help them, began to aid themselves and each other amid the devastation.

From the destruction and the aftermath of Hurricane Katrina emerged an organization called the Common Ground Collective that was built on hope, dedication, and and the anarchist inspirations of mutual aid and solidarity. The story of Common Ground is a story of ordinary people compelled to act for justice in an extraordinary situation.

I have written these words to answer questions (some of them my own) about this organization. What brought me to New Orleans? What brought others? What was our part in the battle for justice in that city? How did we all struggle to resist, to rebuild, to stop the disasters perpetuated in historically marginalized communities?[1] I also want to ask questions that may not have answers, but need to be asked.

In the first three years of the Common Ground Collective, over twenty-eight thousand mostly middle-class and white volunteers aided communities that most had no direct connection to apart from the bond of humanity. What impacts did we have on the future of the communities in the Gulf?

These are my observations and feelings about my involvement in the formation of the Common Ground Collective in its rapid path from an idea to being the largest anarchist-influenced organization in modern U.S. history. It was an organization built in unstable surroundings, in constant, sometimes chaotic, evolution. As Bill Ayers once noted, "Memory is a motherfucker." I cannot remember everything that happened on the ground, everyone who participated, or even what I had for breakfast most days. But some vivid images and intense feelings, from feeding people to the flower that pushed up through the concrete, will stay with me for the rest of my life.

From Common Ground's tumultuous beginnings, people (especially radicals and anarchists like me) came to New Orleans with no prior experience in disaster response. Common Ground went on to engage in protracted social justice struggles side by side with New Orleans residents, First Nations peoples and other members of civil society to regain dignity and control over their lives. Our aims were to aid people in the short term, and for those of us from the outside to support historically marginalized communities in the Gulf in building power for long-term social and political change.

These people had a small chance for justice. In the catastrophe, the state lost its grasp, and some of the walls they had built to keep people out came crashing down. Many who had lost everything were angry and desperate. What else could the state do to them? They could either give up or fight. Many chose to fight.

At the Common Ground Collective we knew from the beginning that we did not need the permission of the state or its resources. We did not need it at all. We only needed the willingness to do it all ourselves—together.

The people who presume to have Power tell us an arrogant fable about how the working class and poor do not have time or interest in solving their own problems.[2] That is a lie. In New Orleans I witnessed what happens when people take action for their lives in a struggle for self-determination. With support from small organizations like ours, communities all over the region fought on many levels to have access to basic health care, to reopen their schools, to have decent jobs, to return to their homes and neighborhoods, and ultimately to decide their own fates.

As I saw it, if there was ever a time and place for those of us with any amount of resources to put our principled political theories into action, this was it. My political and personal history led me to the Gulf. I went to aid comrades of many years that I greatly loved and respected. I also went to support the people, already made invisible by social indifference, who had everything taken away, first by the storm, second by the failure of the levees, and third by the failure of unresponsive governments.

I want to illustrate how our relief work, based in radical social analysis summed up in the slogan "Solidarity Not Charity," was tied into engaging in broader community justice struggles against deep-rooted racism, private developers, and bad government.

I did not go to the Gulf to be a savior; that was against my principles. Hell, I wasn't even absolutely sure of what I had gotten into when the storms rolled back out into the Gulf, leaving water everywhere. I was struggling to keep my balance in the turbulence. I thought a lot about the idea of "white saviors" on my way into New Orleans right after the levee failures, and during the weeks that followed. It was a mindset that permeated government agencies, the Red Cross, the media, insensitive white rescuers, too many religious organizations, and even some of Common Ground's own volunteers. It was an unstated viewpoint that coiled around every aspect of aid within the region, even as many of us struggled against it.

It was our time to cast doubt aside and say: we can and we will do this. As we built more together, we began to realize that, as June Jordan said, "We are the ones we have been waiting for." We weren't the only organization engaged in these struggles. There were many and those stories need to be told, but these are the stories I can tell.

This is my piece of the truth.

It Takes a Spark to Start a Prairie Fire

> I think what motivates people is not great hate, but great love for other people.
>
> —Huey Newton

A Beginning

All stories have beginnings. My story of the Common Ground Collective begins with questions of life and death. Not only my own, but also the lives and deaths of people I knew and loved, and of thousands I have never met, who lived in the Gulf Coast region in the fall of 2005. That was when, following an immense storm in the late summer, everyone and everything in the Gulf Coast region changed forever.

I have deep personal ties to Louisiana. Among them is my good friend Robert H. King, a.k.a. Robert King Wilkerson, whom we affectionately refer to as King. A former member of the Black Panther Party, he was unjustly imprisoned for his political convictions. After serving twenty-nine years in solitary confinement in Louisiana's notorious Angola Prison, he gained his freedom in 2001. He is an outspoken man with a big heart, and deeply committed to social justice. His analysis is honest and sometimes reserved. He maintained his inner strength while locked in his cramped cell. King carries on his body deep knife scars from an attempt on his life when he tried to stop the sex slave trade of young inmates behind bars. These scars— and two of his comrades, Albert Woodfox and Herman Wallace, the other two members of the Angola 3—serve as constant reminders of those days.[3]

When Katrina came ashore, King was living in New Orleans. A few of us stayed in contact with him throughout the storm. The worst of it had missed the city. We watched the hurricane and the aftermath unfold on the television with disbelief. In Texas, where we were waiting, mild fear set in. In the last call anyone received from him, King said that he was all right. He and his dog Kenya had successfully ridden it out just like many times before in his younger days. Hours later, the levees broke. New Orleans flooded, martial law was declared and King was unreachable by phone.[4] Military and police blockades were going up at all access points around the city. Movements in or around the city were being restricted, and an unsparing dusk to dawn curfew was put in place. No one was to be seen on the streets after dark. Shoot-to-kill orders were being given at all levels for the appearance of looting or violation of the orders. They locked New Orleans down. We all became increasingly worried as the situation in the city quickly disintegrated. We feared he was trapped in the deluge along the Gulf Coast. Immediately, my partner Ann began making calls all over the country, trying to find information on King or any of our other friends in the city, even questioning recent evacuees who made it out. However, by the evening of August 29 we still had found out nothing.

Then Brandon Darby called. I hadn't spoken to him in almost a year. He proposed that he and I leave immediately for New Orleans to try to find King. He wanted us to join the search and rescue teams and looking for him while aiding others who were trapped there. Brandon had befriended Ann, King, and me in late 2002. He was a cavalier and difficult man who emphatically claimed he wanted to challenge the ills of the world. He mostly participated at the edge of radical political circles within Austin. New to social justice struggles, he was full of rhetorical fire, proclaiming himself a revolutionary. He seemed sincere, but at the same time misguided and impatient. Over the years, he became adept at absorbing the anarchist and radical political language around him, but not the practices. He tolerated, but didn't believe in, community organizing. He always wanted to go the lone wolf route. His treatment of his ex-partner, his unhealthy views on women, and his incessant monologues led me to repeatedly cut off communication with him for long periods. He always worked his way back to me. He seemed to want to belong to something important.

At first, Brandon's idea seemed far-fetched, but then the plan evolved further. Our decision was shaped by personal and political factors. Most important was that King was family; I had to know if he was all right. As word began to come in that most of our people were out of New Orleans, the uncertainty about King began gnawing at me more deeply. As a Black Panther, he had dedicated his life to the struggle for social justice inside and outside prison walls. King was a part of the fabric of these movements for justice, as well as being my friend and mentor. But this disaster had also revealed the neglected parts of society we keep hidden from view. I had access to resources that could help more people than King alone. As a community organizer who cares about people no matter where they might be, I felt that it was my responsibility to aid those in New Orleans who, already marginalized, now had total devastation added to their burden.

The hard-pressed levees had given way from the severe flooding Monday afternoon. On Tuesday, Brandon found a boat. We called the Red Cross, informing them that we had a boat. They responded, "Come on now!" If all went well, the Red Cross would serve as our gateway to get into the Crescent City. Hurriedly we gathered our supplies. Our survival gear included gas, water, food, etc. We also took a pistol. Our concern was that during times of civil unrest people under duress can do desperate things. Brandon talked me out of taking my rifle, which I would later regret.

But amid all this preparation I hesitated, and I withdrew. There were myriad reasons. It was all happening so fast, there were so many unknowns, there was a low chance of achieving our objectives, and we both lacked experience. Also, Brandon's personal and political history with me showed him to be unstable and difficult at critical times. I was unsure of how this would go. I had never participated in disaster work in my life. I don't consider myself to be a hero, just someone who is motivated to do the right thing when necessary. This was really big. What was about to happen? How would this play out? After thinking and talking for a while, with much pain and some shame, I decided not to go.

Saddened, unsure, and afraid, Brandon took off by himself. After he left, I continued to ruminate over what was happening; I couldn't put it out of my head. It ate at my heart and my mind. Politically and personally I felt as if I was condemning people to death by my inactions. About an hour after Brandon was gone, I called him and told him I was back in. I just had to know about King; I couldn't sit and do nothing. I could hear the relief in his voice when I told him. He waited for me in Houston, and we took off from there into the unknown, quite conscious that we would take the steps that followed carefully.

The highways heading east toward the disaster were virtually abandoned. I didn't even see law enforcement vehicles in our travels across Texas or Louisiana, which is very unusual. As summer dusk gave way to night, flashing warning signs began to appear on the roadside every fifty miles or so. They flickered with ominous messages about New Orleans. I had knots in my stomach. Ours was one of the few vehicles ignoring the messages and heading into the unknown.

We drove until we arrived at the makeshift Red Cross/FEMA office on the outskirts of Baton Rogue. It was just before dawn on Thursday. We were stunned to learn that, two hours before we arrived, the officials had turned away 280 people ready to go in with their own boats, simply because they could not figure out what to do with them. These officials were entirely disorganized and disoriented. There were thousands of people stranded in their attics, on porches and rooftops; some were trying to swim to safety. These boats and people were needed now!

We waited there until daybreak, watching FEMA, the Red Cross, state Wildlife officials and others argue over who had jurisdiction on search and rescue while people were dying a few miles away. The situation broke down even more with disputes between countless city, county, state, and federal agencies. But that is the way Power operates: control first and fore-most, then attend to everything else.

I had a general idea of where King was in the city, or at least where he lived when it was dry. But I didn't know how we were going to reach him. We were not officially sanctioned by anyone in control to go in. Under all that water, the city looked vastly different, with familiar structures distorted into unrecognizable forms. All we had was our boat, our meager supplies, and the determination to find him. So we went in on our own. They could argue over who had more authority; we were on a mission to help people.

We had discovered that no one could get in from the west of the city, due to the government efforts focused on that side. They had choked the only access point into the city center and the flooded wards down Interstate 10. I-10 disappeared into the floodwaters just at the city's edge. I had seen plenty of debris and wind damage, but seeing a roadway I knew go under water that didn't end was disorienting. Neither of us knew the terrain well enough.

This led us to choose the northeastern route, via IH-12 north of New Orleans, down into St. Bernard Parish. This seemed like the only way to get to the east side of the city so that we could find a place to either drive in on the back roads, or put our boat in the water. As we passed the bridge known as the Lake Pontchartrain Causeway, which enters from the north into the city, we found it was blocked as a result of flooding. It was also quite possible that it had missing sections caused by storm surge damage. No one knew for sure, but it looked liked a bridge into the waters of nowhere.

Who Could Imagine This?

I was not prepared for the terrible things I saw as we got closer. The massive devastation went on for miles. Televised reports could not show the full picture. Roadways and bridges were gone; mud was thirty feet high from storm surges; electrical lines were lying everywhere, sparking furiously. The east side was closer to ground zero of the storm, so it had been hit harder. The few people there were standing on the side of the road crying.

There was not much they could do in the emptiness of the areas around East New Orleans. I felt the same way.

It was unimaginable: cars thrown into buildings, whole housing subdivisions completely leveled, now scattered wood ruins with nothing identifiable left. It was as if a monstrous force had flung millions of matchsticks across the ground for miles. Trash, which had previously been the useful contents of these structures, was strewn across the cluttered landscape. Natural gas, with its unmistakable smell and hissing noise, leaked out of massive broken, open pipes—near the live electric lines in many places. As we drove, we saw many empty, destroyed storefronts, some standing under water.

Apart from a very few residents and some emergency crews, we were about the only other people in the area. Most had evacuated days ago if they were able. Death, fear, and despair were in the air for those who were left. Despite the animated pops of the power lines and the constant sounds of escaping gas, the atmosphere was still and quite eerie. It seemed like the end of the world. Was this how civilization as we know it would end?

In the midst of this devastation, we stopped the truck and began to weep. I stopped thinking. I had tried to wrap my head around it, but it was overwhelming. We both just sat and cried deeply. It was all we could do.

We then began to help the few locals with small tasks like searching for people lost in the storm, moving boats which had been stranded on the roadways, giving out water, which was in short supply, and moving lots of debris in searching for intact roadways or back roads to get into the flooded city proper. It wasn't much; it was a start.

While exploring many blocked or destroyed roads that became dead ends, we listened to the only radio station, WWL 870, that was broadcasting for miles. It was our only source of news, though we got most of our information from the people we came across. In one of the most advanced and information-heavy technological countries in the world, we were limited to words from "over the hill" and the radio. I tried to take into account that rumor, conjecture, and fearful speculation were running rampant. Assimilating the information coming in was difficult and became increasingly more so as the days progressed.

When the first rumors circulated about gunfights between armed rescuers and stranded people, we had no way to confirm or disprove them. Who could I trust? Even the law enforcement personnel I met didn't have any better access to information than we did, and were reporting sketchy hearsay as facts. They were scared and confused, too. My internal balance was beginning to shift as we continued to search for a way into the city.

Storms in the Open Waters

On what was left of a small road with cars, boats, and debris scattered all over it, we found two men—a father, John, and his adult son Richard—who agreed to guide us by boat into East New Orleans, where they owned a warehouse they were trying to reach. Before we launched, we had to carry the boats and supplies to the water on multiple trips of about seventy-five yards each, through choking mud up to our knees, with large houseboats beached and toppled all around us. Sweat poured as we moved slowly through the mud. We hid extra water and gasoline in nearby brush for our return.

Finally, we were ready. John and Richard had their own boat, while Brandon and I, despite having little boating experience between us, set out in a fifteen-foot flat-bottom skiff (called a johnboat) into an oncoming storm in the open waters of the Gulf of Mexico. As the storm approached, it exploded with lighting, thunder, and strong winds, drumming up six-foot swells that violently rocked our little boat.

The johnboat is made for the quiet, flat conditions of small lakes and ponds, not for the open sea. We almost capsized numerous times as lightning struck the water near us. My senses had been heightened before, and now they were on overload. The storm became so bad that our guides turned away from the direct path to the city, heading into a canal that led into the flooded Lake Pontchartrain.

We entered an intricate series of flooded waterways. The damage got worse as we advanced. We ended up in the Gulf Intracoastal Waterway, a large channel for massive ships and barges, but the only vessels we saw in it were beached on the shores. In effect, our little boats were the only two craft that were coming in. The few scattered others we saw moving were all coming out. I was bewildered and resentful that the oncoming boats we saw departing the area contained only armed, white law enforcement and white rescue volunteers. Not one evacuee. With all these resources, why were there no rescued people on board?

The two men we were traveling with had unofficial permission from a Wildlife Department search and rescue contact that enabled us to travel upriver. As we passed the departing boats on the waterway we would stop to exchange what little information we had. The stories from these other boats worsened. People were being shot at, boats were being taken, and a rescue helicopter had been fired on. It reminded me of *Apocalypse Now*, how it got psychologically darker and more hellish as they went up the river. The farther they traveled into the unknown, the more the social constructs they had known were broken down. That is how it seemed to us that day. Everything I thought I knew, all of my realities were shifting like the muddy water moving in the currents beneath us. Everything was constantly changing.

As we continued up the canal, we saw whole communities in the water. We saw street after street of houses with all their contents, not flooded, but thrown into the water off their stilts like common trash. Death was everywhere; there were semisubmerged and unidentifiable parts, some from animals and others we believed to be human. I couldn't bear to look too closely. We had to maneuver our boats and our souls slowly and carefully through the waters.

The last boat that we came into contact with was filled with six guys from Texas, rural blue-collar types who had been compelled to do something too. They had just engaged in a firefight with some other men on a bridge who had tried to take their boat. The drawbridge operator had been trapped in his booth for days, waiting for help that was not coming. He panicked when the gun battle had broken out, but the Texans could not reach him. We all agreed that it was our moral obligation to do something, but these guys kept saying "it's not worth it . . . it's just not worth it" as they headed back home. The reality was that we needed to go under that same bridge to get past the breached levees into the flooded Lower Ninth Ward.

But on that day we turned right into a smaller industrial canal on our way to the East New Orleans warehouse. In the distance, thick black smoke billowed from fires in unknown buildings and blew across the canal, while occasional gunfire resounded from remote locations. Machinery from nearby factories and refineries creaked and moaned as if it might explode or collapse at any moment from stress and heat. Smoke filled the air and my lungs with a haze as lonely helicopters creased the misty grey skies. Somehow, cranes and other waterfowl ignored everything around them and continued to hunt for fish on the swollen shores of the canal. Tranquil and oblivious to us, their lives continued on.

When we got close to our destination, we pulled the boats onto the shore for the night, and camouflaged them with brush and small tree branches cut from the shoreline. If we lost our boats, gasoline, or water due to carelessness, we would have been cut off in complete isolation. We would have become part of the problem.

The storm we had fled earlier reached us once more, and rain continued in a steady downpour upon the drowned city. After securing the boats we climbed atop a fifteen-foot concrete levee wall from which we could see houses and apartment buildings standing in water. Water had transfigured the city, creating an unfamiliar landscape. It was everywhere.

In the distance there were stranded people, waving and crying for help, trapped across what used to be a highway that was now submerged. Here we were within less than a mile of desperate people, and we could do nothing. They seemed close, but they were impossible to get to from where we were. After traveling hundreds of miles, we were now within reach of those who were cut off from the outside world. A pang came across my chest. I felt useless. This was becoming a recurring feeling.

I stared at it all for a while, trying to comprehend the totality of the disaster, then climbed down the other side of the levee and waded through a marsh to a road covered in thick mud.

We commandeered an abandoned rusty pick-up truck, loaded it up with the gear and drove to the warehouse to hide from the rapidly increasing armed helicopter presence. John and Richard left us at this warehouse, while they went to another one further down the road where they would stay the night. Choppers were constantly circling overhead. In the morning we would regroup and figure out what we were going to do next.

The helicopters that flew close to where Brandon and I stood were fully armed with large fifty-caliber machine guns or were carrying soldiers with guns. I asked myself why they were aiming their guns down on us, instead of dropping lines to rescue the people clearly stranded across the unseen highway nearby. The gunners trained their weapons on anything that moved, so we stood in the shadows before going in. This country's military could muster enough bodies to shoot to kill but not to send help. What kind of world were we living in?

The nondescript metal warehouse had a few windows around the top edge. It was totally deserted. Nobody could get near it without a boat because water surrounded it on all four sides. It had become an island. There were dead fish everywhere on the ground left from the water that had recently been ten feet higher than it was now. And of course, there was no electricity; there was nothing but standing water and stench. Darkened, full of shadows from the overcast day, the inside was full of cases of small, thin glass bottles of hot sauce. The tall, stacked cases creaked and moaned under their own weight, sometimes falling like trees in a forest and shattering on the ground. As the long day drew to a close, the sun came under the grey sky to meet the horizon, shining beautiful shifting daylight through the transom windows. The light revealed many of these bottles standing perfectly upside down, full of water, on the dry concrete floor. It was like a temporary art installation. It all seemed sacred in the profane world just outside the walls.

The choppers flying near the ground circled frequently, rescuing no one at all, until the sun was gone. We secured the perimeter and soon found ourselves in pitch-black darkness. There were no lights, no reflections: a city with no shadows under a moonless night.

In this total breakdown of civilization, the improbable happened: we found that one lone telephone in an office worked. Through its scratchy, heavy static we could communicate with the outside world. From this phone line, our only connection with a reality beyond our own, we received frequent updates about how unsafe the whole situation had become. The failure of the authorities to evacuate people was causing tremendous and compounding problems. They were still dragging their feet. Their ineptitude had left people to despair without food, water, or hope for what was turning into days. I began to wonder if it was on purpose.

We tried to find some rest from the long day as helicopters and gunfire faded in the distance. Edgy, we took shifts trying to sleep on the ground in the office despite the stifling humidity inside the warehouse. The one who was awake kept guarded watch, pistol in hand.

Bellwether

Early the next morning a call came from the Wildlife Department contact. He said, "Don't go into the city any further." He was quiet for a moment, and then he told us (total strangers) that he had been working for that agency for many years and never shot anybody. Then he said, "But yesterday I shot five people in the course of about three hours. I probably killed some of them." He added, "It was the most horrible thing I ever had to do in my life; don't go into the city any further."[5]

He explained that his group had gone out in their rescue boats to get women, children, and elderly people first. He saw people's desperation to get out. Young black men would push to the front, saying, "Take me first." The armed rescuers replied, "No, we can't, we're taking women and children first." And then the men would pull weapons on them. The wildlife contact said, "We just shot them." The rescue boats would come back to a place two or three times, and people would still come up and do this, and they would shoot them and push them out of the way.

He was not going to go back out into it again; he sounded as if he was in shock. His phone call rattled both of us. Fear, fatigue, and disillusionment had set in heavy. This situation was out of control. I couldn't entirely process what we had just heard. His words pummeled me, but I didn't sink. It became surreal; I had come on a humanitarian mission that had turned into the beginnings of a possible racial civil war. Almost all the law enforcement and rescuers we encountered were white men, while the majority of people in distress were a low-income and black population.

Were the police afraid of real or imagined threats? How much did their prejudices play into pulling the triggers? The long history of failure and neglect by the government had created space for strife that led to overtly racist words from white rescuers and unspeakable actions from those that should have been helping others.

I knew which side I would be on politically. The side that I had come to aid, the marginalized, underserved, and often ignored populations, like the one I came from, within the floodwaters. The average person, however, would not know my intentions. Would they see me in the same way they saw the insensitive white rescuers? I had to ask myself some serious questions. What if I had to shoot someone in our own defense? Would it be worth it to help my friend King and others? We had risked so much to get this far. Were we now going to give up? How much was racism playing into everything around me? Was King safe, or was he already dead? The questions were hard. Some I couldn't answer while others I didn't want to answer. I was sick from the unknowns.

We thanked the two men for their help and left them at their warehouse. Returning to our hidden boat, we loaded it. The sun was warming the air as helicopters circled back and forth on missions unknown, passing close down to us, watching. The fires, unseen as we sat in our boat, still produced smoke across our landscape.

We idled the boat into the middle of the waterway and killed the engine. We had to make a choice: turn one way to the bridge and eventually into the flooded city through the broken levees to further aid those disregarded by the state, or head the way we had come in to make the long journey back to where we had started. The decision was ours alone on the silent moving waters.

With much pain, we decided to leave. It was not worth it to me to hurt someone to aid someone else. It would have been one more travesty in this chaotic mess.

The boat trip back, upon which we were about to embark, would take roughly three and a half hours without any interruptions. It would not be an easy return. Being upriver, I realized that I had psychologically turned a corner, where I was ready to shoot somebody in self-defense. This was not an abstract idea but a truth from my heart. If a boat came upon us too fast, or if anybody started firing at us, we both agreed we would fire back at them. We were ready. The gun was in one of our hands the whole time, loaded, chambered, and ready.

Think about that for a minute: this was not a scenario from a book; this was real life, unfolding out of control. That is how psychologically fucked-up things were at that time. Fear and the unknown had gripped many, and now it had us. It was an undeclared war on many fronts, between many desperate, confused, and frightened people on all sides struggling for survival or control. I placed blame not on the desperate, but on those who had power, or who presumed to have it, who withheld the resources. Their empire was crumbling here, and taking all of us with it.

We would have to pass under several bridges (with potential opportunities for ambush lying overhead) to get back to the open waterway. Tension was high throughout my mind and body as we continued back. Was I leaving my principles and beliefs at the muddy bottom of this flooded city? With doubt and trepidation, we continued on our way.

As we reached the open water that met Lake Pontchartrain I saw what could only be described as a good omen in all this tragedy. In the turbulent waters, a family of dolphins approached the boat, circled, and then swam off. They reminded me for an instant that there could be hope—that there was a chance for life.

When we finally got back to our truck, where we had initially launched, we heard on the radio that the government had called off all search and rescue boats. The authorities had ordered that nobody come in. They had called off all the private citizens and their boats and sealed off the city of New Orleans. It was Saturday. We had been there three days, and through attrition of rescue crews things were destabilizing further. They were going to restore law and order no matter the cost. This left many, many people still trapped without food, water, shelter, or a way out.

A man on the radio was angrily decrying George Bush, FEMA, and the federal government, saying that people were dying that did not have to. He cursed, then he and the announcer both broke down in tears. There was no commercial break. We heard two grown men crying the tears of helplessness we all felt. The announcer gained his breath and said, "Thank you, Mayor Ray Nagin." I couldn't believe an elected politician would say the things he said. I knew he felt it, but I also knew he was covering his ass. It was dire.

Dejected, we headed back to Austin.

A Path Home Paved with Tears

Leaving the Crescent City, I felt guilt, shame, and deep sadness. We had left King there; we had left entire communities there. I used all these resources, access, and my privilege of being white—and what had we done? We left with nothing. Yes, I had helped some people along the way, but it was demoralizing how ineffective I had been in the overall scope of things. There weren't enough of us.

I realized that we weren't prepared for the immensity of the situation, and that people were extremely desperate. Help was not coming. The little help that was getting there was arbitrary and disorganized. The government seemed confused, moving slowly and without preparation. That has since proven to be the exact truth. Their words were empty.

As we traveled out of the city, we witnessed a massive spontaneous evacuation happening despite the authorities. In slow motion, cars, trucks, and trailers overfull with people and what few belongings they might have had made their way down highways littered with vehicles abandoned for lack of fuel. Meanwhile, other masses of people wandered by foot along the roadside, heading away from the danger of the flooded city toward the unknown.

As the civilians fled the disaster, small military convoys were beginning to arrive via these same roads. The armed guards who now appeared were watching over the lines of stranded cars that piled up at closed gas stations along the highway, waiting for gas that might not ever arrive. As we drove home, I kept saying to myself, "This can't be happening here."

My tears would demand more questions of me on the way home. Should I return? But how could I? Before any answers came, we arrived at our destination and collapsed from exhaustion.

Against Forgetting

'Twas like where you're from weren't never there. Where you're going doesn't matter. And where you are ain't no good unless you can get away from it!

—Flannery O'Connor, *Wise Blood*

I am an accidental warrior. I often think that random events dragged me to my place in life. Building the Common Ground Collective was the culmination of countless life experiences, some within political organizing, but mostly ones that were far outside of it. Growing up in the South, the history of social and political struggle for justice outside of electoral politics is hidden to most people. The odds are against you pushing against the grain. I had to dig deep to find it and to nurture it. It was a process outside of college, gained through knowing people and looking down many paths to find the ones that were worth walking.

In my understanding of the world, whether we know it or not, whether we want to admit it or not, we are the sum of everything that has happened to us from our birth on. We are shaped by genetics, families, geography, economics, culture, and politics. Like fish in water, we live in these environments but do not notice them, even as they influence the choices we make today.

These experiences—these times, events, interactions, and places strewn together—make me who I am. They are what make any of us who we are. We can't remember it all, but these fragments are what we call life. With so many memories shaping us, how could we pick and choose which ones have the most meaning? Events, smells, places—even words jog my memory. It is not possible to remember everything, but it is important to remember that our current actions and thoughts come from somewhere. They are built on our pasts.

In the U.S., our inevitable forgetting is reinforced in troublesome ways. We have a long history of forgetting who we are and where we came from.

In our hurry to get to the future, we are often taught to place no value on remembering. Our nomadic lifestyles take us away from our cultural and familial roots, and our deeply ingrained individualism focuses us on ourselves before others.

People, who had been disturbed by the waters of Katrina, came to the Gulf Coast from all over the map to rectify the wrongs of history and provide aid. The reasons were as varied as the people. It was a combination of media hype, a chance for heroics, cynicism at the constant failures of the state, and people's deeper personal and political histories that compelled us to act. I know that my own life experiences shaped how I saw things, how I reacted, the networks that I mobilized—in short, everything I did as one of the founders of Common Ground. They even influence the way that I am writing this now.

Returning to New Orleans and helping to found Common Ground was not an isolated event in my life. It was an action deeply rooted in years of experience, organizing, learning, and thinking. Without those years of building theory, practice, contacts, and meaningful relationships around the country, my participation in the New Orleans struggle would never have been possible.

So just how does a white working-class kid raised on country music in the semirural South end up on the New Orleans porch of an ex-member of the Black Panther Party with a rifle in his hands to face down a white militia in defense of a black community for political principles?

Emily

> Will you say hello to my ma?
> Will you pay a visit to her?
> She's an artist, just as you were.
> I'd have introduced you to her.
> She would take me out on Sundays.
> We'd go laughing through the garbage.
> She repaired legs like a doctor
> On the kitchen chairs we sat on
>
>   —Jane's Addiction, "Then She Did"

I am the only son of Emily Crow. I grew up poor, on what was literally the wrong side of the tracks—first, in the inner city, and, later, near steel and paper factories in an agricultural town.

I was conceived by accident. I have never known my birth father. Throughout my early years, my mother raised me largely on her own, supporting us while she moved from one low-skilled temp job to another.

She loved me deeply. Like many mothers in her situation, she would sometimes go without so I wouldn't have to. She kept that hidden from me. She had grown up dirt farm poor and wanted me to have a better life. I remember the stories she told of her youth. Her experiences of growing up in such poverty followed her for the rest of her life. I have always found this side of her character poignant. I still don't know how she had the strength to climb uphill every day, but she did, for both of us. She has always been a strong woman.

I didn't know we were poor. In my eyes, it was just the way things were. For me, our situation was neither unique nor particularly tragic, but I did notice some differences. Most of the people I went to school with had two parents; I was the only Cub Scout whose mom came to events instead of a dad. Most families owned their own homes; we lived in apartments and duplexes. I went hungry on a few occasions. Most of my extended family was made up of manual laborers with low levels of education who started working at early ages.

I didn't get new clothes often. My mom would buy clothes too big for me so I could grow into them; she would let my pant legs down at the beginning of the school year. We shopped at thrift stores and went dumpster-diving out of necessity and for fun. My extended family wore the same outfits for weddings and funerals.

In the early 1970s, we lived in a mixed barrio, largely black and Chicano, in East Dallas. I attended a free multiracial preschool run by members of the Black Panther Party, Brown Berets, and Young Patriots. There were no Huey Newton posters, guns, or readings from the Little Red Book. There was food, naps, safety, and time to play with toys, away from the rough blocks of the neighborhood. (I find it curious that, starting there, the Black Panther Party became a thread running through my life.)

I was one of the few white kids, but I cannot recall noticing it. That sense of difference came later, with social training. The black and white folks who ran it were kind. They fed us and kept us in line if we strayed. I tasted soap a few times due to my bad language! I enjoyed my days there and was sad when I had to leave. Twenty years later, I moved back to that neighborhood, right down the street from the school. Eventually, I worked with some of the same people on issues that still plagued the neighborhood.

When I was five, we moved to Garland, a town like many in the U.S. Its pastoral landscape had given way to industries such as U.S. Steel and International Paper in the 1950s and '60s; it retained elements of both agriculture and manufacturing when we arrived. Long after I was gone,

Garland would become a sprawling suburb full of low-income housing. The industry moved overseas, leaving workers and buildings abandoned, both ghosts of their former selves. Many of those rural towns in Texas died, or are still drying up, as cities have become huge.

The duplex we lived in sat at the end of a dead-end street on a circle that backed onto an artificially widened creek. It was only fifty yards from the railroad tracks in a treeless neighborhood full of other nondescript gray duplexes. I would sometimes forget which house was ours.

This neighborhood in Garland was also poor and mixed, but it was across the railroad tracks from a poor black neighborhood. I had never seen anything like that before. I played in that neighborhood as much as in my own. The fact that we lived in mixed, low-income areas with Latino, black, and Native American friends wasn't discussed much. It was just where we lived. I was taught to be respectful of everyone and never use slurs. I always felt at home in both neighborhoods.

I think that I was born an empathetic person, with a great sensitivity to the world around me. My mom was always supportive of me in this. The natural world and the creatures in it were intriguing and alive. I was the kid who didn't want to crush insects or torment animals with my friends. I felt it too much.

My mother caught on to the growing environmental movement in the 1970s. Once, she called me over to the TV to see something astounding. People in small rubber rafts were putting themselves between a giant speeding ship with a bulky harpoon and a beautiful whale that was trying to escape. I knew it wasn't the old black-and-white film *Moby Dick* we had seen before. She explained that the people in the small boats were trying to stop whale slaughter. I was rapt at the courage and danger of the scene I was watching. She said, "It's a group called Greenpeace." Watching it made me cry with sadness for the whale and excitement at the actions to stop the slaughter. It was my first exposure to humans saving another species. I wanted to be like that. I wanted do something I believed in, to stop the harm to animals and the planet. But what was on TV seemed distant from where I lived and the people around me. In any case, my mother's awareness and compassion for what was happening in the world was passing to me.

My mother had developed many progressive views, especially around race, despite being white and poor in the South. Her care and support instilled in me a rudimentary sense of fairness, dignity, and compassion.

For two years in the late 1970s, I got support to attend a new kind of school called Montessori. It was like no place I had ever been. The school provided autonomy within a collaborative setting for students. The teachers didn't stay on top of you to do rote work. They let you choose the work you wanted to do, the pace at which to complete it, and whether you wanted to work with others. It was a great degree of freedom compared to my public school days. (It was my first exposure, for example, to vegetarian food, as that was what they provided, reinforcing the idea of compassion for all animals). When I returned to public school, I never seemed to function as well. Montessori helped give me a sense of self-respect and a badly needed chance to dream. Years later, I went back there to thank them for giving me a chance.

Straw Man

> The ones who love us least are the ones we'll die to please
> If it's any consolation, I don't begin to understand them
> We are the sons of no one, bastards of young
> > —The Replacements, "Bastards of Young"

Freddie Haws, the man who called himself my father, was absent most of my life. My mom had married him when I was three. I didn't find out he wasn't my biological dad until I was about eight. Kids on the playground had called me a "bastard child," words that stung painfully when I first heard them. He was the only dad I had.

In the 1960s and '70s, he was a traveling musician in the band of country music legends George Jones and Tammy Wynette. A lot of his time on the road was spent developing a major drug habit. I grew up backstage, meeting country greats like Waylon Jennings, Freddie Fender, Johnny Cash, and the Statler Brothers. I often saw him on TV, which was exciting, but when he was home it could be either great or awful. I looked forward to his coming home; sometimes I felt regret when he was there. Eventually, he left the band. From the 1980s on, he ended up doing fifteen years in prison for numerous arrests for controlled substances and DWIs.

I haven't talked to or seen my dad in over twenty years, but he still occasionally haunts my memories. Sometimes he is still over my shoulder. I have many unanswered questions for him. He couldn't break the cycles of drugs and violence, and the world had no support or use for him. I have had to learn from his mistakes. He taught me what I didn't want to become as a man, rather than how to become a man.

Children of Tragic Histories

The railroad tracks about fifty yards from my house. It crossed the mostly dry drainage creek carved out of limestone bedrock. For kids in the neighborhood, the creek was a place of endless wonder, with its pockets of water where frogs, small fish, and snakes lived. I spent a lot of time down there exploring or playing, building tree houses, and digging out the fossils in the rocks. I also spent lots of time putting things on the train tracks to be flattened by the constant trains. I knew many of the kids in the black neighborhood on the other side of the creek. We often met at the creek for adventures, sat nearby in school, or swam at the city pool down the road in the summertime.

When I was about eight, my cousin Richard and I were walking in the middle of the dry creek when we were surrounded by a group of young teenagers from the black neighborhood, some of whom I had known for years. They circled around us, gathering rocks in their hands, and began to yell at us, throwing the rocks and kicking us to the ground. I had played with some of these kids for years and had never said anything derogatory to any of them.

They told us repeatedly that this was retaliation for what our ancestors did. As white kids, we were responsible for slavery and racism. We had to pay for making their grandparents slaves. I was hurt by the barrage, afraid for my life, and confused by their harsh words. I didn't have any idea what they were talking about. I barely had any understanding of black slavery at that age. I tried to defend myself by saying through my tears that no one in my family had owned slaves, but it didn't stop the bullying.

I was humiliated. I cried for them to stop. Finally one of the kids, my friend Maurice, who had tried to stop them earlier in the attack, finally got them to cease. He was my age and the smallest of them. He stood next to us, pleading with them, taking a chance on facing their wrath too. After a few minutes he got them to break their circle, allowing us to run away in the creek. As we left, they continued laughing, still hurling rocks toward us. I didn't see Maurice again until the next summer, at the swimming pool. I thanked him for standing up for us.

The profound effect of this event on me could never be overstated. The degradation scarred me for years. I didn't tell anyone about it until I was in my teens. As a child, it had forged anger and shame; as I got older, that gave way to wanting to understand. Why had those kids been so angry at white people? In my young mind they were just wrong, confused. As an adult I learned of the legacies of slavery, degradation, and intimidation wrought on whole populations based on skin color and economics. It didn't excuse the brutality of that day, but it eventually gave me a context in which to understand it. My wounds of disgrace, as deep and painful as they have been, only served as a taste of the bitterness that the world had poured on these kids and their families. I would have been angry too.

Where Was Jane?: Abortion and the "Religious Right"

> A bullet came to visit a doctor in his one safe place,
> a bullet ensuring the right to life . . .
> And the blood poured off the pulpit,
> the blood poured down the picket lines . . .
> —Ani DiFranco, "Hello Birmingham"

Sometimes painful decisions in our lives steer us into unknown trajectories that break with what we think we know about the world. At seventeen, my high school girlfriend accidentally got pregnant. Like most terrified teenagers to whom this happens, we didn't have any experience and couldn't rely on our parents for counsel or money. She was always steadfastly certain from our first days together that she would have an abortion if she got pregnant. I supported her and her decision, but the reality was still painful for us. We were both budding atheists still breaking from the religious baggage that permeates the South, but questions still lingered. Were we morally corrupt? Would we be sorry? We were the first generation to grow up in the light of *Roe v. Wade*, even as the conservative climate was rapidly beginning to cast its shadow.

Operation Rescue, the zealous national Christian fundamentalist anti-choice organization based in Dallas, was at the height of its power. They terrified us. They often had huge crowds of people block clinic access and protest at doctors' homes across the country. I used to see them at residences near my school with their bloody signs. When we finally chose a clinic, it was ironically in a building where Jane Roe of *Roe v. Wade* (who had become a born-again Christian) had an office across the hall, and was spending time trying to "save" people. A man in a bulletproof vest led us through a small, self-righteous crowd into a highly secure area. The swirl of it all added greatly to the sadness and anxiety we were already feeling. I hadn't cared for the god worshipped by Operation Rescue before, but now I was afraid of religious bigots and what they might do. Their actions didn't shame us. We carried on with our uneasy decisions. Their hatred fueled my desire to struggle against people with narrow and unreasonable views. It also underpinned my lifelong support of the right of women to make decisions about their own bodies and lives.

Rearview Mirror

Violence, drug addiction, alcoholism, and imprisonment were rampant in my extended family and community. I watched their combination ruin many lives. It seemed normal. This is the way it was in most families I knew, except the ones on TV.

Drugs and alcohol were established coping mechanisms that we used to fight the alienation in our lives. I was arrested for smoking weed at thirteen, and at fifteen I began to experiment with harder drugs like cocaine, meth, and LSD. It seemed like the thing to do. Nancy Reagan's "Just Say No" slogan was useless. It was a pathetic joke from an out-of-touch government.

I remember my final physical confrontation with my dad. It was the last time I tried to stop him from beating my mother. I must have been around thirteen years old. He towered over her, hitting her as she lay on the bed; I clumsily stepped between them, fists clenched. For a moment he and I grabbed each other. He had always kept a loaded revolver in the top of his bedroom drawer; we both remembered it. We looked at the drawer in the scuffle, and I thought of reaching for it, though I had only shot it once in my life and it scared me tremendously. In his crazed state, he was capable of anything. I feared for our lives. The standoff passed and neither of us reached for the gun. He finally pushed me out of the way and left the room. My mom and I grabbed a few things, left with no money, and never went back. I always felt small and powerless against my dad, even though my mother told me years later that I had made him stop by doing what I had done.

That feeling of powerlessness haunted me for years as a teenager. The early violence in my life shaped the way I have almost always sided with the most vulnerable. I always knew I had to intervene, though I didn't always know how.

Seeing nothing good come from the violence and fear in our house, I grew up to be a pacifist, rejecting anger and avoiding violence completely. I thought that reason, negotiation, and nonviolent methods could overcome in any confrontation. I learned to use words to negotiate and deescalate conflicts. In some ways, I went too far in the other direction. I became too passive about stopping violence when I should have. I gave the power of violence to others without question, and thought I was above it all.

Meanwhile, something gnawed at me. I wanted to get away from this dead-end life. One fall, I enrolled in a school/work program that allowed me to leave school early and work while getting full credit. At seventeen I became a full-time stocker at a department store, and then the night stock manager. Working in the adult world, I saw more clearly the nature of the bullshit I had to deal with at school, the petty power plays and demeaning behaviors of students and faculty. I decided to change my situation.

In open defiance of my family, I followed my intuition to quit high school. I wasn't absolutely clear why. Many in my extended family had never made it past the eighth grade. I would have been the first to graduate. Instead, I left to get my GED in the face of great disappointment. My school counselor and teachers said that I would end up a loser at a dead-end job. I already had one of those jobs. Somehow, I knew it wouldn't be like that forever. I had to leave my hometown or die.

I began to openly question the assumptions that pervaded my life, thinking as critically as I could about my world. Wide-eyed, I was opening new doors. It was daunting and liberating. I began to walk a high wire between my gut instincts and what others thought I should do with my life. I just knew some things were not right, no matter what others say. I started to discover that my personal liberty and social responsibility often seemed to counter majority wisdom.

I always sensed that there were inequalities around me but didn't have the words to describe them. I had no understanding of what complexities kept my family, neighbors, and many others marginalized, what kept us in our places. To us these systems had no visible forms. They kept us separated and scraping by, hidden from each other, and therefore isolated and diminished in our own corners of the world. I watched backs and wills broken, with only the splinters of families left. From our births to our deaths, someone else tried to define our worlds. How had this happened?

I decided to escape from this place. I wanted to burn the bridges and never look back. I believed it was my time to realize my potential on my own terms. I didn't have to let anyone define me or box me in. I decided I would rather flounder under my own will than be stifled under others' rules. I ran toward my future and practiced hiding parts of my past, reinventing myself in my language, manners, dress, and interests. I didn't want to be poor, and I didn't want people to know that was my background.

I now know that I can never forget this past, even if it is painful. It is part of me; these are my roots. As I have stated, I believe that everything that has happened to us in our lives affects us in our present situation and our future choices. So I need to remember where I come from. I don't have to dwell on it, but if I forget my history then I will be part of civil society forgetting its history too. That amounts to allowing our history to be written by others, by those who want to maintain the beliefs that everyone is doing just fine and that the poor should pick themselves up by their damn bootstraps.

Rockets' Red Glare

> Buddy you're a boy make a big noise
> Playin' in the street gonna be a big man some day
> You got mud on your face. You big disgrace
> Kickin' your can all over the place
> Buddy you're a young man hard man
> Shoutin' in the street gonna take on the world some day
> You got blood on your face. You big disgrace
> Wavin' your banner all over the place
>
> —Queen, "We Will Rock You"

I became socially and politically aware in the 1980s, during the presidency of that scary, cartoonish man, Ronald Reagan. I grew up fearing nuclear war with the Soviet Union, or that Reagan would accidentally push "the button" and cook us all. Economist Robert Lekachman said this about him at the time: "Ronald Reagan must be the nicest president who ever destroyed a union, tried to cut school lunch milk rations, and compelled families in need of public help to first dispose of household goods in excess of $1,000 . . . If there is an authoritarian regime in the American future, Ronald Reagan is tailored to the image of a friendly fascist." [6]

Reagan and his cronies seemed to relish power and fear as they waged undeclared wars on women, unions, the poor, immigrants, and small nations in Central America. Many of the warmongers of his cabinet would raise their ugly heads again and have seats at the table in George W. Bush's presidency.

Music saved my life during those days, showing me a way out of the life I was living. Without the exposure music gave me to cultural and political information, I would have been at a dead end. I gained access to shared emotions and thoughts that kept me from feeling alienated and isolated.

I had grown up listening to country music and later bloated album rock. Then punk and new wave hit. I was on the outer edges of the small Dallas punk scene, seeing bands like T.S.O.L., Agnostic Front, and Suicidal Tendencies; it didn't speak to my angst. My early political education and exposure came rather from the industrial scene: bands like Disposable Heroes of Hiphoprisy, Einstürzende Neubauten, Test Dept., Consolidated, Skinny Puppy, and Ministry. The combination of clanging metal and industrial beats and the political lyrics inspired me more than fast guitars.

One day, back in high school, I had read an article by Al Jourgensen of Ministry, describing what he called working-class and blue-collar issues. His descriptions of neighborhoods and environments sounded just like my life. It was the first time I had concepts that related to what I had felt, and that exposed the differences between the American dream and my family's actuality. I was so excited that I could not wait to tell my mom when she came home from work. When I explained it to her, she dismissed it as not relating to us. I knew she was wrong. I knew I was working-class. But I was supposed to hate it and pretend otherwise.

After quitting high school, I attended college in a nearby town for a few months due to pressure from my family. I learned a lot being there. Theater and art shows, late night discussions on politics, religion, and philosophy, and some acid trips: the entire curriculum expanded my thinking.

Small glimpses into political worlds of protest opened up. I was becoming more conscious, wanting to be a part of something. I joined the local chapter of Amnesty International, writing letters to political prisoners. It was my first contact with the concepts of political prisoners and prisoners of conscience. I had naively assumed that all prisoners were people who had been caught doing something illegal, like some in my family. It was shocking that people were imprisoned because of their political beliefs or actions. I wrote letters with a passion, but I wanted to do more. I learned of Steve Biko, Nelson Mandela, the African National Congress, and the struggle against apartheid in South Africa. I joined the burgeoning antiapartheid movement and attended my first marches and demonstrations. I was enthralled with the power we found together as people taking to the streets.

Chanting, marching, and listening to the speeches was liberating. I felt we could move mountains. I had thought this had only happened in the 1960s. It was spontaneous, angry, irreverent—and fun! Although I was not yet finished writing letters to power-brokers, I knew that this was what I really wanted to be part of. At one rally, I listened raptly to a reverend making an impassioned plea to end apartheid and racism abroad as well as on our own soil. I discovered that he had been one of the Black Panther Party leaders in Dallas—yet another moment when a member of the Black Panthers influenced me.

Eyes Wide Open

> In the east where the bear is dancing
> in the west where the eagle flies
> in the middle we stand our ground
> while the false leaders pull us down
>
> —Ministry, "We Believe"

In early 1988, my mom maxed her only credit card so we could see parts of Europe. It was her lifelong dream, even if she had to pay for it for the next five years. For me, at twenty-one, it was a chance to shop my band's demo tapes to record labels and to explore what I perceived to be more developed politics and culture.

The governments of Ronald Reagan and Margaret Thatcher held power over the globe, leaving me feeling like an ugly American, fearing that people wouldn't separate me from "my" government. I was fortunate to travel to Europe before corporate globalization came to dominate the culture, with McDonalds and Starbucks on every corner. Regionalism and cultures were fragile but still in place. The Berlin Wall still stood, a reminder of the Cold War.

In four months, I never got a record deal, but I did get a crash course that transformed me into a more politically educated American. I was taken by the beauty of European culture and history. I met wonderful fellow travelers along the way. Throughout Europe, I learned firsthand about the differences between terrorists and freedom fighters. I was almost a random casualty of right-wing terrorists on a train in Italy! In Spain and Ireland, I saw people celebrate their indigenous culture while struggling for their autonomy against a government that wanted them dead and forgotten. In London, I made a pilgrimage to the overgrown Highgate Cemetery where Karl Marx was entombed, and was then swept up in the largest demonstrations I had ever seen: two hundred thousand people of Middle Eastern descent marching against Saddam Hussein's gassing of Kurds in Iraq.

I saw the dirty realities of dilapidated structures, barbed-wired walls, and the military presence. I learned firsthand that our government lied, as I pierced through the veil of the Iron Curtain or walked the streets of living apartheid in strife-torn Belfast, Northern Ireland. In Berlin I saw the beauty within the walls of the Bauhaus Museum and was trapped in an exhilarating three-way riot between hundreds of skinheads, police, and football fans. It gave me my first taste of flying teargas, bottles, batons, and shields. The American privilege I assumed meant nothing in a hail of debris. I met the challenge like a true revolutionary—by hiding in the bushes nearby.

Seeing what the power of people could do in these places, as well as engaging in conversations on the larger political world with strangers had profound effects. These experiences brought me to dissect complicated social and political issues in ways I never could have from my bedroom. Disjointed information became clearer. With eyes wide open, I saw the brutality, corruption, and neglect that governments were capable of. In my travels I learned that people in the Middle East, Northern Ireland, or Berlin were not my enemies; they wanted many of the same things we did.

My travels in the late 1980s were at the beginning of the Information Age, before TV became as globalized and immediate as it is now. CNN was just getting its legs, and the Internet was hidden in academia and the military. Sharing international culture and life was not yet instant. I had never known anyone to travel to or from some of the places I went. I wished they could have; we would have had less fear of the Other.

Unity of Oppression

> There is no America! There is no Democracy! There is only IBM, and ITT, and AT&T, and DuPont, Dow, Union Carbide, and Exxon. These are the nations of the world today.
>
> —From the 1976 film *Network*

Returning home, I decided to promote political ideas and move people to action through music. It had affected me profoundly; maybe I could do the same for others. From the late 1980s until the early '90s I cofounded and fronted two political industrial-techno bands, Lesson Seven and Audio Assault. We had songs produced by MC 900 Ft. Jesus and Kurt Harland of Information Society. We toured with bands such as Nine Inch Nails and Skinny Puppy and performed often with Ministry, Consolidated, Meat Beat Manifesto, and others. It was our platform for tabling and talking about social justice at our shows. Many of the industrial bands at that time highlighted social issues, and their music had influenced me to dig deeper. Now we were touring together, spreading the word.

To overcome my callow analysis, I needed more information. I began reading more, trying to make sense of social, environmental, economic, and international politics. I started with Noam Chomsky, who I found dense and academic. But it was a book called *Friendly Fascism: The New Face of Power in America*, by economist Bertram Gross, that clarified the emerging corporate globalization take over. It helped me understand why jobs had left my home town, why families were sleeping in cars under bridges all over Dallas, and how U.S. international policy was shaped by money.

Gross described an emerging global system he called "friendly fascism" (what we now call neoliberalism). He painted a picture in which undemocratic international corporations were beginning to have more influence over governments, and in which people were willingly giving up their rights and power, not through the traditional fascism of brute military force, but through economic persuasion. "Democracy" and "freedom" had become commodities like everything else in the hands of big business. Emerging multinational corporations were engaging in even more intense domination of the environment, people, and animals than the colonial empires they were replacing.

In 1988, I became a vegetarian. Animal rights was a central issue to me for ethical and environmental reasons. I had come to see animals not as commodities, like cars or houses, but as sentient beings to be treated as such. I had felt this innately all my life. Animal rights also brought into focus other questions about the sometimes invisible, because apparently normal, oppression of women in civil society. I discovered the writings of Carol Adams and Marty Kheel, which helped me connect feminist ideas to animal liberation and ecological struggles. More dangerous ideas! More affronts to what was accepted as normal in the South in the late 1980s!

My band continued traveling, distributing literature, and raising money for a variety of groups from town to town. I spoke from the stage about many issues that I now saw as connected: women's liberation, animal rights, racism, the AIDS epidemic, and the U.S. war machine. The hours were grueling and long, but I felt I wanted to help educate people to take action for lasting change, even if I was unsure of what that would be. I thought that we could protest and vote our way to a better world if everyone got educated on the issues. It was standard old-school organizing. By morally outraging people, we could bring them to act, which meant making an appeal to Power to make changes.

Exit Stage Left

In 1992, after seven years of shows and touring, I left the music industry. It was too much industry and not enough music—or steady income. By this time I had been in a relationship with Ann Harkness for years. We were raising her son Milo together while living back in East Dallas in my childhood barrio. It was now largely a Chicano and Latino neighborhood, along with a decreasing black population, the last of the white people who had moved there in the 1940s, and a few younger white couples like us. It was still a poor, working-class community. I was glad to be back; it felt like home. The daycare I had attended was still there too, transformed into a much-needed private school for low-income kids with good educational foundations. It was still run by former Panthers and Young Patriots.

I got into the antiques business and eventually cofounded a cooperatively run antique store in 1995. We shared our resources and labor equally. The collaborative efforts I had learned at the Montessori school followed me into my business practices: share and take care of each other.

Ann and I were lifelong cultural and political radicals. We were raising a son together while never needing the recognition of the state or religion in our union. We home-schooled Milo. But I still felt pressure to do better financially than my family had done. I wanted to attain middle-class status and have some nice things. I didn't think I was chasing the American dream; I wanted to be secure. I never wanted to be evicted again.

Panthers, Puppets, and Plastic

For all its plastic and concrete surfaces, Dallas is fairly racially and economically diverse. Unfortunately, aside from being known for killing the president in the 1960s and an insipid TV show in the 1970s, there is not much memory among many people about the place. Like other cities in the South, it was rocked by the civil rights movement and uprisings (or riots to some) of the 1960s and '70s.

In the 1990s, some radicals were employed by a self-described Quaker Sufi mystic named Johnny Wolf. He ran an odd theatrical prop business. He was hired to build backdrops for religious churches and for the kids' TV show *Barney*. With great irony he then turned around and used the money to fund social justice and community projects. I am lucky to have befriended people from Dallas's earlier radical movements in Johnny's shop, including former members of the Black Panther Party, the Brown Berets, the Southern Christian Leadership Conference, and the Weather Underground.

From 1971 to 1976, the Dallas chapter of the Black Panther Party was one of the most active in the country. During this time, the Dallas chapter, like many, operated free breakfast and pest control programs, citizen police patrols, a liberation school, and a tenant information center, among other projects. They worked with Chicano and white groups to serve the people and resist the brutality and racism of the old South. Many of the former members still carried on the struggle in different ways. I treasured the chance to get to know these former Panthers in Johnny's shop. It was a great setting for dialogues, and I listened and learned. Their long-term commitments and energy gave me hope.

Through them I came to a deeper understanding of the interconnected systems of oppression around race, gender, and class. It was an informal education based on listening and talking with people. This is a style of learning I have been drawn to and have grown comfortable with over the years. I love to hear stories. These revolutionaries had dedicated their lives to resisting oppression and willingly shared their knowledge of their histories. I didn't idolize them, but I held them in high regard for their commitments and actions.

Their mentorship also taught me the importance of knowing your history. It isn't just black or brown people who have had their histories stolen. To some degree, all of us have. These brothers and sisters exposed me to the antiracist politics that drove the work of slavery abolitionist John Brown, and the Weather Underground. They showed me that whites, blacks, and Latinos from all economic backgrounds had worked together for social justice and still could, even in Dallas! It was in dialogue with them that I learned that my preschool had been run by members of the BPP, Brown Berets, the Young Lords, and the Young Patriots.

For four years, I helped Charles Hillman and Skip Shockley, along with other former Panthers, to organize the Malcolm X Day Festival. I learned to value the background role I had in their efforts. I also learned the importance of being consistent in my commitments to people who had been deserted by so-called white leaders, even radical ones, all their lives.

I could never have learned these histories and this analysis in school. This experience radicalized me. The threads in my journey to understand the world began to come together. The tapestry of liberation gained strength. I was further developing a deeper antiracist analysis and beginning to realize that the systems of politics, economics, and culture that the state and the rich controlled couldn't be voted away. I started to see the status quo and civil society differently. I began to ask different questions. The political rhetoric I had heard all my life now sounded different. I understood state power and violence differently. Power—whether it was the rich, the military, or government bureaucracies—could only be appealed to for minor adjustments to its systems. The centralization of wealth and control in the hands of the few had to be abolished. The symptoms that caused these problems would never be eliminated if we only played by their rules. We needed to stop asking for handouts and build our own power from the grassroots, block by block.

An Anarchist in Texas

> Jasper: I remember the time the Wobblies . . .
> Mack: Wobblies!
> Jasper: You said one big union!
> Mack: Yes, one big union . . . but we ain't annarkists an' we don't believe in violence. No weapons, no force unless you're attacked.
> —Langston Hughes, *Harvest*

In the late 1990s I met Gene Akins, an old anarchist and lifelong member of the Industrial Workers of the World. A Wobbly. He had done time for drugs in the notorious Angola Prison in Louisiana during the 1960s, then had gotten clean and worked for social, environmental, and economic justice pretty much since then. He was a cantankerous agitator with a big heart who focused on community organizing, especially with recovering addicts. Gene shared with me what he called the real history of the IWW. He turned me on to books and pamphlets about the principles of anarchism that demonstrated how personal liberty was tied to collective struggles for justice. He emphasized repeatedly how many in the IWW struggles had been anarchists.

Like the former Panthers, he gave me tools to organize across cultural boundaries. He would say that if you want people without cars or phones to participate, then you help them to participate. I rode around with him in his old van picking up people to drag to meetings and rallies of all sorts. If they had no phone, then we went to check on them. If their electricity was cut off, he helped them get through that month. He was far from wealthy. He showed me the value of supporting people's self-sufficiency.

Through our conversations, I moved deeper into anarchist thinking. Gene was a street philosopher who loved dialectics. We debated and discussed ideas like mutual aid, cooperation, direct action, and dual power. He stressed the idea of "little 'a' anarchism." It was not a dogma; it was freedom of thought. For the first time, anarchy took on a positive meaning in my life.

I had flirted with State Communism and socialism. I had seen the failure of the Soviet Union firsthand in East Berlin. But even after that, I still held Communist-leaning beliefs, largely from lack of exposure to information, and because most of the other older radicals I respected had come from Communist or socialist backgrounds. Gene helped me understand why "big 'C' Communism" had failed. Power, centralized and monopolized by the state, will always fail regular people.

I started calling myself an anarchist. Gene often said, "If it describes you or your actions, just claim the damn thing!" To him, it was a badge of honor, like being a Wobbly. I came to see it as an opening to possibilities rather than a label to box myself in with. I was already doing and thinking many of these things innately. It was a moment of clarity, a political and philosophical homecoming. Anarchism was a cluster of living ideas that spoke on many levels, politically and philosophically, about us as individuals and our collective struggles. Gene and I didn't always agree on everything, but we had good debates and tried out ideas on each other.

Anarchism became the integrated framework I engaged and grew from. Gene had provided the spark for this revolutionary path. In my early years of claiming anarchism, I would spend a lot of time explaining what it was, while dispelling the falsehoods about it in political circles. It was liberating to know others thought and felt in similar ways when the practicalities of anarchism were explained. Part of Texas's unknown history includes anarchist agitators like Robert Owen, Lucy Parsons, Ross Winn, and the Flores Magón brothers. This history and these ideas resonated in my head as well as in my heart. I firmly believe people have the power to make decisions locally and cooperatively. Anarchism is how that is put into practice.

Black Flags and Windmills

Just then they came in sight of thirty or forty windmills that rise from that plain. And no sooner did Don Quixote see them that he said to his squire, "Do you see over yonder, friend Sancho, thirty or forty hulking giants? I intend to do battle with them and slay them . . . for this is a righteous war and the removal of so foul a brood from off the face of the earth is a service . . ."

"What giants?" asked Sancho Panza.

"Those you see over there," replied Don Quixote, "with their long arms. Some of them have arms well nigh two leagues in length."

"Take care, sir," cried Sancho. "Those over there are not giants but windmills . . ."

—Miguel de Cervantes, *Don Quixote*

You're not your job. You're not how much money you have in the bank. You're not the car you drive. You're not the contents of your wallet . . . You're not your fucking khakis.

—Chuck Palahniuk's Tyler Durden, from *Fight Club*

The twentieth century was rapidly winding down. As fear-mongers waited in bunkers for the Y2K apocalypse, I ran toward the global tumult: I hoped for new openings for change where false borders and wars to defend them might grow fainter, where even nation-states might cease to exist. I ran toward where hope grew, where corporations didn't rule and where people were rising up to plant the seeds of better worlds.

I was still part of a successful cooperative antique business. We were featured in architectural magazines and sold expensive furniture to celebrities, museums, and rich people. I was writing a bimonthly column for a national furniture magazine, but my interest in maintaining it began to wane. In the late 1990s, I had been devoting more time to local and national social justice issues. I had committed myself to full-time organizing *and* continued running a business. The worlds of business and activism I was traversing were beginning to separate much more than they had in previous years. For example, on numerous occasions I had protested against Neiman Marcus, one of our biggest customers, for selling fur. They threatened to boycott, causing uproar within our shop. I didn't step back; I kept up the organizing, promising to keep it out of the store. I made sure the heat was directed on me. After a few months of ignoring their pressure, their business returned as if nothing had happened. They had no principles.

In those days, I walked a tightrope from which I fell many times. Our living situation had also grown more communal over the years. We went from a small family to a household with roommates and projects in an affluent neighborhood. This made us odd ducks to many of our longtime neighbors and business friends. It began to dawn on me that I no longer wanted to straddle both worlds.

I began to grasp how wrapped up in the system I was: the house, the car, the loans, all the trappings that make what we call comfortable, liberal, middle-class lives. I knew better. I didn't have a boss, could donate money, go to rallies, eat organics, and take eco-vacations, but I only challenged the underlying relations of oppression in small, isolated ways. I often felt like an impostor when I compared myself to my neighbors and knew I was moving toward something different.

I had grown tired of figuring out how to make money first and everything else second. I wanted to focus solely on how to solve social problems directly. The "hulking giants" of capitalism didn't rest on the horizon anymore. I was running at them, in quixotic optimism, with black flags waved high.

Aiming at Shadows

Two pivotal events stripped bare the contrast between my diverging lives. The first came during the spring of 1999, when an FBI agent from the domestic terrorism office in Ft. Worth came to my shop. He questioned me about animal rights vandalism in front of my partners. This was the first time I had heard of environmental and animal issues being related to terrorism. The Animal Liberation Front didn't kill people, so to me they were not terrorists. They were militants who used nonviolent sabotage against industry. The agent intimated repeatedly that I was involved in attacks on local fur stores. Then he put the pressure on, asking if I would help them out by giving information on animal rights extremists within any group I worked with. Shaken, I respectfully declined. What had happened at those stores was vandalism, not terrorism. It felt like the secret police of some old Communist Guard had just dropped by to warn or recruit me. It was the first time, of many to come, that I was harassed by the FBI for taking socially conscious action. My business partners, who were not activists, were astonished at what had just transpired in our shop. I was embarrassed, angry, and full of unanswered questions.

The second event happened a couple of years later. I returned from an organizing trip to Washington, D.C., where I was on September 11, 2001. I hurriedly coorganized a peace rally to protest reactionary violence against local Middle Eastern communities and the bombing of Afghanistan. This rally was a desperate public action to a dire situation where people I knew were under attack. In retaliation, bricks were thrown through the window of our shop, and I received death threats at work.

That was enough for my partners. We all worked well together and enjoyed the freedom of being a co-op, but they were comfortable with the status quo, letting the wheels of democracy grind slowly from election cycle to election cycle. I was doing more. My views were more radical: my consciousness had shifted from voting for change to fighting for change. These events showed me it was time to make major adjustments.

Stray lines from a Talking Heads song played over and over in my head:

And you may ask yourself: What is that beautiful house?
And you may ask yourself: Am I right? Am I wrong?
And you may ask yourself: Well, how did I get here?
And you may say to yourself: My god, what have I done?

I started making plans on how to exit that life while reaching for something truly aligned with my values and principles.

Leaving my business wasn't just quitting a job. It was leaving my security, my ego, and families who all interdependently counted on each other. We sold our business in 2001. Ann and I made a plan to relocate to Austin. Around the same time, she left her advertising job. In a way, I had returned to the uncommitted path I had embarked on when I was younger. But now I had the analysis and perspective to dig in and fight harder.

Through years of organizing, I found that I wanted to get to the root causes of change, not just the single issues that are often the focus within activism. Bandele Tyehima, an old-school black socialist revolutionary, once said to me that if you want to improve people's lives, you can't help people one by one. You have to change the systems that create these situations.

I was learning how to work on issues within the larger alternative glo-balization framework, which included *everything*: people, the environment, and animals. "Framework," a word I had never heard outside the context of carpentry, became a way to interpret every problem as I worked toward solutions. The alternative globalization movements and the influence of the Zapatistas fit my growing anarchist views. Both depict the world and its elements as connected. Oppression of one means oppression of all; I have worked to develop practices that reflect that.

Furious Seasons

The only limit to the oppression of government is the power with which the people show themselves capable of opposing it.

—Errico Malatesta

To return to the late 1990s, in Dallas and Austin at that time I rapidly cofounded, affiliated with, and participated in numerous, sometimes overlapping, groups. I engaged in political education and action in a wide context, addressing issues of forest and environmental defense, immigra-tion, living wage, prisons, and the death penalty, police brutality, animal rights, white supremacy, and war.

I traveled across the country, working professionally for Greenpeace, and the Ruckus Society. Locally I worked in Texas for the Ralph Nader cam-paign, ACORN, and Rainforest Action Network. I attended major political convergences and participated in smaller actions. In between, I traveled to cities all over Texas, helping smaller groups with their projects and in developing better organizing tools. Through these engagements, I was able to help build cohesive networks to engage in street actions.

It had taken a lot to get to this point in my life. Ann and I had sacrificed security and comfort. I was in my thirties, she was in her early forties, and our son, Milo, was now a young man. He left for Northern California to work on forest defense with Earth First! and to be on his own for the first time.

Since 1985, I had moved within political systems and outside of them, from national and international groups to small community and affinity groups. I tried every tactic I knew of, from voting locally to direct action. I carried puppets, ran in black blocs, chained myself to objects, and built blockades of all types to stop business as usual. I hung off tall buildings with banners, sat in tree platforms, gathered petitions, wrote letters, wore suits, and gave testimony on issues while visiting electoral and corporate representatives, all to change the minds of decision-makers.

I was growing weary of shady nonresponsive electoral politics, but I helped build the emerging Green Party in Texas. At the time I felt that the Greens had the potential to move beyond voting: I wanted to build a movement wing within the party. I will even admit that I voted for Ralph Nader! It was the first and last time I voted. I caught hell for it but have no regrets.

Working on a living wage campaign (first with the Greens, then for ACORN) was the end of my illusions about electoral politics. Behind the scenes, very modest proposals were eroded down to nothing to appease business interests or politicians' fears, and those who needed the support were cast aside. I was sick of electoral politics and parted ways with it to focus on a radical culture shift.

Watching the organizing against the World Trade Organization meetings in Seattle in 1999, I saw the ascension of anarchist ideas to the forefront in an all-encompassing web of movements against globalization or "friendly fascism," as Gross had called it. That people from indigenous communities and labor, environmentalist and anti-corporate movements had gathered in one of the largest protests in the United States to challenge these undemocratic, secret, and powerful financial institutions received barely any attention from the mainstream media—until some anarchists put bricks through the windows of corporate stores. The property destruction didn't solve the problems, but it became front-page news. Undemocratic institutions like the WTO and World Bank were in the limelight, and anarchy had its coming-out party, spawning an anarchist renaissance in the United States. It was clear that I needed to get back to full-time political organizing.

In the spring of 2000, Milo and I attended the World Bank/IMF protests in Washington, D.C. We wanted to be in the exciting resurgence of people in the streets inspired by the growing alternative globalization movement. The experience of being unlawfully jailed and pepper-sprayed, sitting on blockades in the streets, and the teach-ins and camaraderie all reinforced my convictions. I left D.C. with more determination than ever to fight unjust systems.

Upon returning, Ann and I cofounded a collectively run organization and a collective house called UPROAR (United People Resisting Oppression and Racism).[7] It was our first attempt at building a group with an anarchist horizontal structure. We were the only direct-action group that had operated in Dallas in years.

We used nonviolent direct action and education within an anti-oppression, anti-globalization, and anti-capitalist framework. It was our attempt at anarchist praxis, from how we shared power within our organization to the way we framed our political actions. We addressed issues using the resources of larger national groups, who hired us to do actions for their campaigns; this, in turn, funded our local work. We also provided support to low-income groups of people of color, including former Panthers.[8]

UPROAR soon joined The Continental Direct Action Network (CDAN). It was the first explicitly nationwide anarchist network I had ever participated in. We were the only group from the South. I was able to learn valuable skills and network with great people through that project. In its short but bright life, UPROAR was influential in effecting new strategies behind the scenes of the antiglobalization movement. For a while, it worked very well. But UPROAR took on too many projects without enough resources. There were too many emergency actions and not enough planning for the future. It ended in flames, but we all drew lessons from the ashes, taking them to other groups.

From 2000 to 2003, I participated in Stop Huntingdon Animal Cruelty (SHAC), a highly controversial but extremely effective militant campaign to stop animal testing. It was like nothing before it in the animal rights movement. SHAC incorporated anarchist practices of decentralization and direct action within a campaign framework. It focused on the executives behind the corporation, holding them responsible for their decisions while raising the economic costs of business as usual. It got so bad for the corporation that they couldn't trade on the stock exchange, find investors, or buy toilet paper. Huge multinational corporations were afraid of our actions.

Unsurprisingly, the state and private security forces reacted harshly. Many individuals faced high levels of repression, including friends of mine who eventually went to prison for conspiracy to commit crimes under the rubric of "terrorism." During my involvement, I was strong-armed by lawyers and threatened by armed private security, as well as the FBI.

With the rising tide of committed individuals focusing on social change in Texas, some of us perceived a need for regional trainings for activists and community organizers to build skills and develop campaign strategies. Rene Feltz and I cofounded the Radical Encuentro Camp modeled on trainings offered by the Ruckus Society or Greenpeace that drew more from anarchist underpinnings. Each of the camps, held all over Texas roughly twice a year, drew hundreds of participants. Beyond the skills trainings, they are also gatherings where people from different places share their struggles and ideas.

Since my time with Amnesty International, it has been my goal to free political prisoners and prisoners of conscience. I have also worked to abolish prisons and the death penalty. Members of the BPP have always been there to guide me. Among them are Robert King and his two comrades, Albert Woodfox and Herman Wallace, known as the Angola 3. In the early 1970s, they were members of a Black Panther Party chapter at Angola Prison in Louisiana. With the complicity of the FBI, they were targeted by prison officials and put into solitary confinement longer than anyone in modern U.S. history.

Soon after King was released in 2001, Ann befriended him, becoming one of the main advocates for the Angola 3. Eventually, we all became family. Our support of the A3 connected us intimately to Louisiana, and specifically to New Orleans. There we formed many bonds with other activists, including Malik Rahim. Our support has ranged from working with King on his candy business to helping him write his autobiography. Ann and I coproduced a documentary film called *Angola 3: Black Panthers and the Last Slave Plantation* to help bring attention to their plight. The Angola 3, and all political prisoners are inspirations for holding on to your convictions against all odds.

In 2003, taking cues from my work on the SHAC campaign, I cofounded Dirty South Earth First!.[9] Our goal was to pressure the Maxxam Corporation, based in Houston, to stop deforesting the last remaining old growth redwoods. The DSEF! campaign was an attempt to escalate, in Texas, a struggle that had been going on for nearly twenty years in California. In this two-year campaign, we adapted many SHAC strategies, such as decentralization and militancy in language and actions. We took the struggle from the forest in California to the homes of Maxxam executives in Texas. None of this had been done before in the environmental movement. Longstanding executives stepped down, and some moved away; Maxxam finally began its withdrawal from the forest. We were criticized for our militancy, but our strategy brought about much-needed debate within radical environmental circles. Ultimately, despite our successes in forcing long-term decision-makers to step down, and further blemishing Maxxam's image in the local media, the campaign lost steam due to heavy state repression. The confrontational tactics weren't adopted by others.[10] Before it was over, we all parted company and I began to focus on other issues. In Austin, I joined Anti-Racist Action, a decentralized network of antifascist groups across North America that have effectively confronted white supremacists in public places since the Reagan years.

Our chapter focused on three goals: developing better horizontal organizing models within an antioppression framework; using direct action and self-defense as tactics; and building a militant street antifascist movement for liberation. We recruited mostly white youth, educating them on issues of race, class, sexuality, and gender. We defended abortion clinics, confronted white supremacists, and organized massive street mobilizations.

The militancy of the ARA network was something I had not seen outside of the animal rights movement. Their willingness to confront fascists of all stripes without relying on the approval of civil society or appealing to Power was impressive. ARA incorporated self-defense as a practice in its framework; for some of us, this meant arming ourselves. It only took a little history and some altercations to understand that this was important. White supremacists from Greensboro to Nevada had killed antifascist organizers over the years and our lives were being threatened in Austin. Though often cowards draped in thugs' clothing, they were not afraid to attack those they saw as their enemies. It was during this time that I learned to overcome my fear of guns. I purchased a rifle that I learned to trust and use well. I also developed my tactical analysis and practice of armed self-defense. I had come a long way from the fear of violence in my household to where I now stood. Armed self-defense was a necessity in our community.

Despite their best efforts, ARA as an organization inherited many old organizing models that perpetuated hierarchies of oppression and refused to address the problems this created across the network. Many in ARA could not see the problem with focusing on the small neo-Nazi threat, instead of the insidious forms oppression often takes, such as sexism. This led to one-dimensional struggles, where we weren't allies to marginalized or underserved peoples and lacked broader community support. There were times when it felt vanguardist. It was easier to get people to the gun range than to confront our organizing models. I left after four years. I believe ARA still has the capacity and framework to be one of the most effective anarchist militant organizations in the United States.

From I to We: Collective Liberation

These years transformed me. When I was knocked down, I got back up, even when I didn't want to. I learned from it. I savored the struggles, the learning, my comrades, the commitments we were making, and the velocity at which change was happening. I was engaged and alive for all of it. I have wanted to turn back. I have wanted to give up. I couldn't. I was too curious and too stubborn. I had to see how things turned out.

In my life, and in movements around the world, anarchist and cooperative ideas were in the ascendant. I realized that these were *our* days to do something. Social libertarian principles were taking root and multiple overlapping and interconnected movements grew from them. No one was the boss; no one was the leader. We would all do our part. Once I grasped that, I felt more stability, more strength. I didn't have to have *all* of the answers. I could be part of something, make mistakes, and learn from them as I went, because others were doing the same.

Power could not continue to hold us in place with either the carrot or the stick when we connected our commitment, time, creativity and materials. My belief in what we could do showed me that we didn't need some elected official or generous corporation to do the right thing. We could create change and resist the destruction that they wrought on the world. I felt joy and hope in all the possibilities we could continue to create, rebelling against their hallowed message that we should give up and give in.

I had to climb the hillside to see what was on the other side. Once I did, I saw the giants everywhere. I continued onward with curiosity and courage. I saw others doing the same and many of us walked together in mutual support. The giants that had seemed like overwhelming forces before began to look less daunting.

These furious seasons would inform my decisions in New Orleans in the autumn of 2005.

A Battle in Algiers

The very first question people in this country must ask in considering the question of revolution is where they stand in relation to the United States as an oppressor nation, and where they stand in relation to the masses of people throughout the world whom US imperialism is oppressing.

—The Weather Underground, from "You Don't Need a Weatherman to Know Which Way the Wind Blows"

On September 4, I was back home in Austin, resting uneasily. My first trip to New Orleans had drained me. I received a call from Malik Rahim, who, unknown to me, had also remained in New Orleans. The phone line crackled: ". . . we got racist white vigilantes driving around in pick up trucks terrorizing black people on the street. It's very serious. We need supplies and support." He and his neighbors were being harassed by armed white men and by the police. He had been interviewed for a piece that appeared in the *San Francisco Bay View* that explained his grim situation in detail.[11] Now he was on the phone because he had heard I was just in New Orleans looking for our mutual friend King. He hoped I would come back to New Orleans to give them support and use it as another opportunity to search for King.

Malik Rahim is a serious man with a broad smile and a big laugh. A former Black Panther, he was defense minister of the New Orleans chapter. He has continued to work for social justice since then. His life story has intertwined with those of the Angola 3. He and King had not only been Panthers together, they had also been childhood friends in the Algiers neighborhood.

After living in Oakland, California, for years, Malik had settled once again in Algiers. One of the oldest neighborhoods in New Orleans, it is situated across the Mississippi from the French Quarter. Malik had waited out the storm at his home there with a close friend named Sharon Johnson. While Katrina left massive damage in its wake, it did not flood his neighborhood. Malik had no electricity and no water, but his phone still worked. When he called, I knew it was critical to move quickly.

The Deluge

Since the first mission, I had been haunted by a story that King had related about a flood in a small town he lived in when he was young. His grandmother had gone to work, leaving the younger children (including King) in the care of the older ones. The story circled in my head and wouldn't let go; it now seemed like a painful prophecy.

> I remember a deluge: Water—seemingly with a desire for retribution—literally poured from the sky. And the water rose. More than three feet high, it covered our porch, and beyond . . . The land on our side of the highway was much lower than the other side, where whites lived . . . I began to inch my way toward the end of the porch. I really didn't intend to go off the porch . . . The water did the rest. It was polite enough to pull me right off the edge of the porch . . . Then, from what seemed like a mile away, I heard Mary yelling: "Oh look! Junior is drowning, Junior is drowning." They all hurried back as fast as they could, and pulled me to safety. I was numb with fear, but most grateful. I remember hearing William say: "We ain't goin' tell Mama about this, y'all hear?" Mama never found out . . .[12]

"All right," I said, "I'm going to go back there to deliver supplies and get to King." This was a chance to try again, to find out what had happened to my friend. I only knew that he had been trapped in his house, surrounded by dirty water, for eight or nine days. This man had been in solitary confinement for twenty-nine years in a six-by-nine-foot cell. I could not let him sit there any longer. I felt a duty to try and get to him—if he was still alive.

On my way out of Austin, I stopped at a meeting called by local activists who were organizing local aid for evacuees. I tearfully shared my stories and the frightening realities I had encountered. Then I asked if anyone in the circled crowd of sixty would come to New Orleans, knowing what might transpire. There were no takers. The prospect of potentially using arms provoked serious discussions. Some said it was crazy. Others who professed advocacy for armed self-defense made excuses for not going. My heart sank. Brandon and I would be the only ones heading tumultuously into the unknown on that trip. I left Austin disappointed, exhausted, and anxious.

As we traveled, I thought it over. I *knew* why people were not going. They could not grasp the immediate need, or the absolute destruction that had happened. I couldn't either, until I had arrived on that first trip. Now more uncharted waters lay ahead. I wondered if I had done a terrible job of communicating at the meeting. I think that fear was a major factor in people's decision not to go. I wondered: was I doing the right thing?

After the first trip to the Gulf, we both had a better idea of what to bring: water, food, candles, matches, ammunition, and guns. The first time, we were outgunned. Not this time. As I headed back, fear of what was about to happen crawled under my skin. I knew the situation was getting more desperate as time passed. Was a race war going to erupt? How many people had already died needlessly? In my first trip, I saw the disregard and lack of empathy that some white rescuers had shown to desperate people. It had made me deeply angry, but I had mostly kept my mouth closed. I was torn between doing the basic work of helping people, and espousing my political ideals in the face of ignorance.

I recalled a conversation with my *compañero* Greg Berger about Mexico City after the massive earthquake in 1985. He recounted that, in the early days, the state prioritized a return to law and order and minimizing negative media coverage instead of using its resources to get people to safety. When the people realized the state had failed them, they began to help each other to survive. This self-organization eventually led to the emergence of new grassroots movements. That moment catalyzed all the currents that had been underfoot. Would we be able to do the same here in the United States? Was New Orleans going to be ground zero? Brandon and I continued to drive.

Our truck sped along the highway, our thoughts in a tumult. Few cars moved our way, apart from the occasional military vehicle. In the other direction, the roadway was overflowing with evacuees. They began to look like refugees from another place. People were piled into and on top of vehicles, carrying with them the remnants of their lives; others walked alongside the roads. They were trying to go anywhere that was away from the inundation. On the radio, a voice repeated, "Order will be restored." But what people wanted to hear was that the government would do whatever it took to get everyone to safety. It was a modern-day exodus, caused by corruption and unresponsiveness. It didn't have to happen.

I asked myself, "What the hell am I getting into?"

We changed course to go along the lower southwestern coastal route, traveling into what increasingly resembled an occupied territory. We saw military vehicles and personnel at every turn. We had made doctored passes to get us past the bureaucracy we knew was already rearing its head; I wondered if they would work. The soldiers and officers only understood badges and uniforms; they wouldn't let civilians help. Many of the young soldiers looked stressed and distant as we closed in. They grilled us about why and where we were going. Half-truths got us through. After the last checkpoint, we drove headlong onto the empty causeway. I let out a sigh of relief. We were the only truck on the expansive concrete road above the city. When we reentered the empty city streets, we ignored the few useless stoplights that were working and headed to Malik's.

So Much Water Close to Home

> Within the war we are all waging with the forces of death, subtle and otherwise, conscious or not—I am not only a casualty, I am also a warrior.
>
> —Audre Lorde, "The Transformation of Silence into Language and Action"

Algiers is situated in an area called, ironically, the West Bank. Like the other West Bank halfway around the world, it is home to an apartheid system and two unequal populations. Before the storm, the West Bank was home to seventy thousand people. It had a largely poor and working-class black population and a small, wealthy white minority. People in positions of Power rendered the larger group invisible in daily life. Would a storm make it any different?

Huge housing projects and surrounding neighborhoods were already burned out or empty from neglect—and now, from the storm as well. There had been no social services for decades; when the last clinic had closed ten years earlier, it remained shuttered, as did many schools. Algiers was surrounded by massive concrete levees on the Mississippi sides. These levees had not given way, despite nearly being crushed by an enormous barge run aground by the storm. This was why it hadn't flooded, even though the river had swollen to the top of the levees. After the storm, most residents were gone, with only about three or four thousand remaining behind. Many were people who simply could not leave. They had no money, transportation, family support or were elderly and in ill health. The storm had made an already terrible situation worse.

The police command structures in Algiers were in shambles. There was scant military help. The city center, where the profitable businesses were, was the first priority for those in Power. They had to get New Orleans open for business; they neglected everything else. There were dead bodies on the ground. Buildings smoldered in flames. Like the rest of New Orleans, Algiers was only a remnant of its past self. It was isolated geographically and psychologically from the north side of the river and the eyes of the world.

What was called law enforcement at this stage was erratic and disorganized. It was made up of city, county, state, and some federal officers; mostly, it was Louisiana-based. If they had a plan (beyond acting like thugs with impunity) it had not yet been revealed. As in ordinary life, laws were enforced subjectively. There were different standards for middle-class whites and for everyone else, and the level of threats from officers varied widely in severity. They were accountable to no one but themselves. The military had set up heavily fortified military zones and checkpoints around the area, but nothing inside. Residents and anyone else were left to fend for themselves, sometimes against the police.

Trapped in this situation, cut off from the rest of New Orleans and the world, Malik Rahim, Sharon Johnson, and a few nearby neighbors struggled to provide basic aid to each other. They started with a rudimentary delivery of MREs (Meals Ready to Eat) and water provided by the military. They only had one busted-ass car, with precious little gas, along with what they could siphon from abandoned cars. To get anything you needed a vehicle and access to gas. Gas was not close by: you had to drive twenty-five miles to a remote military outpost, wait in a long line under armed security, and hope you would be let back into your community before the dusk curfew without being shot. The ordeal would take the whole day. There was no Red Cross, no FEMA. There were no other options.

Tableau of Violence

> The police are not here to create disorder. The police are here to preserve disorder.
>
> —Mayor Richard Daley (at a press conference defending police misconduct during the 1968 Democratic Convention)

Upon our arrival at Malik's, everyone pitched in to unload the supplies we had brought. Then Malik took us down the street to cover up a bullet-riddled corpse with a piece of sheet metal. The bloated, putrid body had been there for days. We could smell it as we approached. We hoped someone would come and get it soon. But was anyone looking for this man, unknown to any of us, including the kids who found him? His image haunts me among the string of deaths I encountered during my time in New Orleans. He met an ignoble death, left to decay on the sun-baked street. Death can be undignified, but I felt he deserved something more than to be forgotten.

Our first real accomplishment was establishing our own security, and that of the closest neighbors. As Malik had reported, something else had happened in the interim since our first arrival in New Orleans. While Power was in momentary crisis, white militias had formed in Algiers Point and in the French Quarter.

These vigilantes were barely more than an organized lynch mob. From the backs of their trucks, they stated that, in the absence of the police, it was their job to secure law and order. The militias in Algiers seemed to be made up of drunken fools and racists from Algiers Point, a small, very wealthy, white neighborhood that is about ten blocks long in each direction. It is part of the broader West Bank, which is overwhelmingly black and poor. Algiers Point was the only neighborhood on the West Bank where, traveling down the mostly abandoned streets, we saw signs like "You loot, we'll shoot" and "Your life ain't worth what's inside." Signs like these were put up by the vigilante types who stayed. It was as if the dam of civil society that kept them from acting out their most racist tendencies had broken enough to allow their hatred to emerge.

This white militia, acting in the role of a paramilitary, rode around armed in low-income black communities and meted out intimidation from the backs of their trucks. What they called defense amounted to harassment of any unarmed black person on the street. They acted tough, never offering to help anyone but whites. I found myself asking, "What kind of people are more interested in their private property and security than the well-being of another human?"

On principle, an armed group of people gathering to defend themselves in the absence of the state is something I am usually in favor of. Ultimately, though, in their racism they were no better than Klansmen straight out of the old Deep South. Our conflicting ideas of what community self-defense meant were on a collision course.

In the days just after the storm, the Algiers Point Militia openly threatened and possibly killed desperate unarmed civilians, foolishly bragging about their exploits to anyone who would listen. Local authorities, with their racist attitudes toward the communities they were supposed to protect, stood by and let this militia function. There were bullet-riddled bodies of black men in the street, including the one that we tried to get picked up for days while it continued to decompose. Who killed these men? Was it the vigilantes? Was it the police? Those corpses were on different streets, near nothing of value.[13]

On the streets of New Orleans, militias had killed people! They were accountable to no one. At this thought, anger arose in my heart. With each
shot, with each bullet, they had further shattered the veneer of justice.
According to the neighbors' stories, the vigilantes regularly drew their
guns on, and shot at, innocent people who were unarmed, poor, and black.
Malik said they mockingly called him "the mayor of Algiers," pointing guns
at him as they drove by, threatening to "get 'im." The police did nothing
but close their eyes to this, while continuing their own harassment. The
lines between authorities and thugs blurred, leaving everyone else with
nowhere to turn.

Undercurrents

From the moment I had set foot in Algiers and spoken with Malik and
Sharon, I realized that this was going to be a more difficult and more dangerous undertaking than anyone had thought. They were exhausted from
having to both struggle for survival and be vigilant about the militia and the
police. There had been no help. Although Algiers had not flooded, it had
been ravaged by the storm. The water was still high along the levees down
the block. Spirits were low in the streets, but there was some desperate
hope among the remaining residents. This had always been their home.
They didn't want to leave.

I had been here a few years before with Malik and King, who showed
me their old stomping grounds as young hustlers before they became
Black Panthers. Now trash and abandoned cars littered the empty streets
and vacant lots. When I arrived, passing the armed, sandbagged turrets
at the intersections, I asked myself what damage was new and what had
been that way for a long time. This place had been occupied by a police
force before. Now the outskirts were occupied by an army that watched
from bunkers without helping the people within. Military vehicles were
patrolling the city streets. It resembled low-intensity warfare against a
civilian population. It reminded me of what I had seen in Belfast and East
Berlin.

Immediately after delivering the water and food we had brought with
us, we spoke with people from the neighborhood. They were fed up with
the militia and the police. They were mostly men, young and old, with
little or no resources. They told us the stories of their lives and why they
had stayed. Some were forgotten veterans; others had seen prison time
for trivial offenses; some were quiet and deeply religious men. They had
all stayed because they had to. They had long family histories within their
city blocks; many houses were intergenerational. They cared about where

they stayed and what happened to their neighbors. They worked together to make the most of a bad situation. These were people who had been reduced to statistics, characterized only as poor, black, and unemployed, branded as hoodlums or drug addicts, and now they were being called looters by the media.

Our small group discussed what we might do to defend ourselves if it became necessary. There were conflicting opinions on how the police might react, but we felt we had no other choice. We inventoried what we had between us. Who was in? Who would have nothing to do with carrying guns? Eventually Brandon, Reggie B., Clarence, and I began the first watches, standing or sitting on Malik's porch and waiting, armed. There was no machismo about this. I was anxious and honored to be among some of these people. To me this was solidarity with people affected by real threats to their lives.

Being there was an expression of my antiracist principles and my revolutionary beliefs. I had been asked for support and did not make my decision to come blindly, but based on principle. I was ready to defend friends and strangers in the neighborhood. The authorities had given them no choices. It looked as if they had been left to die. I had to at least help give them a fighting chance for survival.

I was a community organizer from another city who believed in the right to self-determination and self-defense as fundamental to just communities. Dismantling the systems that hold people down takes various tools; sometimes, it involves defending our communities, even if a violent world is what we want to work against. This is one of the hard realities that our movements must face while proceeding toward liberation. Self-defense is our right whether the Constitution says so or not.

I took inspiration from the George Jackson Brigade and the Weather Underground in their efforts to be allies to others' struggles for self-determination. I was resolved in what I was doing. I was also terrified. Before I arrived, my practice of self-defense had been tested on a much smaller scale: resisting neo-Nazis, confronting police brutality in the streets during protests, and facing threats from private security. This was unlike anything I knew. I was taking a conceptual framework of armed self-defense into a reality with many unknowns.

Friends of Durruti[14]

The midday humidity hung heavy; helicopters continued their constant noise overhead. A few neighbors were with us at Malik's, a narrow shotgun-style house built in the 1930s that sits high off the ground, with a tall concrete porch behind a rusting chain-link fence. The white vigilantes came around the corner in their truck, and, as before, slowed in front of the house, talking their racist trash and making threats. But, this time, it was different. We were armed. However nervously, we held our ground. There were five of us, three from the neighborhood; we held the high ground. We had more firepower, a better firing position, and we were sober. Finally, Brandon told them to move on down the road. Clarence added that they would not be able to intimidate or threaten any more residents "'round here." Time was standing still. Each moment passed slowly. A hail of bullets could have suddenly turned everything for the worse. My finger rested on the trigger of my rifle.

We had all agreed earlier that some of us would hold the space, though it was unclear what that meant. This was one of the most unnerving situations of my life. A few more words were exchanged; the truck drove on. My heart was pounding. By opposing them, we had made our presence known. My head swirled. How were the authorities going to react? Was this the right thing to do? What if the situation continued to escalate? Would any movements support us? What if I had shot someone, or, worse, killed him? Would it have been worth it? Some of the men in the truck were known to Malik and his neighbors. It was as if a veil of legality had been lifted and they felt free to kill as they pleased. But it had become apparent that they had no real power once they were challenged. As they left, there was guarded joy and relief among us. We feared that they might continue their attacks on the neighborhood. Over the days to come, a handful of volunteers would sit on Malik's porch and keep watch. We also began rudimentary neighborhood patrols, to keep the militia, and to a lesser degree the police, at bay. Our refusal to leave in the face of repression made us all enemies in the eyes of law enforcement. It also made Brandon and me race traitors to the militias.

I had come to help, not to end up on a porch with guns facing down a truck full of armed men. But, like the others, I was ready to die defending the community. It meant something to them—especially at that time—that white people would come to their aid and put their lives on the line, as more would do in the days to come. We had all taken the first step to rebel against giving up hope.

Under siege, we stayed. As I have said, there was no Red Cross and no FEMA. There was no protection except what we were willing to organize ourselves. The presence of whites and blacks working together against the militia would later be cited by locals as one of the factors that helped ease tensions in that difficult time.

By Any Means Necessary?

> One last word to the cops
> end of the club that's where the buck stops
> you can turn in your badge, uniform and gun
> and get with the people when you're ready to get done
> diplomatic channels have been exhausted
> people are sick of paying the cost
> we all say we want the violence to cease
> well no justice motherfucker and no peace
> —Consolidated, "Guerillas in the Mist"

In the days following our first encounter with the racist militia, their presence diminished significantly. Facing armed opposition from our small, band, the militia's power seemed to be dwindling. Many feelings surfaced in those days. I felt guilt, pride, and fear about using armed self-defense. Most activists on the Left have been indoctrinated into codes of nonviolence, which is usually seen as the only legitimate practice for social change. In the U.S., many of us have the privilege to avoid violence or thinking about using self-defense for liberation. This question is reserved for other communities in other countries, not us.

Although I had used self-defense in minor ways before, this incident challenged me profoundly. My words have always been my weapons of first choice against violence, and the use of force a last resort. The mantras of nonviolence at all costs so often repeated in our movements lingered in my thoughts. The Leftist history I grew up with had been whitewashed. It claimed that struggle against oppression is illegitimate when we defend ourselves with violence. I had wrestled with this history in political organizations that were almost dogmatic about it, as well as in groups like ARA, whose tactics came under fire from other activist groups.

Over the next few weeks, rumors spread about the stand-off and about our armed patrols, both within the newly formed Common Ground and in the neighborhoods. I found myself of two minds: I was afraid to talk about it, but I also needed to in order to reduce the burden of the trauma from what we were still clandestinely engaged in. My language was awkward, skirting around analysis, exhibiting distress, fear, and foolish bravado. I wondered if we would get into trouble. Or, worse, bring more violence upon us. The neighbors who had taken up arms receded into the background. They had to do so to protect their families and communities from possible backlash from the militia or the police.

As more volunteers arrived from afar, some weighed in with unsolicited opinions about the tactics we used. I found the second-guessing tiresome. I believe critique is important, but the "should have, could have, would have" language some assumed in early conversations was hard for me to digest while the trauma was still fresh. I wanted to have a theoretical dialogue, but later, not in the midst of crisis! I think that the discussion on self-defense should be about when to use it, and how to minimize it, not about whether it is appropriate.

Like conflict resolution, gardening, organizing, or any other skill, self-defense is a tool. It is not the most useful tool, but it has a place. Power has more tools of oppression than we can shake a stick at. In certain situations we have the moral obligation to resist violence with something other than protests and passive resistance.

In contrast to the Left's whitewashed history, what I learned from people who had to struggle against being erased had revealed much about resistance. For example, there were the stories of rural blacks protecting themselves from attacks by the Klan, small-town sheriffs, and white business owners. The armed self-defense tactics of the Deacons of Defense and Robert Williams stopped immediate violence and thwarted future attacks. Those who assumed Power and their henchmen could no longer openly enact violence, and were forced to hide behind white sheets under the cover of night, their power diminishing as people fought back.

While the SCLC (Southern Christian Leadership Conference) and the NAACP (National Association for the Advancement of Colored People) derided *any* use of self-defense to stop violence in Southern communities, groups like SNCC (Student Nonviolent Coordinating Committee), who first turned a blind eye to it, later begrudgingly embraced self-defense after activists who traveled to the rural South experienced violence. Law enforcement rarely, if ever, protected them from racists, so they had to protect themselves.

Somewhere along the way, though, the mainstream and the Left distorted the complex history of the civil rights era into clear, quick and bloodless victories. Although I agree that the movement gained incredible ground with the tactics of noncooperation and nonviolence, the sanitized vision of Martin Luther King Jr.'s "revolution" that appears on postage stamps today simply never existed. It took what we now call a diversity of tactics to achieve the goals of the civil rights movement: legislative appeals, legal defense, protests, economic boycotts *and* self-defense.

If we only use nonviolent resistance and noncooperation in the struggle for change, the state and corporate interests have already won. They will allow us to scrounge for modest scraps, while they get to keep the bank. We will never get true revolutionary change, that change which stops the disenfranchised in our world from being exploited. We will only get reform.

The state has always claimed the monopoly on violence. Its legislators define what counts as violence. Its military can preemptively bomb the hell out of some defenseless place or storm your house, threaten you, and call it justified. But when we defend ourselves as communities, we are portrayed as criminals. It is said that the state's violent actions are always warranted, and civil society often backs this up without question. Why do we allow politicians to define who can use violence?

The Political Is Personal

Here I want to recall an incident that, over ten years ago, brought home for me the complex nature of violence as part of our struggles. A woman living across the street from me was being beaten in her front yard by her large, drunken boyfriend. I had seen it before and offered little real support. I had seen scenes like this repeatedly, and they always triggered old fears. Sometimes a neighbor would call the cops; they would both be arrested; then, once out of jail, the violence would begin again. It bothered me deeply. I wondered who should take responsibility. The woman? Me? The neighbors? The police? All of us?

That day, I assumed personal responsibility. With a baseball bat in hand, I walked across the street. In a calm voice, I told the hulking figure now looking down on me to stop. I kept my stance and voice firm. I was shaking inside, mostly with anger. He stopped hitting her and she left. He then threatened and cussed at me, but, after a few minutes, he looked me over, and said, in a quieter voice, that he would never do it again. Stunned, I walked back to my house. The next day, he moved out; I didn't see him around for years. The woman thanked me, as did my neighbors and my housemates. Even those who disagreed with what I had done were grateful.

I am a skinny guy. I had not been in a fight in my entire adult life. But at that moment it was clear that I had to stop him to defend her and our neighborhood. That event moved me from thinking about self-defense to practicing it. I couldn't ignore the contradictions between the hypocrisy of the state's "legitimate" violence and the Leftist movements' aversion to self-defense.

When I stood there, facing him, I saw multiple realities playing out. Socially, I was defending women, many of whom are subjected to daily violence. Politically, I was defending our neighborhood from being emotionally held hostage by the violence and the guilt of not doing anything about it. Personally, it was the unfinished business of a child once again defending my mom from my dad. But then, the disconnects dissipated; the political became personal.

That small step, taken with only moderate care and a little righteousness, allowed me to grasp that if I could do something, then we all could. In my house and on my block, we had conversations about the police and agreed that people only called them because it was easy. The police have the backing of the state to use force. This does not mean they are good at dealing with conflict, necessarily reducing violence or solving problems. This is why self-defense is relevant.

Charlotte's Web

Eventually, I recognized that in our larger struggles, our strengths are intertwined. From marginalized voices to privileged voices, we are connected as if in a web. Violence affects all of us, directly and indirectly. It affects us in our homes, in our communities, and in our struggles. We should all recognize that violence affects us all, and work to eliminate it, as well as defend ourselves from it. We have the power to do this ourselves without letting politicians and bureaucrats set the terms.

Self-defense opens up the possibility of changing the rules of engagement. It doesn't always make situations less violent, but it can help to balance the inequity of power. I am not calling for us all to rise up in arms but to rethink how we defend ourselves under attack.

We can dream, we can build new worlds, but to do so we must not forget to resist on our own terms.

Barbed-Wire Hopes

Hope is the conviction that struggling makes sense.

—Gustavo Esteva

The harried days after the storm and levee failure felt like lifetimes. I had already made two trips to the Gulf Coast. In the stress of those days, I struggled to think through the unstable situation. What did it mean? What could we do to change it? Full of adrenaline and exhausted, I stole time to reflect. In the midst of chaos, I started to reexamine the histories of those who resisted injustices and built ways to make life better. I needed inspiration and a language for my actions. I was convinced that we were going to have to do something or more people were going to die.

It was getting to be late afternoon as we discussed what to do next. We divided up. Brandon decided to search for King across the river in central New Orleans; Malik, the neighbors, and I stayed in case the militia showed up again.

I sat with Sharon and Malik at his small kitchen table as the sound of helicopters and gunfire echoed in the distance. Still shell-shocked from our earlier encounter, we sat and talked, discussing ideas for expanding the severely limited aid a few neighbors were attempting to provide to each other.

I took out some crude notes composed over the last few days and painted a picture of how we could build a revolutionary aid organization. It would be based on the principles and practices of other groups: an organization of residents and outside volunteers with support from larger civil society, one that engaged in aid work without government interference. I referenced the Zapatista rebellion and Black Panther street organizing. Naturally, I also took inspiration from my anarchist path, building on the hundred-year history of anarchists engaging in mutual aid in varying types of disasters, such as wars, failed economies, and environmental destruction—in particular the Russian Revolution, the Spanish Civil War, and the anti-nuke indigenous land defense movements of the 1980s. These were, after all, some of the foundations that had brought me to New Orleans in the first place. Our circumstances and timing were different, but our goals were similar: to struggle for survival, justice, and self-determination. I knew we could do better than the bloated bureaucracies of the government and the Red Cross. We would create mutual aid from street to street, block by block, neighborhood by neighborhood, throughout the flooded city and beyond.

We agreed on some goals. First, establishing security and checking in again with the closest neighbors about immediate needs. Next, establishing first aid and food distribution stations. We needed to move quickly. Lives were in the balance. We needed people and supplies to support this endeavor. My hope was that we would build survival programs and resistance from the ground up with members of the surrounding communities and the ad hoc solidarity networks that we had access to around the country. Once projects and programs were stable, most of us who were not from New Orleans would leave, and support the programs from a distance. (At that time I thought that people would return within a few weeks to start again. I was wrong!)

As our conversation continued, I drew up a proposal on a scrap of paper for a framework based on dual power. We would resist any further annihilation of the community. We would also work together to create counter-institutions for the long term. Malik's humble kitchen became electric with the possibilities and the daunting scope of what we were embarking on.

Still shaken by the earlier events, Sharon committed to the proposed project, whatever it was. She said that we couldn't wait. Days earlier, she had been working at an office job. Now, with great courage, she was about to embark on something very risky, well outside of her previous experience. Malik was reignited. He wasn't about to give up. With a big smile, he said these ideas gave him hope and a spark he had not felt in a long time.

Standing on Strong Shoulders

The communities in New Orleans and the wider Gulf Coast Region have a long history of resistance to domination by traders, settlers, plantation owners, segregationists, Klansmen, and the police. First Nations peoples, blacks, Cajuns, and others fought for survival even before New Orleans existed. This history ranges from the first indigenous and slave uprisings to groups like the Deacons of Defense, the Black Panther Party, and the John Brown Anti-Klan Committee. These people organized themselves to resist annihilation, sometimes with outside support from white communities. In their resistance, they used many tactics, ranging from strikes, sabotage, and sit-ins to armed self-defense.[15]

Although there have been many gains against systemic racism, the culture of oppression still runs deep. And people have never stopped fighting for their dignity and liberty. Before the storm in New Orleans, many projects and spaces fought oppression and corruption.[16] Although their organizing centers and homes were underwater or in pieces, they were not gone; they were waiting to return and fight again. Given their rich past, it is no surprise that, when the levees gave way to chaos and disorder, ordinary people and local community organizers resisted on many fronts. They always have. These communities, many of which had been neglected for generations by government policies and civil society, were not going to give up. They wanted to make their neighborhoods better and to hold the state accountable for its past and present neglect. In some areas they were already self-organizing regardless of our presence. Other areas would need much more support, from getting a single family's life back together to establishing badly needed services for the community as a whole.

Here I have tried to scratch the surface of a deep and rebellious history in the Gulf Coast, opening spaces for stories only others can tell.

To Serve the People

As I have mentioned, Malik Rahim, who was born and raised in New Orleans, had been a member of the Black Panther Party. He had returned from Vietnam disillusioned with the racism he experienced on the battlefield. The unjust war against people of another nation was mirrored by the treatment his fellow black and brown soldiers within the U.S. military. With his eyes now opened, he saw his own country differently. Malik wanted to make life better for those abused by Power in this country. He saw the commitment of the Panthers to helping his neighbors and joined the New Orleans chapter in 1970.

Malik contributed to running survival programs within the most affected areas of New Orleans: the Desire and D.B. Cooper Housing Projects. These are two of the poorest blocks in the country. They were tenement housing, built in the 1940s, and poorly maintained by the bureaucracies who controlled them.

After a few months of working in the area feeding children, stopping drug dealing and helping people to feel safe in their community again, the New Orleans chapter came under scrutiny, then attack, from a fearful police force. Armed officers raided their office twice on the pretext of evicting them. (The Panther office was open seven days a week across the street from the Desire Housing Project.) These raids were shows of force linked to the unjustified criminalization of the Panthers. They were coordinated with behind-the-scenes assistance from the FBI, who used the local police to do their dirty work. Similar raids happened at Black Panther houses from coast to coast. During this time, many young Panthers were killed due to J. Edgar Hoover's obsession with destroying the Party.

The first time, Malik and his comrades stood in armed resistance. After pelting them with sniper fire from across the street, the police came forward, heavily armed, to raid the small house. The Panthers fired back. The shootout lasted for twenty minutes. No one was killed. When the smoke cleared, the Panthers, unscathed, agreed to leave the building. They defiantly walked out, fists raised, shouting, "All Power to the People!" to a gathered crowd. Malik was swept up, along with twelve other members, and taken to Orleans Parish Prison. They faced many serious charges for defending themselves.

Luckily, the Desire Street house had been fortified with sandbags to protect against such attacks. Party members such as Malik and Geronimo ji Jaga were decorated veterans who had returned from Vietnam with military training. Most chapters had some defense precautions to prepare for these kinds of raids. The Panthers knew what levels of violence the state would go to neutralize them. In New Orleans, Panthers such as Althea Francois and Betty Powell had been branded enemies of the state for their uncompromising engagement in survival programs.[17]

Following the first raid, some of the Panthers who weren't arrested went back to the house, serving kids breakfast, holding political education classes, and patrolling the neighborhood. Former Panther Marion Brown later remembered how the community saw them out there everyday working for the people: "It was beautiful."[18] While one group of Panthers was being held in prison, the police returned to Desire Street, intent on wiping the rest of them out once and for all. They brought 250 armed officers with rifles and a tank to serve a second eviction notice on the twelve people inside. This time, the community in the housing project, who had benefited greatly from the Panthers' survival programs, rose up three thousand strong and surrounded the Panther house. The outpouring of support stopped the police and military from eliminating the whole chapter in a hail of tear gas and bullets.

These raids interrupted the daily work of the Panthers, but they didn't stop it. Each time the police harassed them, more people showed up wanting to become involved. When asked years later why they fired back, Malik responded, "Our position was that African Americans should no longer be lynched or beaten or attacked and have their rights taken away without any form of resistance. We believed that you had a right to defend yourself. You had a right to defend your community. You had a right to defend your family. And you had a right to defend your honor as a human being."[19]

Gangsters and Revolutionaries

> Each entering the courtroom with a chant of "Power to the People!" and many with a smile on their faces . . . the judge charged them with an array of charges including criminal anarchy . . .
>
> —New Orleans live TV news report on BPP Louisiana
> Chapter court hearings, September 1970

In Orleans Parish Prison, Malik and the other Panthers were beaten. They were kept barefoot, away from other prisoners, on a cell block the guards mockingly called the Panther Tier. Below them was another tier of "thugs and bad brothers," according to their keepers, including Herman Wallace, Albert Wood, and Robert King. These three men were confined on the tier below because they had all escaped separately from the prison within the last few months, only to be recaptured, and so were considered dangerous flight risks.

Hoping for a violent war between the two groups of men locked in the overcrowded cell blocks, some guards told the Panthers they were bringing up the gangsters from below. They suggested that they wouldn't be so tough once these "thugs" got through with them. Then, the guards went below, telling Herman, Robert, and Albert, among others, that the Panthers said they were going to fuck them up.

When the "thugs" were brought upstairs, the Panthers got ready to be assaulted. Tensions were thick in the quiet of the old, dirty jail cell. After a pause, the first person to walk through the door was Albert Woodfox. Albert raised his arm in a fisted salute and said, "All Power to the People!" The Panthers returned the salute, and the tensions were gone. To the guards' dismay, everybody began laughing. Soon they all became comrades. Unknown to the prison authorities, Albert had escaped to New York, was jailed with Panthers there, and joined the Party before coming back to New Orleans.

Robert King, who had watched the Desire shootouts unfold on TV from behind bars, was ready to join right then. He knew it was "his moral obligation to liberate himself from the slavemasters' shackles by any means necessary and the Panthers were doing it."[20] In the cramped cells, Malik and the Panthers taught Herman, King, and Albert about the Little Red Book of Chairman Mao and the principles of the Party. They began having political education classes, explaining why they should fight for their people. It made perfect sense to men who had been victims of the criminal system since their youth. In turn, Herman Wallace taught Malik how to read. The New Orleans Panthers were soon exonerated and released from jail, while Herman, Albert, and eventually King would be transferred to Angola Prison. In 1972, they formed a prison chapter of the Black Panther Party there and began working to improve prison conditions and educate their fellow prisoners. They would remain in solitary confinement for over thirty years for their political activities.[21]

After the Party Was Over

Within a year of the Desire Street shootout, the chapter folded. Malik and other members moved to Oakland, the BPP's home base. At this time, the Panthers were consolidating chapters across the country to Oakland to focus on local issues there. As the 1970s wore on, the Party finally ceased to exist. Most of the Panthers moved on with their lives. Malik, who had left the organization in the mid-1970s, continued to carry the principles with him in his social justice work in other organizations. While living the San Francisco Bay Area, he organized tenants and fought for affordable housing for low-income people, established housing co-ops, and worked for prisoner justice.

Upon returning to Louisiana in the late 1990s, he hit the ground running. Malik ran a program that helped former prisoners readjust to life on the outside. He cofounded Pilgrimage for Life with Sister Helen Prejean, advocating against the death penalty. Upon discovering that the Angola 3 were still incarcerated, he cofounded the National Coalition to Free the Angola 3 to bring attention to their case. It was widely assumed that most of the activists who had been imprisoned during the social justice struggles of the 1970s had gotten out, but there were over two hundred who hadn't. The Angola 3, like many other revolutionaries, had become political prisoners. They had been forgotten.

The ideology and the social programs of the BPP spawned many other groups, black, brown and white who continued their work in the years after the Panthers ceased. They had a profound effect on Malik's life. He saw connections between America's racist international policies and its domestic structures. He channeled his energies into fighting unjust systems for over thirty years before Katrina came ashore. The BPP had given him, like thousands of others, a political education, a sense of dignity, and the idea that self-determination is a right.

Passion, Fire, and Grace

On September 5, 2005, a day of trials by fire against hope, Malik, Sharon, and I cofounded the Common Ground Collective. Dreaming with emergency hearts, we laid the plans for an organization whose vision was to render visible the long history of invisible disasters in New Orleans: long years of neglect, and centuries of racist policies. Those who assume Power would not be able to turn their eyes away or cover up what was happening. We would show their illegitimacy by "doin' for ourselves," as Malik said. While they waged wars and built prisons, we would aid people until they could get their footing and do it for themselves. Despite our lack of resources, we would do more than them. We would help communities to tell their stories and we would tell ours, so as to move people to action.

We were seeing, in real time, what slowly filtered out to become painfully apparent worldwide. The state was off balance and unresponsive. The entities within it were failing to grasp the developing issues. The Red Cross wasn't doing any better.[22] They were raising *billions* of dollars while people were still suffering. For me, it was the closest thing to seeing those in Power lose their stranglehold of control. We interpreted this as an opportunity to create an autonomous space where residents could establish self-determination over their futures, be treated with dignity and respect, and have access to basic services that hadn't existed in years, if ever. We would begin relief work, without reliance on or interference from the state or professional aid agencies. We would prefigure the civil society we would like to see in the future.

Rhizomes

I knew we would need access to resources. We needed support from civil society, as well as its protection, if we were going to survive. The Zapatistas' appeals to civil society served as examples of ways outsiders could provide solidarity: this included volunteers and material and monetary aid, as well as raising awareness in other areas. This solidarity could protect struggles like ours. Past movements used this support to create autonomous spaces in regions that were out of sight for most people. The importance of networks in providing aid and acting as protective shields has always been great.

The alternative globalization movements have built networks that have converged strategically at major events such as the 1999 WTO uprisings in

Seattle or the 2010 G8 riots in Toronto. In the fifteen years since then, there has been a huge growth in networked and decentralized groups, projects and programs rooted in horizontal and cooperative models of organizing. Many of these groups took direct action. They organized shutdowns of institutions that were doing harmful things, started community gardens, fed people, created alternative media outlets, and formed cooperatives to share the work and benefits. These disparate projects had been drawn together by the common goal of creating new worlds from below, worlds where those who are historically neglected and their allies pulled together in solidarity for the benefit of everyone. Around the world, there are many traditions that incorporate these ideals; in the global North, anarchism is the political philosophy that encapsulates them.

These networks of support include medics, legal aid, food, and housing, provided by community organizers and activists from all over, even across national borders. Networks allow groups to cross over, intersect, and overlap but keep their autonomy and connection to others with common purpose without leaders or parties dictating from the center. They converge to create temporary autonomous zones. These alternative globalization networks also support struggles for autonomy around the world.

Our engagement was going to be built upon these many networks. Many projects and ideas like these had blossomed within the last ten years. I wanted to build on these ideas to make them more permanent. Could street medics and their temporary first aid stations become a permanent clinic or hospital? Could groups who served food once a week set up long-standing free kitchens? Would we be able through alternative media be able to tell the deeper untold stories that countered mass-media sensationalized hype?

Among the Watery Ruins

While we spoke in Malik's kitchen, Brandon left alone in his truck. There would be little communication when he crossed. The atmosphere was tense because it was not clear what he would face. On the highway, flooding and debris brought him to a dead end. He got out, climbed down from the bridge embankment, and stared into the water. It was murky and full of debris. (The government and the media were constantly calling the water a biohazard, a "toxic soup.")

Brandon called me one last time, too scared to step into the dark water. I told him that we would come looking for him if he didn't return. He hesitated, then waded in, his phone held in the air. He hadn't gotten far when

FEMA agents saw him. They yelled through a bullhorn that he couldn't be there and told him not to move from his spot. They were coming to get him. He refused to budge unless they would check on King. Finally, they relented and dispatched a boat to go look for him at the address Brandon gave them. Luckily, it was very close.

Understated

> It's been a long, a long time coming
> But I know a change is gonna come, oh yes it will
> And then I go to see my brother
> —Sam Cooke "A Change is Gonna Come"

When the FEMA agents pulled the boat up in front of King's house, they found him sitting on his front porch. He had been there off and on since the levees broke. He knew this boat was different. They knew his name, and they told him to bring his dog, Kenya, which he gladly did.

I got the call back at Malik's with the great news. We both started crying. It was one of the most moving moments in my life. I had almost given in to hopelessness, feeling he could not have survived. Now he would be here within a half hour. Calls were made to the outside, and soon everyone worldwide knew that King was safe.

The FEMA personnel dropped King and Kenya off on dry ground near Brandon's truck on the bridge. When he walked in the door covered in what smelled like swamp water we all cried, laughed, and shouted with elation. Our celebration of his return could be heard throughout the neighborhood. Later, King, in his understated way, simply said, "I knew y'all would come." When we finally settled down we listened to his story of those days.

King had decided to ride out the storm with Kenya. Like many along the Gulf Coast, he had been through hurricanes before. When Katrina struck the city, the storm had violently shaken their home, but passed without much damage. When the levees gave way, the water rose quickly. One foot . . . three feet . . . within twenty minutes it was lapping at the top step of King's porch, eight feet higher than it had been only minutes earlier. His basement was completely submerged. The water had risen so quickly that he and his neighbors who had stayed could not get away.

Fortunately, he had filled his bathtub and the available containers in his home with clean water to accompany his stockpiled food. Still, it was a limited amount, enough to last only a few days in the late summer weather. King decided to ration his meager supplies. He loved his dog; she was a great companion to him, and he fed Kenya better than himself.

He waited through the sweltering heat of the long days and the pitch black of the silent nights, punctuated by occasional helicopters, search-lights, and gunfire. He had many years of practice waiting. He had waited for justice while working for his freedom to be won. Now he waited patiently once again for an unknown way out of this disaster.

After a few days of living in the watery hell, rescue boats finally began to appear. These boats would pull up to King's porch to get him, and he would ask the people one question: "Can I bring my dog?" The answer was invariably no, so King would tell them that he would wait. The rescuers would shake their heads in disbelief as they pulled their crafts away.

Although immersed for many years in inhumane situations, King's compassion for humanity and animals held strong. They couldn't beat it out of him in prison, and his resolve held firm in the floodwaters. He had been hearing horrible rumors about the Superdome from the rescuers, and he was going to stand by his dog. There was no reason to go to the Superdome and he sure wasn't going to leave her.

Now that King was back on solid ground we would soon get him away from what was left of New Orleans.

But Who Will Take Out the Garbage?

It was in Barcelona, after the Spanish civil war, when the memory of the anarchist syndicates still remained, unutterable, under the iron heel of the fascist regime. City bus #68 was making its rounds when the driver slammed on the brakes at an intersection. He swore in angry Catalan, and, opening the bus doors, stomped out.

The passengers watched in shock at first, and then began to protest anxiously. One of them stood up and started to honk the horn, but the fed up ex-bus driver continued on his way down the street. For a full minute, the riders sat in silence. A couple stood up and got off the bus. Then, from the back of the bus, a woman stepped forward. Without a word, she sat down in the driver's seat, and put the engine in gear. The bus continued on its route, stopping at its customary stops, until the woman arrived at her own and got off. Another passenger took her place for a stretch, stopping at every bus stop, and then another, and another, and so #68 continued, until the end of the line.

—from the CrimethInc pamphlet *Fighting for our Lives*

The following day, I initiated more conversations with some people who were nearby, asking them what more we could do to help them. What could have a small impact on their lives right now? This scene would play out in neighborhoods repeatedly in the weeks and months to come. I thought the responses might be difficult for us to live up to, given the situation. An elderly woman asked us to clean up the rotting garbage on the streets. Its stench was awful after days without electricity. The rot was quickly becoming a large-scale health hazard. Her suggestion met with nodding approval from those around her.

Her request cut two ways. First, it was an achievable goal; second, it reminded me of the skeptics who claim anarchist ideas are pipe dreams. "People will never do anything for themselves without government or coercion, especially the dirty work." I could hear the tired old mantra: "If there is no state, who will take out the garbage?"

An answer resounded among us: we will! King, Malik, Sharon, Reggie, a deacon named Rev. Powell, and I began to pick up putrid garbage. We stockpiled it down the road, away from the houses on the block, to reduce the health hazard and the overpowering smell. We had no supplies, no gloves, and only a little jug of water to wash our hands with. I hadn't eaten meat in almost twenty years, and here I was, in one of my worst nightmares, handling rotting meat among the debris. Within a few hours, we had made another difference in these people's lives.

I had years of experience in organizing with people outside of my own cultural experience. I have always thought that it is important to use my privilege in solidarity with historically marginalized communities. Most of my experiences with such communities had been positive, but on a rare occasion I had been criticized for not working with *my own people*. I would listen, and, if necessary, honor the legitimacy of this critique by removing myself. I had also learned that sometimes, there was no critique: it was people's personal baggage coming out in political language. Then, a discussion was necessary to bring our personal issues to the table and work through them. In these rare cases I would listen to the will of the group on how to proceed.

Moving Forward, Looking Back

Although Malik and I now had a plan of sorts, I decided that I needed to return to Austin. We needed to get King out of there. He had been stranded for almost nine days with few supplies, and was now subject to rampant abuse from the authorities given who he was. It wasn't safe for him to stay any longer than necessary. I had to get back to gather more equipment and people. It was a difficult decision. The vigilantes had been quiet in the neighborhood since the day before, but we still heard gunfire often. King,

Brandon, and I delayed our departure to the last minutes of twilight before mandatory curfew. We left at dusk, with military Humvees in pursuit as we disregarded the clampdown. The military escort on our tail finally turned away as we reached the bridge that would take us out of Algiers. After nine days, King was safely on his way out the deluge. We spent a long night of driving in the darkness back to Texas. We cried, shared stories, and sang Sam Cooke songs by the light of the radio to pass the time.

In a few days, I would rejoin Malik and Sharon. Brandon wanted to return to Texas. He wanted nothing to do with forming an organization. He had never organized anything in his life. All of this was beyond the few demonstrations he had been to. His sole interest had been to find King. He wanted to go home and then maybe come back in a few weeks to help out if we got something going. He didn't return to the devastated region until late October, after Common Ground was up and running with over a hundred volunteers on the ground.

I couldn't stop thinking of the organization that we were planning, pulling ideas and experience from my past. There wasn't enough between the three of us to do what we intended, but we knew that, somehow, we would make this happen.

Of Anarchists, Panthers, and Zapatistas

> I rock hard like Palestinian children holding slingshots
> I'm with every single kid that's down for hip hop . . .
> I'm on the side of the workers, the teachers and lunch ladies
> On the streets with brown mommys raisin' our brown babies,
> I'm with Abu Jamal. I'm with Assata Shakur
> I'm with the compas in Immokalee getting a penny more
> I'm for immigrants, activists, unions and freelancers . . .
> For dj's mc's bombers and breakdancers . . .
> I'm with editors, engineers and indymedia
> —Rebel Diaz, "Which Side Are You On?"

My thoughts on political orientation, organizing, and some of my inspiration in building the Common Ground Collective have been shaped by many factors, but I want to focus on models offered by three distinct political tendencies in particular: the philosophies, political underpinnings and history of anarchism (specifically what the Spanish anarchists had achieved before and during the 1930s civil war), the Black Panthers of the 1960s, and the Zapatistas. These three diverse tendencies figured into everything I was thinking as I grappled with how and what kind of an organization we would build. My aspirations were that these would provide strong frameworks to expand toward collective liberation on our terms in our given situation. They weren't perfect, but all of them had opened spaces for people to do extraordinary things in given circumstances. Reflecting on them since, I have distilled what they offered to me as an organizer and how that translated to the Gulf Coast in the fall of 2005.

Combining self-organization and outside support for underserved communities, these political tendencies opened up possibilities for meaningful change. The commitment to collective liberation of those engaged in these struggles went beyond a helping hand in communities historically met with repression and exploitation. They integrated ideas, practices, and programs that engaged the dispossessed to meet their own needs themselves. These diverse revolutionary practices worked to overcome repression and hardship, seeking to create new, more inclusive worlds within the decaying shell of the old.

In each of these political tendencies, people rose up to create initiatives that addressed complex and interrelated problems. They didn't follow prescribed blueprints for revolution; they reimagined and reconfigured them. When they made mistakes, they learned more about themselves and the evolving situations around them, so as to be more effective. They were motivated by the love of humanity that drives us to create something better in the face of cynicism and repression.

All three of these living revolutions actively resisted annihilation by the state. They were a threat to those who maintained the monopoly of Power: FBI director J. Edgar Hoover, for example, who had it as his priority late in life to destroy the Panthers; or Spanish military dictator Francisco Franco, who had thousands of anarchists imprisoned or killed during and after the Civil War; or Ernesto Zedillo's Mexican government, which sought to eradicate the Zapatistas' autonomous communities.

As told by those in Power, history distorts the stories of anarchist movements, or ones like the Panthers or the Zapatistas. In these stories, popular movements are reduced to nothing more than the work of violent zealots, or criminals out to overthrow governments and take power for themselves. We have not been allowed to see past these misrepresentations to their commitment to creating grassroots power.

To correct the distortions in the historical portrayal of these political tendencies would take volumes of writing. Without putting them on a pedestal, I simply want to hold up a reflection from my own mirror, sharing their influence on my continued revolutionary path, as well as the effects they have had on contemporary movements.

A Reflection of You, Me, and Everyone Else: Anarchy

> Anarchism . . . has but one infallible, unchangeable motto, "Freedom." Freedom to discover any truth, freedom to develop, to live naturally and fully.
>
> —Lucy Gonzalez Parsons, in "The Principles of Anarchism"

Anarchism has had the greatest influence on me. It is a broad set of ideas that, historically, have never been represented by any single person or group. Its fluid and dynamic incarnations and its inherently revolutionary nature have influenced many social justice projects. Its rich past consists of a tide of movements that have ebbed and flowed across continents, ranging from the Russian Revolution of 1917 and the Spanish Civil War to American groups such as Black Mask/Up Against the Wall Motherfucker in the 1960s, the antinuclear movement of the 1970s and '80s, and to the many currents of the contemporary alternative globalization movements. These many open-ended transformations of civil society have given me much to think about.

For me, though, growing up, the word "anarchy" was associated with a punk scene that I was always at the edge of as a teenager. I associated it with the extreme individualism of those involved. I saw them as reactionaries with a sharp narcissistic edge. These people could have just as well labeled themselves nonconformists or nihilists. They were against everything and for nothing. They were far from what I now see as anarchism.

Aside from its misrepresentation in subcultures, anarchism was also successfully maligned by the state and mainstream media. Chaos, disorder, and violence are the first things many think of when they hear the word "anarchists." "Hide your babies and lock your doors, the anarchists are here!"

This prejudiced view made me hesitate to associate myself with anarchism as an adult in a conservative state. In my political development, "radical" was somehow an acceptable term; to call myself an "anarchist" seemed like inviting trouble. After learning more about it and seeing the value of its practices, I decided it was time to shock the political system. I embraced this orientation to challenge what I saw as stagnant thinking in the political environment around me. I knew there must be more ways to change or challenge the systems around us, and anarchism offered previously unknown possibilities.

Anarchism is practical and relevant to all of us engaged in social change as it opens possibilities and challenges assumptions. It allows us to see that we are more than just voters, activists, or consumers in our lives. It has appeared under countless names, such as libertarian socialism, mutualism, communalism, and horizontalism.[23] Under these and other names, it has a great number of historical precedents that illustrate how free communities have functioned and challenged Power in all its forms. These precedents show that we all have the ability to make decisions without appealing to some established authority or perceived power broker. To recognize our power, that is, and to use it to take action.

How many times have we all done something that was technically illegal, even something small, like walking at a crosswalk when the light is red? We do things like this because we have all the relevant information and make a decision that is in our best judgment. It is a form of common sense: doing what we know to be in our best interest, without harming anyone else or waiting for authority to grant us the permission to act. These things that we do without permission daily, probably without much thought, hint at the potential of what we could do together in larger numbers.

Trusting and acting on what we know innately without being told is the kind of common sense we are born with, not the kind that is forced on us. It is a mosaic of ideas that are ultimately based on seeing the complexities of the world differently, as active participants with common goals, hopes, fears, and dreams. In this sense, anarchism means caring about our survival and that of those around us.

Individual action gains strength when it is undertaken in tandem with others for the benefit of everyone. Anarchism means acting cooperatively for the benefit of all, as well as our own self-interest. Autonomy and cooperation—these motivations do not have to be mutually exclusive. I spent many years in the antique business. It is largely a cash economy, built on mutual trust and cooperation between people, based solely on their word. There are no lawyers or written contracts. Your word is everything. Most of my business decisions were collaborative in some way. They took into account my interests and those of the people I was doing business with. There was more to the equation than the profit motive. There were multiple bottom lines that included fairness and ethics in an economy based on mutual trust across informal networks. I made business deals across the world on handshake agreements that were reciprocally beneficial and supportive.

Something similar happened earlier in my life, working with club owners and promoters to book shows for my bands. Shows would be set up across the country based merely on our words with each other. There was an implied contract based on benefit, not coercion. In both of these situations, across many years and hundreds of interactions, everything worked out more often than not. It was a form of mutual aid. Neither of these cases is unique; they were multiplied thousands of times by many others. Anarchism and mutual aid, for me, eventually became names for what I had been involved in then.

Common Sense

An abundance of literature has been written about anarchism over the last hundred years. How it is organized? What could it look like? What are examples of it in practice? Is it achievable? There are also complex critiques and analyses of it, but, for me, anarchism is just a point of reference, a political description to get one's bearings for starting conversations that challenge our assumptions about the way the world is and the way it could be. It describes an opening up of possibilities for changing ourselves and our communities. It describes a set of guiding principles and ideas, serious and playful at once, without being stuck in a rigid ideology. It is a reflection of you and I, of everyone, when we want what is best for all of us. So, I will write about anarchism as it has related to my life, as what I see as common sense: as a living embodiment of cooperation and self-organization.

I have come to trust that any group of people can decide what is best for them in any situation if they recognize their political will. This can be done without hurting others, or waiting on someone far away with no firsthand knowledge of the issues to make the decision for them. All my life I have found that people can be accountable to themselves and to each other without coercion at every step.

Given this trust, anarchism seems like a set of common sense behaviors, thoughts or actions wrapped in political language. It is the recognition that we, as individuals shaped by different thoughts, cultures, and histories, can form a functioning society without the state. It is also a set of philosophical and political methods that can allow us to find common strengths for acting collectively, with our own power, so the voices of the many can decide our future instead of the voices of the few. This means creating worlds that can look different everywhere you go, respecting social, economic, and ecological diversity as important to healthy living.

Indeed, anarchism can be illustrated with the example of ecosystems. Both are comprised of separate but interdependent living organisms that evolve in endless variations to meet their needs. In the case of anarchism, the evolving elements are its ideas and practices. Forests in different bioregions, for example, may all look similar from a broad view, if not the same. Upon closer inspection, though, each forest's makeup is different: we find endless variations, of trees, fungi, insects, and animals that are interwoven with their habitat. Compare an old growth sequoia forest in Northern California to a pine forest in East Texas: each has a similar composition, but they are vastly different.

The realizations of anarchist ideas and practices are like sociopolitical ecosystems. Local versions resemble each other, but they are endlessly adaptive and everywhere different to meet their needs in their environments. Anarchism can be adapted to meet the culture, economics, ecology, and politics of various people or communities. That's the beauty of it.

Sphere of Influence

Anarchy has ascended in influence, whereas state socialism and Communism, just like capitalism, have failed people worldwide. We are in a political, cultural, and philosophical anarchist renaissance, seeing its influence across a wide spectrum from workers' self-management to arts and community gardens; from black bloc resistance to farmers burning fields of genetically modified crops; from prison abolition to reemerging housing and child care collectives to schoolyards and ways we think about ourselves. Unlike older political ideologies, anarchism has been embraced and grown organically from necessity and practical exercise. People have always wanted autonomy and direct democracy, a say in their lives. Anarchism provides a framework for communities to build their worlds locally, instead of a top-down party, leader, or corporation to enlighten or control us.

I believe we are at an important time in history, when collective libertarian thinking, political tendencies, and grassroots movements have the greatest potential in many localized, decentralized, and networked places on the planet. Capitalism built on exploitation and oppression that takes forms such as patriarchy, racism, and empire is absolutely linked to our divided modern civilization predicated on profits. Capitalism has brought us to the brink of extinction in our lives, our communities, and the planet through ecological and economic disasters in the name of Power. Capitalism, the dark horse of Power, cannot be reformed; it must be destroyed while creating alternatives. A kinder, gentler capitalism cannot exist. Anarchy, whether we call it horizontalism, libertarianism, flat structures, or call it nothing at all, opens spaces for us to reimagine ourselves and our worlds and also gives us some signposts to move toward these spaces. The conversations are underway; revolt of the dominant systems and self-organization is happening all around us as collective democracy has taken root and is growing globally. Underneath corporate globalization, an alternative globalization has gained ground against the state, authoritarian Communism, and our own misgivings. Horizontal structures are the future, rooted deeply in the past.

In sum, some important elements of anarchism we seek to create, are:

- *Autonomy*: To open the capacity of individuals, groups, and communities to make informed, uncoerced decisions about their lives independent of the status quo or Power.
- *Beyond capitalism/anti-capitalist*: To create social structures and exchange that challenge, subvert, and make inert the economics and power structures of capitalist accumulation that require unjust,

oppressive, and exploitative social, political, and cultural systems to turn everything in the natural world into commodities to be bought and sold.

- *Collective liberation*: To create social-political movements and communities that share power and resources and are free of any kind of unjust oppression and exploitation of others or the world around us.
- *Direct action*: To recognize that it is essential to take actions in our lives without waiting for an authority or Power to give us permission; to recognize that means breaking unjust laws of governments if necessary.
- *Horizontality*: To value and encourage the decentralization and sharing of power within groups and communities; to minimize or eliminate existing hierarchy and power imbalances so that all people involved can directly participate; to allow for personal autonomy within a framework of social equality.
- *Mutual aid* or *cooperation*: To value and encourage voluntary, collaborative work and action to accomplish more together than any single individual, group, or community could do alone; whether in specific projects or while developing a long-term vision, it's all of us or none of us.
- *Solidarity*: That those with access to power or privilege share those skills and resources with those who have been marginalized and exploited under these current systems, in order to support them in strengthening their lives against the exploitation of Power.

¡No Pasaran! The Spanish Anarchists

In the late 1800s, *the idea*, as anarchy was being called, came to Spain where it continued to develop for the next few decades among sympathizers involved in unions, small businesses, farms, housing, health care, and education. As these movements grew, the Communist Party worked to gain influence in these same places, setting the stage for future conflicts.

In 1933, a military coup (eventually controlled by General Francisco Franco) fought to seize power over the Spanish republic, sparking a civil war between military-backed Fascists and the libertarian opposition made up of anarchists, Communists, and socialists. The anarchists, who had been organizing all this time, began to create new counter-institutions and expand the ones they had already created to rebuild civil society without the state to meet their needs. In their resistance, they organized huge national general strikes to shut down cities while also recuperating factories and creating autonomous areas within the cities with armed street blockades

From 1933 to 1936, millions participated in collectives and communes of all sizes and stripes in a network of autonomous neighborhood councils, unions, and individual businesses to recreate the infrastructure of civil society that was being systematically destroyed by the Fascist armed forces and horrific military battles throughout the country. It was living anarchy, as communities engaged in these efforts had similarities based on common ideals of mutual aid, but varied to reflect the population's individual needs. Men and women made decisions together, challenged assumptions of patriarchy and sexism, and affirmed women's roles in revolutionary struggles. Instead of central committees telling people how to live, people in decentralized areas decided how to determine their futures in conjunction with those around them. The Spanish anarchists thus showed that anarchy was more than idealism—that its open-ended liberatory ideas could be realized and practiced involving huge populations across vast areas to achieve freedom in many forms on many simultaneous fronts. It was far from perfect, but it showed the world new possibilities and realties on a modern scale in both in rural and urban areas.

What was the reason for its demise? It was not that anarchist ideas didn't work. In short, Soviet-backed Communists, who had gained a lot of power but continued to want more support, denied anarchists desperately needed supplies to continue the fight for liberation. This weakened armed units and starved out thousands of people as food and medicine was scarce. Eventually, the Communists outlawed anarchist collectives and communes, killing many anarchists who refused to submit to them. This internal battle, the lengthy war itself, and murder by Fascist forces destroyed the revolutionary forces at play.

All Power to the People: The Black Panther Party

I came to understand and embrace anarchism in my late twenties, as I matured politically. Before that, however, the legacy of the Black Panther Party had a significant influence on me. They represented something I often felt was missing from our movements. Their approach to social justice in the U.S. had served many communities and affected a whole generation of social justice activists.

Their analysis and the broad social programs they built in the most oppressed communities reverberated throughout the neighborhood I lived in decades after they were gone. At the time, I didn't understand the complexities. I just looked around me and there was no one like them in the political landscape. Activist groups were fragmented, working separately on competing single issues. Local community organizing was splintered from regional or national issues. People were either trying to stop international wars or the invisible wars at home, on the poor, LGBTQ, women, and the working class. No groups I knew of were addressing the issues in a cohesive way. The Panthers' model tried to address the myriad issues in an integral way by feeding people, defending communities from police brutality, offering education, and providing basic health care. With these first steps, people could get a footing and become their own agents of change.

The Black Panther Party, cofounded by Huey Newton and Bobby Seale, was born from a whole generation of young black people raised on the shortcomings of the civil rights movement and integration policies. When the laws were passed, their situations didn't change: people were still hungry and schools were inadequate. At the same time, police brutality and racism were still rampant. Taking cues from Malcolm X and the emerging Third World liberation movements, the BPP wanted black and oppressed communities to liberate themselves on their terms. They saw themselves as agents of change that didn't need or want to wait for the white power structures to do something.

The Panthers composed what they called a "Ten-Point Program" that could connect with the person on the block. When I first read this document in the late 1980s, it struck me as something powerful and memorable. It is a straightforward document, unlike the esoteric words of longwinded manifestos put out by any number of radical groups. It lay bare the BPP's principles, synthesizing many complex social ideas, distilling them into a form that could be understood and talked about by anyone.[24] It was a statement that advocated the liberation of all oppressed people from the racist Power structure, prisons, the military, and all political offices that were run by the dominant culture. The Panthers knew the key to freedom was more than racial liberation. They understood that systems of Power and control affect marginalized people in different ways. With this guiding document, the Panthers showed that they wanted to create programs to address the issues facing many marginalized communities in comprehensive ways. Instead of fighting for liberation struggle by struggle, they wanted to resist *all* oppression, and build power for creating a just world.

Furthering these ideas, they developed their advocacy of self-defense, survival and aid programs, and ongoing political education in the communities they served. All of these were key components in developing political consciousness. These programs were vital in shaping how BPP members saw themselves in relation to Power in their struggle for dignity and self-determination. They wanted power for the people—all the people.

Survival Programs

Early in its existence, the BPP developed survival programs. These programs were free services to their communities: breakfast for children, grocery and clothing giveaways, legal aid, sickle cell anemia testing, martial arts, medical clinics and ambulance services, pest control, education, child development centers, prisoner and prisoner family support, and more. The programs were necessary to support people in meeting their immediate needs until they could build social and political power and do it themselves. The survival programs weren't always radical or direct challenges to Power, but they were the backbone of many chapters. Huey P. Newton, minister of defense, said this of them:

> We called them survival programs pending revolution. . . . They were designed to help the people survive until their consciousness is raised, which is only the first step in the revolution to produce a new America. . . . During a flood the raft is a life-saving device, but it is only a means of getting to higher ground. So, too, with survival programs, which are emergency services. In themselves they do not change social conditions, but they are life-saving vehicles until conditions change.[25]

During their time and after they ceased to exist, the example of the BPP informed liberation movements across the country. Many radical groups were inspired to run similar programs in their own communities, including the American Indian Movement (Native Americans), Brown Berets (Chicanos/Latinos), Young Lords (Puerto Ricans), and Young Patriots (poor whites) creating a ripple effect that enhanced the lives of those forgotten by or invisible to the rest of civil society.

Self-Defense

The Black Panthers were known for their patrols, armed with guns and law books, against police intimidation and brutality. They were among a few political groups that had taken up arms in self-defense. It was a time when rural sheriffs turned a blind eye to a white man in the South killing a black man just for the color of his skin, when the police in the cities routinely brutalized black men without consequence, and when the FBI was intent on stopping any political groups they perceived as anti-American or communist. Oppressed communities were under attack and the BPP decided to defend themselves. In their eyes, the history of neglect and marginalization amounted to an undeclared war. The Panthers' strong rhetoric around police brutality and armed self-defense challenged status quo assumptions about our rights as humans and citizens.

Guns were no more a legitimate or effective strategy in the struggle for a better world than survival programs, but they were an important component in the overall struggle for self-determination. Power understood the implications of an armed and resistant populace. The Panthers used arms to build confidence among the communities; they could resist and protect their communities from the injustices of the police. Where the state's overt violence ceased or communities at least gained some protection, the Panthers put the guns away and focused on survival and education programs.

What frightened the state so much about the programs run by Panthers? It was that they advocated that people take power into their own hands through food programs, educating themselves, and defending their communities from police assaults and harassment. If they had been an unarmed church group, no one would have paid attention; but they were offering underserved communities tools for creating dignity and self-determination in the face of oppression. Because of their advocacy of self-defense and their successful survival programs, Hoover labeled them "the greatest threat to the internal security of the country."[26]

Leadership Not Leaders

Although the Panthers were able to achieve much in a short amount of time, one of their biggest challenges in addition to COINTELPRO was the organization's general adherence to hierarchical structures and charismatic leaders surrounded by cults of personality. Reliance on these structures aided the state in its war against the Party, aimed at destroying decision-makers and preventing the emergence of new local leaders. Taking out a central node within the organization could—and did—crush local chapters. Additionally, divisive personality conflicts within the movement were exploited by the state to successfully foment internal divisions, all to the Panthers' detriment.

From Mao to Intercommunalism

I have learned a lot from the rich history, politics, and people of the BPP, and I think there is much more to be learned from them. But there are places where our political philosophies and practices diverged, such as their Communist-inspired authoritarian organizing, or the sexism within the Party. As progressive as they were, they were a product of their time. We can see now, through their publications and words, how they struggled with these issues and developed their thinking as they progressed. We have the hindsight they didn't have under pressure. Had they not been under constant attack, what would the Party have looked like?

The BPP's direct-action approach to building programs to help people and the analysis around them has been an inspiration and a major reference point for me in learning to provide necessary support to people. Health care, education, food, shelter, economic independence, and self-defense are cornerstones for any healthy civil society.

We Have Come to Exercise Power

As the new millennium was appearing on the horizon, I was straddling worlds, engaging in grassroots organizing inspired by the Panthers and some last forays into electoral politics while developing anarchist practices. Then, another political tendency began to shape my political orientation: it came from a rebel group based in Chiapas, Mexico, called the EZLN, or the Zapatistas. Their cries, *Para todos todo, para nosotros nada* ("Everything for everyone, nothing for ourselves") and *Queremos un mundo donde quepan muchos mundos* ("We want a world where many worlds fit") were clarion calls that reached me in the far corners of 1990s Dallas. Their words and their actions fit with my developing libertarian ideals.

Unlike my dialogues with former Panthers over the years, most of my understanding about the Zapatistas has come from reading their words or through conversations with comrades who have spent extended time in their rebel communities.

The Zapatistas are an unusual revolutionary group made up of some of the poorest rural indigenous people along with a few *mestizos*, people of mixed descent. Together, they initiated an armed uprising on January 1, 1994, to fight for their basic human rights, defend their land and gain autonomy. At the outset, they were labeled terrorists by the Mexican government. Since the original uprising, they have continued to fight for their rights nonviolently. After the initial armed struggles, they engaged international civil society in dialogues on revolution and autonomy.

Since then, they have created autonomous communities by recuperating land, building health clinics and schools, providing clean drinking water, and forming horizontal decision-making councils. People worldwide also began to connect their local struggles to theirs, forming networks of mutual support and solidarity. Zapatista communities have reshaped their lives with support from Mexican and international communities.

Zapatismo combines aspects of libertarian socialism and Marxist analysis, brought to the region by mestizos schooled at city universities, with the indigenous population's long history of participatory social and political culture and resistance to conquest. The Zapatistas learn from each other, recreating the idea of revolution. They propose a revolution that is fluid, dynamic, quixotic, fallible, and even humorous. It is as much about their hearts as it is about their minds. It is deeply rooted in their history, even as they struggle for their futures. Their living revolution shows a willingness to learn from their mistakes and change from within. I see the Zapatista struggle as a living synthesis of two disparate methods for liberation: the Black Panther Party's integrated programs and the open-ended horizontal practices of anarchism.

Their foundations are in pointedly sharp contrast to older revolutionary models in which dogmatic principles and strategies are laid out like maps by self-appointed leaders. There, everything good for the people would only happen "after the revolution." There, leaders never give up control, trading one form of authority for another. People were to sacrifice and toe the party line, ignoring the leaders' hypocrisy and the inefficient programs, even as their lives churned toward collapse. The leaders must remain unquestioned, or you are cast as a traitor to be silenced. Static revolutions of this sort ended up replacing one bad centralized economic, social, and political system with another. Like the Panthers and many anarchists before them, the Zapatistas created a living revolution, changing people's lives now *and* after the revolution.

When people rose up in Chiapas, they told those of us on the outside to look at how all our struggles are intertwined: *Todos somos Zapatistas* ("We are all Zapatistas"); *Nuestra lucha es tuya* ("Our struggle is your struggle"). With those slogans, they reached out for support but also showed that our struggles must continue until there is peace with justice everywhere. They didn't create a new political ideology as much as new ways to see ourselves and the power of our actions in the world. Their project suggests to me a living anarchism, not only of communes and small temporary projects, but also of community self-defense, autonomy, and the appropriate inclusion of survival projects and services that build for a future without the state.

Much like the Panthers' Ten-Point Program or the underlying principles of anarchism, the principles of Zapatismo projected powerful and understandable ideas across many cultural boundaries.

Some evolving principles of Zapatismo:
- Lead by obeying
- Everything for everyone, nothing for ourselves
- We wish not to seize power, but to exercise it
- Asking questions while walking
- The defense of memory against oblivion
- Our struggle is your struggle
- We want a world where many worlds fit

Living Revolutions

The Zapatistas have shown that, in a living revolution, one can ask questions and try out various programs and projects. If a program fails, one can admit it, dissecting its failure while moving on. No one has to be perfect, just accountable and honest.

This idea could liberate us from some of the psychological weight of what we embark on in our struggles. In our hypermasculine American culture, women and men are trained to be confident, to have all the answers, and to be sure of every step. We are constantly pressured to go forward no matter what the cost. (Just look at the fiascos all of the confident American leaders have gotten into since the inception of this country!) I had learned similar ideas from the Women's Liberation Movement, which sought to break free of the broken concept that the *ends justify the means*. The Zapatistas have reinforced the same concepts in a broader spectrum. We can own our political and personal mistakes in the public eye; we can learn and grow from them. This doesn't have to be demeaning or judgmental. Honesty and transparency can be liberating for all of us, allowing us to be human with all of our complexities.

Our Words Shape Our Dreams

The Zapatistas, mostly through the words of spokesperson Subcomandante Marcos, have transformed the language of revolutions, civil engagement, and the narratives of modern politics into forms that are beautiful, engaging, and poetic, filled with history, humor, questions, hope, and dreams.

Their words have inspired me to consider how important it is to redefine or recontextualize our own political language. The Zapatistas have sought to create new paradigms for thinking about how we speak, unburdening the loaded baggage and misconceptions built into most political communication. Many radical political movements are mired in what I call *political speak*: loaded, bloated words that haven't changed over the years, with stagnant ideas attached to them. This has left us with a political vocabulary that often doesn't speak to anyone outside of our own subcultures. "Liberal," "class war," "masses," "minorities," "capitalist class," "conservative," "working class," "proletariat," "minority," the list goes on. Some of these might be useful in a local context, but they remain terms that don't speak to our humanity, our depth, or that of the communities we belong to. Take identity terms, for example: I may be a privileged white, a hetero North American, a male anarchist; I am also a father, son, neighbor, worker, Texan, volunteer, and any number of other things.

And, beyond identity, what about broader society? Who are "the masses"? We live in an atomized, multicultural society made up of many types of people, with many backgrounds, with different goals, experiences, and references. How can we organize with these people if we cannot speak to them? A single language based on "the revolution" does not fit all. Many people close their ears to it.

This often leads to the disconnection of social movements from broader society, as well as misconceptions and sectarianism among us when we speak together. What if we were to shed some of those constraints of language to move forward together? Not to invent new terms but to broaden our vocabularies to include other terms, to allow more words to represent our ideals and our actions.

At Common Ground, we intentionally set up a culture to speak from the heart about liberation in more human and encompassing terms. We used terms like "traditionally marginalized communities," "historically neglected communities" or "impoverished" as ways to refer to various types of affected communities, instead of standard, one-dimensional terms. Any community is made up of smaller overlapping or separate communities with complex relationships, different socioeconomic subtleties, family dynamics, and rich cultures. Our terms referred more broadly to various groups within civil society who have been exploited, pushed to the margins or left out. They may share the experience of some common overarching discrimination, or hold values, goals, and power as a group, but they also have divergent views, histories, and voices.

Our language was an attempt to be more inclusive for those involved and less exclusive for everyone else. We wanted people who were directly affected to maintain their dignity while allowing those from the outside to see their own varied experiences in our narratives.

Many Worlds

Zapatista struggles for autonomy, land, and dignity have been referred to worldwide as the first postmodern revolution. They have transitioned from an armed insurrectionary uprising to an inspirational movement, tying land, ecology, regional autonomy, and local indigenous issues into broader alternative globalization movements. I believe their arrival on the international stage has helped anarchism by providing a living example of horizontal structures, autonomy, and self-reliance, with a focus on the relation between the local and the global.

Connections

The three political tendencies discussed in this chapter span timelines, geography, and circumstances. From each of these struggles for social, cultural, and economic justice, however, a few common threads emerge that are key to creating revolutionary frameworks for social organizing:

- *Autonomy and self-determination*: That individuals and communities have the right to determine our own futures without interference or coercion from outside forces.
- *Community defense*: That every person and community has the right to self-defense by any means necessary with appropriate tools.
- *Dual power*: That every action must both endeavor to stop oppression and exploitation and aim to build collective liberation for the long-term future.
- *Intersectionality/connecting the struggles*: That all of our struggles on this planet are intertwined and we must connect them to gain freedom for us all.
- *Narrative*: That each of these political tendencies has challenged narratives of resistance and tells us stories of impossible revolutions, daring us to dream.
- *Liberation/revolution*: That systems of Power cannot be reformed but must be challenged and dismantled in creating collective liberation.
- *Participatory democracy*: That every voice counts in deciding our futures together and that we must listen to and value each other's perspectives as we move forward.

Once the fog of our assumptions about these concepts clears, we can use them as a reference to create desired futures. Given time and development, they might even become commonplace in our collective growth.

"You're Not from around Here, Are You?"

A small but important detail, not often discussed in the stories of these three political tendencies, is that the people involved in them were from varied socioeconomic backgrounds. Throughout history, people born into privilege have joined in revolutionary struggles with those who have been oppressed. Driven by the ideal of a just world for all, they join to support and lead the struggles of those made invisible by Power.

Many know of Subcomandante Marcos, for example, who is mestizo—but numerous other nonindigenous people have joined the Zapatista struggle. The Panthers were joined by many middle-class students, and in Spain people came from all over the world to support the anarchist struggle. This can serve as an important reminder to those with relative privilege not to consider their positions from a place of shame but rather as something of great service to collective endeavors.

Our Hearts Beat in Revolutions

My comrade Geronimo ji Jaga once reminded me that revolutionaries are motivated by a great love for a better world they are willing to fight for. Governments have always feared that. I believe that feeling forms part of the roots from which struggles grow. These three movements, in their own ways, embody that revolutionary love.

Love drives what I call our *emergency hearts* to action and change in the face of repression and against all odds. The emergency heart is the feeling of empathy and compassion that motivates us to act now to end oppression and destruction. An emergency heart gets people into the streets to resist injustice and create something better. It should never be underestimated in our quest for social justice.

Something Beyond

Beginning as small groups of concerned people, the anarchists, the Black Panthers, and the Zapatistas erupted to become movements beyond themselves and their conceptions. They captured people's attention, and eventually their imaginations. Their actions challenged status-quo assumptions, pushing through implied and real barriers for personal and collective liberation. They showed us how we, as broader communities, could make change. They advocated something different—something better. They we were willing to fight or die for it. I think we sometimes forget that. We have been taught to forget them or to marginalize their contributions to other movements. Even in radical circles today, we can forget the significance of these movements on our current engagements. But if, for a moment, we allow ourselves to get past the lies, we can see their struggles. Although disparate in many ways, they were inspiring, challenging, beautiful, and effective.

Where I once saw concrete and monoculture
in the social and political landscapes of our lives.

*Empty worlds of **I** and **I** or **YOU** and **YOU**.*

I now saw fields of rebellion growing.
*Fields where **WE** and **US** now informed our resistance,*
our collective movements.

Our collective lives toward better futures
for all generations who make it so.

Like Flowers in Concrete

We are united by dissatisfaction, rebellion, the desire to do something, by nonconformity. History written by Power taught us that we had lost, that cynicism and profit were virtues, that honesty and sacrifice were stupid, that individualism was the new god . . . We are united by the imagination, by creativity, by tomorrow . . . We left skepticism hanging on the hook of big capital and discovered that we could believe, and it was worth believing, that we should believe—in ourselves.

—Subcomandante Marcos

Now back in Austin, I frantically made calls across the country to get people to the Gulf. I went to stores to gather any supplies still on the shelves. And I kept working on the founding documents of what would become Common Ground.

Malik and I called to recruit anyone who would come, and asked everyone we contacted to also contact others so as to spread the word far and wide. Around the country, people still could not believe the severity or the scale of the situation, not just in New Orleans, but also across Louisiana, Mississippi, and Alabama.

On TV there was a media fog of images and endless banter without connection to the reality being lived; it had all become nothing more than a horrific spectacle. Watching disasters unfold on TV has become regular fare in this country. We have become immune to it. The news allows us to see the horror, but gives us no tools to process it, much less to do something about it other than give money to the largest relief agency in the world. We had to make people overcome that helplessness.

When Malik and I started contacting people around the country, we spoke of desperation, but also of the vision to fight it. We weren't giving in. We wanted to motivate people to come to the Gulf Coast Basin. We knew that if people had a way to directly provide aid, we could provide a framework to do it. But we also wanted them to begin to build revolutionary change in the U.S. Some of this was wild-eyed bullshit, but if we didn't dream big, we would have nothing. Cynicism and apathy are hard obstacles to overcome in this country. People and money were nowhere to be seen at this time. The sole exception was the Red Cross, which had already brought in almost a billion dollars, but was doing nothing. We needed to capture the attention of people to get them there. We had to replace cynicism with hope, and spectacle with action. If we didn't, more people would die or be displaced.

I sent the first communiqué on September 9 to e-mail lists around the country. It was goofy, but it spoke to that time. The visions we spun were idealistic, meant to inspire people from all walks of life to come and be a part of what became Common Ground.[27]

While I was contacting people, I was also stockpiling supplies. I quickly found that, all across Texas, store shelves were bare of basic survival necessities. In our "efficient" economy, shortages were happening hundreds of miles from the disaster zone. This failure revealed the fragility of the commerce and distribution systems within this country. The big box warehouse inventories were stripped bare, leaving distribution systems collapsed in a five-to-six-state region in the South and Midwest. There were no options for people who wanted to bring supplies to those trapped in the Gulf. The same problems plagued the Red Cross and FEMA.

But some supplies did trickle in. Small grassroots organizations and concerned individuals in Austin pitched in with what they had. Borrowed two-way radio communications equipment arrived overnight from Sky King at Greenpeace; eventually, it allowed us to set up a communications center that could reach across the city. Two friends from Houston helped me to bring the Hartford, Connecticut, chapter of Food Not Bombs to the Gulf.

It seemed that the government was determined to stop any aid to the region that they had not sanctioned. As we were sending in supplies, they would question and search volunteers. So we began to create clandestine supply lines. We often hid the supplies that got through with media and aid personnel.

During the brief nights of preparing to return to New Orleans, I finished the first draft of the framework of our emerging organization. I knew we needed a roadmap to build from, a set of ideas and principles to inform the creation of an organization from scratch with the help of many diverse people. This would keep us from arguing or burning into ashes from a lack of clarity about who we were and what we were trying to achieve. It didn't even have a name! Here are our first vision and mission statements, as drafted on my coffee-stained notebook:

VISION
Our aim is to provide relief, aid and support to underserved/marginalized communities. We want this community empowered project to give hope to the hopeless and help regain power for the powerless. Our goal is to be community-led and responsive to their needs.

MISSION
Our mission is twofold:

One, to provide first response relief to marginalized communities in the Gulf Coast Basin.

Two, to build or rebuild infrastructure in communities affected by the disasters of the hurricane and the long, slow history of abandonment and neglect.

The ways we would implement our aid would challenge the state directly and indirectly. Over the phone, Malik said to me, "It's gonna be dangerous and they ain't gonna like us." I continued to move forward with the ideas. In less than three days, I returned to the Gulf for a third time.

Rhizomes

> Rise like Lions after slumber
> In unvanquishable number,
> Shake your chains to earth like dew
> Which in sleep had fallen on you—
> Ye are many—they are few
> —Percy Bysshe Shelley, from "The Mask of Anarchy"

The list of projects we wanted to engage in immediately were rudimentary and centered on survival. But we also wanted to supplement the ongoing grassroots projects that exist in many radical communities, even in New Orleans before Katrina, and help bring them into the future. I am referring mainly to the overlapping informal networks that had grown from alternative globalization movements, first around the world, and then in the U.S. since the late 1990s. In this short time there has been a huge growth in groups, small and large, employing horizontal, self-reliant, and cooperative models for organizing. This includes groups such as Food Not Bombs (who serve free food), street medics (who provide free basic medical help at demonstrations and events), Indymedia and Infoshop (grassroots alternative media sources where anyone could tell their story), and Yellow

Bike (who provide free bikes as well as education on bike repairs and safety). Most of these groups have long been part of organized resistance to undemocratic businesses and institutions, and their work has included planting community gardens, feeding people, creating alternative media outlets, and forming cooperatives to share their work. They are just some of the examples of the participants in larger networks that allow groups to intersect and overlap while maintaining their autonomy.

Many projects like these had blossomed within the alternative-globalization and anarchist movements around the world in the last ten years. We wanted to make them more permanent. Could street medics and their temporary first aid stations become a permanent clinic or hospital? Could groups who served food once a week set up longstanding free kitchens? Would we be able to use alternative media to communicate untold stories that countered the sensationalized hype of mainstream media?

I had been part of many different organizations over the years. In this endeavor, I was determined to not repeat historical mistakes. Unfortunately, most of us do not grow up in communities that teach us to be cooperative, so new groups spend inordinate amounts of energy reinventing the wheel of organizational structure. Would we, in this situation, be able to avoid these pitfalls? I told myself years ago that I would never be a part of an open collective without clear structures again, but this situation was already going to be challenging on that front. We didn't have the luxury of time to build broad consensus among ourselves or the affected communities, which can take years of good organizing and alliance-building to do. It was going to take experience to battle the unknowns in such a desperate and unforgiving situation.

Another complication: most of the grassroots groups led by people of color in the region were displaced. Their ability to communicate inside the region was limited and their infrastructure had been severely hampered or destroyed. It would be weeks before many of them could regain balance. This diaspora shaped the political dynamics in New Orleans as the weeks passed and outsiders became more established there.

With the idea of incorporating the networked anarchist projects, the "to do" list grew: picking up garbage, serving hot food, setting up first aid stations and eventually medical clinics, starting free schools, providing free bicycles and trailers, planting community gardens, building affordable housing, and launching worker cooperatives. We looked into land trusts because we already knew there was going to be a land grab before the water dried up. How these kinds of ideas would be implemented was unknown, but Malik, Sharon, and I knew it could be done. I scribbled note after note, filling up pages. The clock continued its countdown.

Triage

One of our immediate goals was to get a medical clinic open in Algiers. The first doctor we tried to get in was denied entry multiple times at military checkpoints, apparently because he was black. (I knew some white volunteers were getting in, because, from Austin, I had already coordinated a few food drops into Algiers.) This man, who had credentials on him, cried on the phone from frustration and anger. I thought, "Is this really happening?" It was an ordeal that took hours. I apologized profusely for sending him to those dead ends. From hundreds of miles away, I tried desperately to find him another route, outside of military control. It was as if they had set up an apartheid system to determine who come into the area. Unfortunately, his story was being replicated everywhere. I felt helpless.

Just before we left Austin, some good news arrived. Malik called to tell me that an anarchist collective called Mayday D.C. had just arrived in Algiers in an old rust-bucket of a van. Mayday D.C. was an ad hoc group of anarchists mostly from Washington, D.C., that worked on homeless and housing rights issues. They were quickly setting up our initial first aid station in the Teche Street mosque where Malik attended services. The group was made up of three street medics: Noah Morris, Roger Benham, and Scott Mechanic. They had EMT, wilderness, and first aid training. There was also Jamie "Bork" Laughner, a housing rights advocate. Between them, they had years of experience aiding activists with medical emergencies during mass political demonstrations around the country. Before leaving D.C., they also had the idea of creating a first aid station. It was a natural fit with our plan to open a free clinic.

My phone rang again. It was a woman named Natasha, from a California group called the Bay Area Radical Health Collective. They would have medical personnel, including a doctor, arriving within a few days. She wanted to know how they could plug in with us. Her call meant we would be able to move beyond basic first aid to a full clinic within the week.

Always Arriving

> The idealists and visionaries, foolish enough to throw caution to the winds and express their ardor and faith in some supreme deed, have advanced mankind and have enriched the world.
>
> —Emma Goldman

The supplies and equipment had been gathered. There were two vehicles this time: a passenger car and a truck with a trailer. They were fully loaded with provisions: cases of food and water, radios, water carriers, gloves, bags, bleach, batteries, hygiene packs, and two hundred bicycles donated from Austin's Yellow Bike shop for use by residents and volunteers. Our truck and trailer looked like it came from TV's *The Beverly Hillbillies*, loaded to the hilt with bicycles and other equipment dangling in all directions. Five resolute souls had committed to come with me.[28] I stopped one more time at the local meeting to recruit volunteers. I felt that no one believed we could do anything substantive in New Orleans. So why go? It was disheartening that, of all the creative and committed people we knew, more didn't come. But it was only to be those who had already committed that went.

At daybreak, we left for New Orleans. We had manufactured documents that, we hoped, would get us past the ever-growing military forces choking off all access in or out of the city. We made good time on our uneventful drive. As we reached the Louisiana border, traffic heading our way came to a dead standstill—including the mile-long military convoys headed east. We were delayed several hours coming in. When we finally came to the first checkpoint on Highway 90 at the edge of town, I took a deep breath. I pulled up to yet another edgy young soldier who looked as if he had just come back from overseas. I showed him my documents. It was a tense moment. He looked at them and then waved us through. We were elated and relieved. We were instructed to put our papers on the front windshield to get through the next set of checkpoints.

Upon arriving in the cloudy, hot afternoon, we quickly and covertly unloaded the supplies in the misty rain, putting everything under tarps, out of sight of the military and police patrols.

One of the five who had come with me was Jackie Sumell. She was also a friend of King's. Around this time she remembered a talk he had given that summer about exploitation and our commonness. He had said something like, "People are always exploiting each other, exploiting property, exploiting capital, exploiting differences . . . we are so focused on exploiting things . . . If we as people are going to exploit anything it should be our *commonness* . . . those things that we all have in common."[29] Recalling King's words, she suggested a name for our organization: "Common Ground." Malik added "Collective," because the spirit of the endeavor was that of a committed group working together.[30] He and I came at the meaning of collective from two different worlds: he had lived in collectives or cadres with chains of command in the Panthers: my experience was in anarchist organizing, where collectives were horizontal. In any case, agreeing on a name made it easier to get materials to and from us. We were on our way to being a real entity.

Dream the Future

> The Zapatistas . . . defeated the government not with guns but by
> using their imagination and creativity to transform their struggle
> in ways that have outflanked and bypassed the state's repressive
> measures.
>
> —Harry Cleaver, "Nature, Neoliberalism and Sustainable
> Development: Between Charybdis and Scylla?"

Sharon Johnson, friend to Malik and lifelong resident of New Orleans, had no community organizing experience prior to the storm. She threw herself into our work wholeheartedly, despite the deep grief that hung on her from the death and disappearance of family members. "We have to do this," she had said. Of slight build, she took on critical organizing roles such as overseeing the launch of our original aid distribution center from morning until night. She shouldered great responsibilities with the incoming volunteers and logistics. She was quiet at first, but firm in her resolve to help her neighbors and anyone in need, growing into the leadership role thrust upon her by the storms of circumstance. Her inner strength, ability to listen, and tireless work inspired those of us around her.

She and Suncere Shakur, a community organizer who had recently arrived from Asheville, North Carolina, worked late into the night organizing the limited supplies we had brought. Suncere, a dreadlocked man with a tattooed tear in the shape of Africa under one eye, took on many tasks, delivering aid when we were few. He had great fortitude to be an armed black man in New Orleans on the early patrols against the white militias. He also brought a tireless conviction, sincerity, and humor with him to help "his people."

On September 13, we were ready. We rose up out of hiding and unfurled our tarps on the fenced-in yard of Malik's house, opening the gates to the public. Our humble distribution center (which we shortened to the *distro* center) was set up mostly in Malik's driveway in a makeshift tent we constructed from plastic pipes and tarps. Tents started popping up throughout the tiny backyard of his house, the vacant neighbors' lots, and at the clinic. (Soon there would be people sleeping all over the yard—a tent city!) When the gates opened, a small crowd of neighbors that had gathered came in. We sent patrols of volunteers throughout the neighboring areas, some of us armed, to make our presence known. A few blocks away from the distribution center, the first aid station at the mosque that Malik and others had been setting up also made itself known. They went door to door by bicycle looking for shut-ins who needed medical attention, offering basic care, but mostly checking in on people who had been iso-lated for almost two weeks. Bork painted "Common Ground Collective" on some old plywood that was lying around. She nailed one to the front of our distribution center and another to the First Aid station.

I imagined I felt a sliver of what the Zapatistas might have on their January 1 uprising: facing our unknown future head on as we moved from clandestinity to visibility. We didn't know if we would be shut down, jailed, or killed. Instead of pitched armed battles, we set about going door to door. On the mostly deserted blocks, we shared boxes of food, water, and simple hygiene kits. We delivered what supplies we had and told people there would be more. We found the elderly or disabled shut-ins who hadn't seen people for days, as well as people on their porches waiting to see who might come by. Some were wary at first, but their concerns gave way to need and companionship. I talked with many of them, sharing their tears and their stories. I listened to stories about the common traumas of the storm and everything that came after. My heart ached.

On these patrols, we also gave out our crude flyers, talking to people about dignity and self-determination. One of our goals was to create an autonomous area within the city blocks where we were. In this area the community could be safe, fed, and receive medical attention; it would also be free from vigilante and police harassment. Once we established that, we would broaden the scope.

We continued our calls on civil society through sporadic e-mail com-muniqués and phone calls. We requested reinforcements and protection from government agencies that were actively trying to shut us down and ready to shoot us if given the chance. State workers told us off-the-record that we weren't supposed to exist. This area was supposed to be empty. It seemed that they wanted to starve out or remove the remaining residents. But our small-scale insurrection had disrupted their plans. People wanted to stay in their homes and face whatever was going to come their way. They had all heard the stories from the Superdome and knew that friends and families were being shipped to unknown parts of the country. The govern-ment's agenda was simple: clear the area of people by force or starvation.

In a trickle at first, people started to come by to get supplies and basic first aid. Many people were wary of the mostly white volunteers in their neighborhoods until they realized we were not FEMA or the Red Cross. Reggie and Rev. Powell, who were both Malik's neighbors, became some of the first ambassadors into these communities, going through the streets to let people know we were there. Some said they had seen us, but thought we were just more white vigilantes. Instead, they eventually found caring faces.

I knew that I was an invited outsider in these communities. I was always clear about this, even though we were welcomed with open arms. I knew that only together could we work to make things better for everyone, but it was always going to be tenuous. I was working for the people of Algiers and New Orleans and stated this in many of the early communiqués. I was determined to use the privilege of my access to resources (people, materials, money, and media) to begin the process toward a forgotten kind of movement in the U.S. I wasn't kidding myself: we weren't like the Zapatistas, the Panthers, or the anarchists in Spain, but there were many comparisons to these groups that could be made in the ways we were going about our efforts. If you asked residents there was little doubt that our small revolution was a spark of hope in those days.

When Power Is Naked

But, at the same time, desperation was increasing. The militias and the rogue police were still in force. We were struggling to maintain ourselves and to keep lifelines open for others. The long days were already wearing on us. The authorities took notice of us almost immediately, circling helicopters above us and doing drive-bys in marked and unmarked black vehicles with increasing frequency. They carried out unwarranted stops of volunteers in the community. They also interfered with our incoming supply lines. But we continued to be open about having arms over the next two weeks—hell, many locals were still walking around strapped! I was still apprehensive that they might kill us. Who could know?

Our direct-action aid tactics and agenda of resistance contributed to the state targeting us as the days progressed. I am convinced that our stance and practice of armed self-defense protected us from being "dropped in the street": this threat was heard from the voices of law enforcement on more than one occasion. Those in Power don't like to loosen their grip on the use of force, but they don't want resistance either. We weren't going to disappear or fade away when the water receded.

We tried to communicate with the hostile police and military personnel about our work, but they wouldn't hear of it. Our stance was that we didn't want their help or interference. To them, we were a threat to their authority as an occupying force in this place. They wanted to shut us down as if we were insurgents in some foreign war. We were not legitimate in their eyes. We were outside of their experience. Our existence and the refusal of residents to leave delegitimized their power.

In one of our messy altercations, one officer seemed to hear that we were trying to overthrow the government. We *never* aimed to take state power. In our communiqués and media interviews, we were careful in our wording. We neither needed nor wanted to overthrow their power. It wasn't a goal or even within the realm of possibility, except in the minds of corrupt governments and FBI provocateurs. I have never advocated the overthrow of the state because it is strategically unfeasible at this point in history; such a project would be a complete drain on the valuable but limited resources that we have. Our aim at Common Ground was to exercise popular collective power. We needed to build our own power as an organization if we were going to support people.

Programs Take on Life

Within a week, Common Ground grew from a handful of individuals to almost fifty people divided between two centers. We were joined by more volunteers, including nurses and other health practitioners. They were gladly welcomed, but they were not enough even to just cover the immediate area. Supplies and people were still critically short. Many sick and elderly shut-ins had yet to be reached and at least two unidentified dead bodies still lay in the streets in Algiers.

Then we were visited by two groups, the first of many to come, who were instrumental in providing vital material aid. The first was Secours Populaire Français, a fifty-year-old French aid organization that had been rebuffed by FEMA and the Red Cross. They stocked comprehensive medical supplies in our first aid clinic and provided the rest of the necessary hardware list for the communications center, which was not yet fully operational. The second was Veterans For Peace. They had been put in charge of almost a million dollars raised by filmmaker Michael Moore on his website. The Vets were all volunteers, many new to organizing; Moore had stipulated that they had to administer this money quickly and responsibly. Common Ground became one of their main beneficiaries. Without their vital support during this time, we might have collapsed from lack of supplies. They set up camp north of New Orleans in Slidell, and began to run limited supplies into Algiers daily. We gave them lists of critical and noncritical items such as food, water, tarps, tools, fuel, and medical supplies. It was slow going at first, but VFP volunteers eventually traveled to far reaches to find us the supplies. They even found us a small johnboat for continued search and rescue both within New Orleans and in the outlying areas along the coast. In addition, we secured electrical generators to keep our operations going. Electricity was vital to keep radios, fans, and lights on in the hot days and nights. We also shared the power with residents: we would set one up in one backyard and run extension cords to multiple houses. Generators were the only sources of power for months in the Seventh and Ninth Wards, as well as the coastal areas.[31]

Next to arrive was the Bay Area Radical Health Collective. They were worn out, but they immediately jumped into the work at Teche Street. They brought with them a wide variety of holistic health workers and our first official doctor. Our First Aid station in the Masjid Bilal Mosque quickly became fully operational as the Common Ground Health Clinic. People started to flood the space. The clinic was staffed primarily by out of town volunteers, but a few residents who returned started to pitch in too. The (mostly white) street medics continued to put their lives on the line, defying police orders and combing the streets on foot and bicycle, even going into areas the police wouldn't go before the storm.

In addition to the doctor, there were nurses, street medics, massage therapists, therapists, and herbalists on hand. We provided vital services to people with ongoing health issues who weren't getting their medications or hadn't been able to check in with a doctor for weeks. The clinic also provided a place for people to relieve their emotional traumas with the help of others who listened and cared. In short, we provided free holistic health care to communities on the West Bank who hadn't had access to it in years. This was a major accomplishment given where we were just days before. People wept from a mixture of trauma, anguish, and joy at the care they were given.

Our goal was to perform triage in order to take care of immediate needs and, in the long term, establish a permanent clinic. Each day we were establishing strength, infrastructure for survival, and space for hope in these neighborhoods.

After much consultation, Malik begrudgingly left New Orleans to speak at a national antiwar rally before a hundred thousand people that was being held in late September. This was followed by a few weeks of crisscrossing the U.S., raising much-needed funds while speaking at community centers, churches, and universities. He brought the realities of what was happening in the Gulf to the doorsteps of thousands of people, making the abstractions of the government disaster real. It was an important contribution to Common Ground. We needed the connections, people, and funding these events would bring. Malik forged ties with labor groups, churches, small community-based organizers, environmental groups, and international movements. Between trips, he was back in the streets with all of us, often shirtless as was his habit, cleaning debris, moving boxes, and getting supplies to people from sunup to sundown.

After the touch and go of the first few days, the programs and projects within Common Ground swiftly gained momentum. They arose simultaneously, spreading throughout many corners of the city and pushing up like flowers in the concrete. Our organization's growth and evolution, as we were to find out, was not linear. It was an organized chaos of changes where ideas and actions sprang to life from necessity, resistance, and our optimistic creativity.

Solidarity Not Charity

> If you have come to help me, you are wasting your time. But if you have come because your liberation is bound up with mine, then let us work together.
>
> —Aboriginal activist group, Queensland

Common Ground's motto was "Solidarity Not Charity." The Common Ground Collective always saw itself as more than temporary relief—more than charity. Charity alleviates symptoms caused by unjust systems, but doesn't challenge basic inequalities in our world. It is just a bandage. Through charity, governments, nongovernmental organizations, and we as individuals allow problems to persist without acting on their root causes.

Solidarity, on the other hand, is the view that service work is a support to those directly affected by injustice, aiding them in taking charge of their lives. Solidarity aims to solve the deep-rooted issues. Solidarity links us together across geography, economics, culture, and power. It is more than dressing a wound; it allows all involved to be active participants.

Let's take the example of feeding the homeless. We can feed the homeless today to keep people from going hungry. What about tomorrow? If we don't analyze why people are homeless and set up programs to change the interconnected larger issues that cause it—drug and alcohol dependency, mental health issues, lack of good education, jobs with dignity, safe and affordable housing, etc.—then hunger and homelessness will always persist. And if we create ways for the homeless to participate in the change themselves, then we are truly supporting deep and lasting change.

That said, charity and solidarity are not mutually exclusive ideas. It ultimately comes down to the practice: how you administer programs, how much power and agency affected communities have in them, and how an organization sees itself. Churches fed people for decades, but in the 1960s, when the Black Panther Party or the Brown Berets began similar programs, they combined them with analysis and actions that challenged systems of oppression and inequality. Feeding people *and* looking for ways to empower those that were hungry to change the systems that caused hunger, they made it possible for people to see the causes of their situation and ways out of it.

The Common Ground Collective sought to analyze deep-rooted problems as we developed our programs. Our intentions were to create permanent and sustainable solutions with and for those who were the most affected. We didn't see them as faceless or helpless victims. We saw them as active participants in the struggle to make their lives better. Both activists from afar and locals could see firsthand, through the struggle, how they mattered to each other in ways that neither had thought of. That consciousness came from the many forms of working together: from standing up to a government that was failing to recognize that people who receive aid deserve respect as much as anybody else. The phrase "Solidarity Not Charity" refers to this broad framework.

Voices Carry

After getting the clinic and distro center up and running, our next priority was to establish a communications and media center. Malik's next-door neighbor William donated the use of his evacuated house to set it up. It was a cramped one-bedroom shotgun house, half of a duplex; the other side was boarded up.

We were in the middle of a largely abandoned city. We needed to communicate both within and outside the region. Electricity was intermittent at best. Cell phones, and even Malik's home phone, which had been a lifeline at one point, were spotty. Portable generators were all that kept us from shutting down at night. We needed functioning phones, Internet, and two-way radios, and we wanted to build a website and a microradio station. It was going to be a challenge, given the intermittent electricity and lack of wireless networks, to build something stable. In some ways it felt like a preindustrial society, where communication was mostly by word of mouth. The news we were getting that way was unreliable at best and harmful at worst.

We had a team of computer and radio tech volunteers, and grassroots media activists.[32] Together, they assembled a functional media infrastructure out of parts donated from all over. What they designed was ingenious and low-cost: we piggy-backed wireless Internet and landlines through temporary cell phone towers and telephone company vans (these had been set up in the region to provide limited service). We were able to connect one computer to the network, then daisy-chain a series of computers and two phones through it. We now had a connection to the outside world.

Next, we set about setting up communication on the ground between the clinic and the distro center as well as the roving mobile teams. Due to our early experiences, we understood the necessity of being able to mobilize ourselves quickly. We had too many unsafe situations where people were alone and in danger without anyone knowing their whereabouts. For this we used old donated UHF radios and a central base. Thanks to the skills of some radio volunteers from the Midwest and Canada who had been rebuffed by FEMA, we accessed transmitters that had already been set up before the storm by amateur radio enthusiasts. In a sense, we constructed a roving analog web that reached across the city for miles on both sides of the river with equipment most would consider obsolete junk. This was especially useful when the first teams started crossing the river into the Seventh and Ninth Wards in late September.

In addition to the safety component, our center was the hub for grassroots media activists and journalists arriving in the area. Grassroots media is produced by individuals and small nonprofits for the benefit of all. It is an active, participatory media that allows access for many voices, opening spaces for communities that are marginalized and allowing them to express views and tell stories shut out from the mainstream. It also allows for the development of deeper stories, giving much more context to events in real time without worrying about advertisers or the financial bottom line.

From the first days after the storm we got major support from a grassroots anarchist news site called Infoshop.org, founded by Chuck Munson. It is a site that has been publishing anarchist news online since 1995. Infoshop provided constant updates of Katrina stories that were being underreported or not reported at all. They also provided Common Ground with critical support by publishing our updates and narratives. Infoshop.org was influential in our ability to reach out to numerous anarchist networks across the nation early in the aftermath. As Common Ground developed, Infoshop.org became a place for people to debate and discuss the merits and shortcomings of anarchist organizing, as well as racism and gentrification in New Orleans.

In addition to Infoshop.org, the Indymedia movement helped tell the deeper stories of New Orleans. The Independent Media Center, or Indymedia, is a grassroots, decentralized media network that came to life during the Seattle World Trade Organization meetings and protests in 1999. Over the next few years, Indymedia grew into a global phenomenon of activists and journalists covering thousands of stories and events without any hierarchy. As events unfold, reports are streamed on the web, updated and added to by numerous people. Instead of one official story, many accounts are presented. Indymedia centers are extremely flexible low-tech endeavors that can be set up at mass demonstrations like those at the G8, WTO, and World Bank meetings within a few days. Indymedia has been an amazing example of anarchist principles in action.

It has connected disparate voices (making it possible, for example, for workers striking in Korea to be known in England), uncovering stories that have been ignored (such as a multinational corporation trying to privatize the water supply behind the scenes in Bolivia), and giving voice to the global movements fighting corporate injustices (such as Indian farmers burning genetically modified rice seeds being forced on them).

In the Gulf Coast we needed grassroots media to tell the stories that were being ignored. We needed coverage without the spectacle and racism that abounded after Katrina, when the desperate were criminalized as looters. We needed people to see that horizontal grassroots resistance was happening amid all of the horror stories coming out of New Orleans. We also needed the protection the media provided. We hoped that the presence of cameras might provide some protection from the harassment of the military, police, and vigilantes. It was also important for us to tell our narrative in our way as much as possible. We engaged with all sorts of independent journalists, but people within the Indymedia movements were our greatest allies.

Journalists had been coming to Algiers immediately after the storm, most of them only staying a short amount of time after collecting the information for their stories. It was an odd scene: being desperate for supplies and volunteers while almost as many reporters stood around as people doing work. Sometimes I wanted them to change their roles, to ask them to put down their equipment to help us. A few brought us supplies such as water when they came. Most just observed, watching the events unfold without intervention.

Indymedia's vast networks kept an influx of journalists coming into the region. They kept the stories of the continued travesties around us alive in the alternative press long after mainstream media had moved on. It also showed the collective's evolution, shortcomings, and accomplishments in real time. After our media center came to life, many Indymedia activists who came for stories stayed around, getting their hands dirty, helping us with our aid work.

The next task on the media list was setting up a lunchbox-sized micro-radio transmitter. It was an FM radio transmitter that would broadcast for about twelve miles. (Indymedia activists had set up and used this little device to help evacuees inside the Houston Astrodome to find family members and transmit updates. It was initially approved by local officials but later shut down by FEMA and the FCC, simply because it was an illegal microradio station.) It arrived with a crew who set about installing it.[33] Meanwhile, in the scorching sun, a team headed up by Jackie Sumell assembled scrap wood into a janky tower on Malik's rooftop. Free Radio Algiers was on the air at 94.5 on the radio dial. A cheer went out from those of us down below. Hundreds of flyers were printed and posted all over telephone poles in the West Bank, telling people to tune in to the station. Our round the clock radio broadcasts, combined with the flyers, helped spread the word of our services and other resources. We also broadcast independent news and live music.

The communications and media space was humming with activity almost twenty-four hours a day. At night people packed the floors, some sleeping all over the place, while others worked late on their projects. The model for this hub was based directly on the Indymedia centers. It became a place where people edited video and audio and uploaded photos. Common Ground volunteers started various projects to help people record their own stories using all types of media.

The center was open to everyone. This included people from the Red Cross, who didn't have access to the Internet two weeks after the storm. We helped people locate family members and other resources, navigate the nightmarish online FEMA maze for benefits, or just call someone they loved to cry on the phone.

During this time we also created a website to let people know about the situation and our presence. On September 14, CommonGroundRelief. org went online. Almost immediately we were flooded with e-mails of support.

Our goal for the communication space was to make it more long-term, eventually setting up computer equipment, free wireless networks, and tech support. We hoped to set up centers in public places so that people would have access to the Internet long after we were gone. We weren't just operating a media center; we were building infrastructure that had never before existed in these neighborhoods.

Tin Soldiers

We sometimes saw military jets screeching across the sky, and helicopters constantly passed overhead, but it was rare to come into contact with military patrols on the West Bank. Most of the massive military deployment for restoring the city was across the river, in the city center. That changed when the government, and by extension the military, realized that some residents in Algiers and other areas were not going to leave and that others were defying the law by returning to their damaged and often nonfunctional homes. That is when the military began its first forays into our neighborhoods. Fresh-faced National Guardsmen and battle-weary Airborne Infantry began to occupy the space, patrolling the streets in Humvees, with weapons trained on everyone as they cautiously approached us in our daily activities. Their first priority was occupying and securing these areas.

I had a few conversations with these soldiers. I felt sorry for many of them. Many of them had just returned from active duty in Iraq or Afghanistan, or, worse, they had just been released from the military only to be called back into active duty to come to the Gulf. Many looked exhausted from being in hellish situations. Although they didn't want us there, they only hassled us occasionally.

Within a few days, a battalion began to contribute to clearing the streets of debris, plus some small-scale trash removal and limited distribution of supplies as they drove through the streets. The way they handled many of these activities seemed propagandistic to me. Their mini-convoys slowly passed up and down largely empty streets. The Humvees had giant loudspeakers on them, blasting a squeaky blipping sound followed by a recorded message in which a male voice loudly offered some service at their faraway complex. Residents would often peer out of their houses to hear the messages and shake their heads. We found it quite humorous to hear the squawky noise and the muffled voice coming closer and closer, reminding us of ice cream trucks as they crept up the street.

But the squawky boxes, despite all of their resources, never brought much relief. For instance, they announced that they would be putting free tarps on houses to protect damaged roofs from rain. Trucks drove around for two days blasting the message announcing the program; on the third day soldiers spent just two hours putting up tarps; then the program was finished. In that short time, with all of their labor, they completed about five houses out of the hundred requests. Common Ground volunteers were tarping houses from sunrise to sunset, arriving at the center just before curfew, on all three of those days. This pattern repeated itself with further tarping, along with their free clinic days at St. Mary's (a Baptist church in a huge old renovated grocery store in Algiers), their very limited water distribution, and their street cleanups. They would announce it all with huge fanfare to the neighborhood, only to provide very little aid.

Eventually, as different military units would leave to be replaced with incoming ones, they began to drop off their unused supplies with us. Few residents were able to pick them up at their outposts, which were located far from most of the remaining population. With all of their military intelli-gence and experience, they couldn't seem understand that people could not get to them. They soon turned their free clinic space in St. Mary's over to us.

Get on the Bus

Late one afternoon a call came from Malcolm Suber of the People's Hurricane Relief Fund (PHRF). He was on a "dirty ol' hippy bus" with the Pastors for Peace, a direct-action, faith-based aid organization, headed into Algiers with a ton of supplies. Our trickle of aid was on the cusp of becoming a torrent. Some longtime New Orleans organizers convened an emergency meeting of local and national grassroots organizations in Baton Rouge after seeing the government's complete indifference. Their plan was to work on redeveloping collapsed activist networks within a framework of justice and dignity.[34]

People's Hurricane Relief Fund was established as a coalition of about forty groups. Eventually, this number grew to over a hundred. The emergency meeting was a gathering that included many sorts of groups: housing rights, prison support, living wage, relief aid, radical feminists, and black nationalists. Common Ground couldn't attend the first meeting, but we sent our support. PHRF was made up of mostly New Orleans-based, people of color–led, grassroots organizations such as Community Labor United, INCITE! Women of Color Against Violence, Ashe Cultural Center, People's Institute for Survival and Beyond, ACORN, and Critical Resistance, together with radical and multicultural grassroots organi-zations from outside New Orleans, such as the Malcolm X Grassroots Movement, Southwest Workers Union, the Catalyst Project, and us, the Common Ground Collective.

PHRF concentrated on a long-term framework, developing agendas for giving voice to people's right of return, holding the government accountable, and rebuilding a just New Orleans. It was the beginning of a valuable and sometimes rocky coalition that yielded many positive results for the oppressed communities of New Orleans. We were all in insurrec-tion against the established order, heading toward a revolution against the oppressive institutions of Power in the Gulf Coast. Here is an excerpt of PHRF's mission statement of September 2005:

> PHRF is working to build a People's movement—a movement of grassroots persons disproportionately impacted by Hurricane Katrina and the dehumanizing treatment they received from local, state, and federal officials.

By grassroots, we are referring to those members of our community who are: (1) surviving families of people who perished; (2) surviving families of those who are still missing family members; (3) survivors of the Superdome & Convention Center; (4) survivors of those left on the interstates & the Crescent City Connection; (5) survivors of sexual and law enforcement violence; (6) homeowners in the 9th ward (both upper & lower); (7) renters who are being evicted and; (8) low income displaced people/survivors of the New Orleans and Gulf Coast Region.[35]

It was great to hear Malcolm's voice and to know that a good quantity of supplies was coming. My friend Brackin had called the Pastors when I had first arrived in New Orleans, telling them we needed supplies. I had worked with the Pastors years before, sending bikes to Cuba in violation of the U.S. embargo. The arrival of the bus was definitely a psychological boost to our small crew.[36]

This shipment, our largest so far, expanded our capacity. We took some of the supplies to St. Mary's. We had established good relationships with Pastor Brown, sharing supplies and volunteers at the church. They shared their volunteers and supplies with us in turn. The military eyed us warily. St. Mary's had become an official supply storage point for FEMA. The back wasn't open to the public. In the front, there were cases of MREs. St. Mary's was the only source of ice in a region largely without electricity and blisteringly hot days. Their church had a quite a few members who hadn't left Algiers.

As I mentioned, the military was supposedly running a First Aid clinic out of there, but they were only there two hours a day, two days a week. It was not nearly enough. Within two weeks, they left all the medical aid to us. We were now operating two clinics within a radius of a few miles. We helped St. Mary's volunteers with their relief efforts and provided medical check-ups. Pastor Brown asked us to set up wireless computer terminals to help people negotiate with FEMA and the Red Cross. We installed computers and provided volunteers to help with the time-consuming process and tech support.

Early one afternoon, I drove a truck over to St. Mary's to drop off our regular supply load. Their volunteers helped with unloading, and I was set to leave, when I realized the truck was blocked in by a Humvee full of young-looking soldiers. I stepped out and cordially asked the driver to move forward so I could back out. The vehicle didn't move. The driver stared through me without moving or acknowledging I had spoken to him.

Then the blank stare changed to a disturbing facial expression I had seen on many faces recently. I thought, "Is he going to shoot me?" Suddenly, a ranking officer stepped off the curb to the driver's side, barking at their car, "Soldier, this is *not* Iraq! We do not control the streets! These are American civilians! Now move your ass—immediately!" Instantly, the driver turned and the vehicle moved. The officer waved me on. Stunned, I drove away. That shell-shocked look was in the faces of many of the young soldiers who were cycling through, fresh from Afghanistan and Iraq, to the hell in their own backyards.

Meanwhile, television reporters were appearing more frequently on our side of the river. They had heard rumors about a small relief group that would not work with FEMA or the Red Cross. They wanted to see what we were about.

> Oddly enough, a group of anarchists from across the country came into the Algiers neighborhood . . . simply because, of course, they don't trust the government from the get-go. And because of all of those differing opinions coming from the federal government and the state, local—and the state government and the local government, they all came here and converged . . .
>
> So, depending on your sense of humor or your sense of irony, the anarchists have come in . . . and things are running very smoothly. . . . They're the good anarchists.[37]

Word was spreading in the media and through informal networks that a mostly white anarchist organization was fighting for New Orleans without going through official channels.

Our small crews were in the streets, cleaning up large debris and garbage. We also picked up dead animals. Some of the gunshots we heard at night were the police killing dogs that had been left behind, now roving in packs. When people fled New Orleans, only those who had the means could take their animals. Everyone else did what they could, locking their dogs in their homes or yards with little food. In the houses, the dogs died of drowning, dehydration, or heat exhaustion in the first few days; we found them for weeks afterward. After the flooding, FEMA wouldn't allow anyone to take animals. For some people, leaving animals was like leaving family members behind. There were thousands of them, slowly starving to death.

At first we only saw occasional strays and fed them with donated pet food. As time went by, there were more of them. It was a city full of dogs, predominantly large pit bulls. Some were sweet, sad animals while others were quite frightening. Without shelter or food, they turned into starving, growling flesh on bones, desperately wandering in packs in search of food. You couldn't ignore their haunting yowls in the night. They were ravenous, eating garbage, and even each other when they were desperate. Daily you could hear the pop, pop-pop of gunfire, then yelping confusion, running, barking, silence. Daily we removed their bodies from where they lay in the middle of streets. With constant decay all around us, the smell was overwhelming.

It became one of our main objectives to remove the carcasses and aid the animal rescue groups beginning to arrive to catch some of them. We assisted a woman in Algiers with her efforts, but she was hampered by lack of space, food, and her own injuries (she had been bitten numerous times within a few days). Even though many people came to rescue them in the coming months, thousands of dogs died in those first two months.[38]

Who Watches the Watchmen?

> Do they protect those who don't have the wealth
> Think about that and then ask yourself
> What protects a rich man's property and status
> Answer, the repressive police apparatus
> —Truth Universal, "Serve and Protect"

As our outreach expanded, the police became increasingly volatile. They continued their harassment of our distribution center at Malik's house and the clinic at the Mosque, and of our volunteers delivering supplies. They pulled us over to accuse us of all sorts of things, from stealing and selling supplies to running guns (especially the local black volunteers). It seemed as if the whole community was under siege. The dusk curfew was in full effect. Who was going to police the police?

All of us were subject to having guns randomly drawn on us, and being threatened with death. Longtime residents had lived with this all of their lives. The mostly white volunteers, on the other hand, were targeted selectively. As for the locals who had little support from us, the police would go after them with impunity. The refrain from their mouths was, "You are part of the problem, not part of the solution."

One mid-September afternoon, two New Orleans police cruisers rolled up on me as I was walking. Startled, I found myself lying face down on the hot pavement in the middle of the street with guns pointed while they yelled for me to "get the fuck down." The policemen, one black and the other white, questioned me about what I was doing. I was on foot, in broad daylight, two streets over from the distribution center. I had just started delivering food, water, and hygiene kits door-to-door to shut-ins. I had my rifle strapped behind my back for protection. It wasn't an anomaly to see armed civilians at this time, especially white people. Carrying my rifle, I felt some confidence, but I was always wary of how the authorities would react. Compared to the vigilantes, I carried my gun timidly. I didn't wave it at anyone.

The two officers detained me and accused me of stealing the supplies, peppering me with questions. Who was I? Where was I going? "What are y'all doing over there [referring to the distro center]?" They couldn't believe I was delivering aid. They asked me why I had a gun. I said it was for protection (I didn't tell them from whom). They kept me prone for ten minutes while asserting their power. My mind was flickering and I was aware of my heartbeat. I was afraid they would take me to jail and no one would know where I was, or worse, find a reason to shoot me. At the same time, I accepted all this; I had already been through so much. Out of nowhere, they received a radio call, let me go, jumped in their cars, and left. Shaken, I walked back to the safety of the distribution center. I was mad at them and at myself. I had made the mistake of traveling alone. It was the last time I would do that. Why did they let me go?

About a week later, Jimmy, a seventeen-year-old volunteer who had just arrived, was dumping trash at an abandoned civic center which had become an unofficial collection site away from people's homes. The military and other agencies were also adding to the pile. The police arrived to question him, even though everyone had been arranging an orderly pile of trash there for over a week. Another volunteer who drove by saw what was happening and radioed me for backup. David A. and I arrived to find two officers at the scene. Upon my arrival I noticed a white officer we often had problems with; one of the same police involved in the previous incident. He was hostile and demanding every time we were in his presence.

I left my gun in the truck so as not to escalate the situation further. He immediately drew his gun and put all of us on our knees at the curb. "Get your hands behind your fucking heads!" he ordered. He waved his gun near our heads, lecturing and threatening us. He was like a gangster from a bad movie. Jimmy was visibly shaken; the kid had done nothing wrong. The cops ran the litany of why we should leave. Oddly enough, I was more confident this time than in my previous encounters with them. I was angry, but I stayed forceful and calm, while David A. tried to talk nicely with them. This cop was a racist hothead. He kept telling us, "We could take you in . . . we could drop you in the streets . . . you make our jobs difficult . . ." In every encounter we had with him, he was demeaning, angry, and explosive. I just asked, "If we aren't under arrest, are we free to go?" After a few minutes, they let us go. We had people on the street filming them.

I was a little dazed; Jimmy and David, although shaken, took it in stride. I was already beginning to suffer from stress, but had no outlet or time to deal with it. I was in emergency mode and just stuffed it down and went on to the next crisis but I constantly worried that tensions would escalate as the days passed. Our communications and ability to mobilize had worked this time. We established new protocols for safety: no one should travel alone; vehicles need to carry a radio; no one should risk traveling at night; and any incidents should be reported.

I think that events like these were part of an ongoing plan to shut us down. Even though we knew our chances of facing death had increased, we still had some protection due to the number of our volunteers, our cameras—and our being white.

Eight Days a Week

The floodwaters were still standing in a thick, soupy mix in the neighborhoods across the river from us. In most of the city, stoplights were not working. Most businesses were still closed. In the scattering of small convenience stores that were open twenty to thirty miles away, there were shortages of staple goods. Without electricity, refrigeration and air conditioners did not work, so food was spoiling quickly. These stores were often under heavily armed security and had to deal with constant power outages.

Thousands of abandoned and flooded cars and hundreds of boats littered the streets and sidewalks. The cars, like the houses, were discolored by watermarks and mud, rotting from the inside. Trash, dead animals, and unknown chemicals mixed with the salt air of the coastal waters into a pungent odor.

On streets we identified clogged sewer drains, lifting the heavy iron grates to remove the years' worth of collected debris that was stopping water from escaping down below and causing chronic flooding throughout much of New Orleans. The city had failed long before the storm; one could see the difference starkly between wider Algiers and Algiers Point.

From the rooftops where we worked one could see that in these neighborhoods many houses had already suffered from lack of regular maintenance. I don't mean lack of care: there was plenty of pride in home ownership. There was, however a gap in resources to maintain homes. New Orleans is like a banana republic: low wages are combined with systemic political corruption that eats up funds from programs like those that aid poor communities to maintain homes. Of course, indifference and corruption happen all over this country; they just might be more prevalent in the Gulf Coast.

The forces of nature exposed and accelerated this condition. The most basic public works infrastructure, from sewers to sidewalks, was in no better shape, again due to mismanagement of the city's money and its long history of indifference to underserved areas.

The distribution center at Malik's house had developed into a bustling headquarters. His small and narrow yard was filling up with incoming volunteers. It was a ragtag crowd of younger anarchists and radicals in their twenties, mixed with handfuls of older people. As one volunteer put it:

> Common Ground Relief can boast one of the most multidisciplinary of all teams. There are (categories not mutually exclusive) nurses, doctors, psychiatrists, pharmacists, anarchists, herbalists, acupuncturists, community organizers, journalists, legal representatives, aid workers, neighborhood members, EMT's, squatters, gutter punks, artists, mechanics, chiropractors, clergy, and so forth involved. A huge sign outside the door reads, "Solidarity Not Charity," and this statement exemplifies the perspective of those involved.[39]

At the same time, a small convoy of buses and other assorted vehicles of all makes and conditions was starting to line the otherwise deserted street.

Tents were popping up in every available space. Sleeping bags and the people in them were everywhere inside the house and all over the yard. Our encampments were spilling into the yard and porch surrounding the media and communications center, across the street in an empty lot, and in the vehicles that arrived with volunteers almost daily. At the clinic, volunteers slept on the floor or in nearby abandoned housing. Some residents put volunteers up in their homes. By now we had over seventy people in those cramped quarters. Donations of supplies and equipment were stacked under tarps in every available corner. Before the morning meetings, we had to put all the tents away to make room for the day's activities.

Our days started at sunrise. After waking up, we would all gather for the 7 a.m. meeting before beginning the day's work. The clinic and distro center personnel would get together to check in, assess the needs and projects for the day, assign crews, introduce new volunteers, and identify any crisis that may have erupted over night. The meetings were vital in keeping information flowing, quelling rumors, and informing each other about what was going on in the different projects. Also, given our horizontal organizing, many people were making decisions simultaneously. No single person was making decisions for everyone. The meetings were not just a way to stay informed; they were also a time for dialogue and debate.

As the weeks progressed, there were soon too many people to speak in the limited time we had. So we shifted to a spokescouncil model. It is an organizational model where everyone met, but the coordinators responsible for the programs in the clinic and the distro centers reported back to the other volunteers in the larger group. Coordinators would also lead facilitated discussions of gaps, needs, and the goals for the day for their project or program. Our volunteer meetings were always open, even as we went from ten to fifty to eventually hundreds of people. This was done in the spirit of keeping communications as transparent as possible.

After the morning meetings we ate MREs for breakfast, if we had time. Those two-thousand-calorie MREs fed all of us in those early weeks. They were the only consistent food source. (I remained a vegan under all of these circumstances, which was extremely difficult. I never wasted food and recognized the privilege to choose among the little food around. Sometimes I wondered if I was holding myself to an unhealthy expectation, especially as I started to lose weight.)

From there, we went on to sixteen-to-eighteen-hour workdays. We were removing trees from the streets and numerous caved-in rooftops. It was a slow and arduous task, done without the proper equipment. Debris removal was followed by putting tarps on houses to keep the elements at bay. Our two clinics were operating at full capacity. Sharon and a steady crew were moving tons of food, water, and medicine through the distribution center, which operated from 7 a.m. until curfew, seven days week. Hundreds of people were visiting our little place, with needs greater than we could address.

After curfew, we had an evening meeting, and then a project organizers' meeting. After all that, I continued to work out the internal processes, structures, and culture of the organization on my worn-out notepads. At midnight or 1 a.m., sleeping on the floor felt like heaven.

Of the many internal problems, access to toilets and running water were at the top of the list. Between the two houses, we only had two toilets. There was always a long wait. We constructed two makeshift composting toilets and put them in the back of Malik's overcrowded yard. This only slightly alleviated the problem.

As the weeks progressed, feeding ourselves also became an internal problem. Eventually, in the limited space at the back of Malik's driveway, we set up an outdoor kitchen staffed by a rotating cast of volunteers. Eventually some fresh vegetables and other substantial food arrived in large donations. We were eventually able to give up the MREs, but it was all incremental.

Every day we were facing rapid growth problems in addition to the crisis around us. We needed space, facilities, and storage. It would take us another month to address the issues; until then, we were overcrowded and busy with our aid work.

Collapsing New Constructions

> If you want that good feeling that comes from doing things for other folks then you have to pay for it in abuse and misunderstanding.
> —Zora Neale Hurston

In between my many tasks, one of my major objectives was developing some internal processes for Common Ground, especially as we were growing. Our volunteer base was made up of a constantly shifting set of people. Many of them were college students, radicals, and anarchists. Among these mostly white volunteers, there was a wide spectrum of exposure to antioppression theory and practice. This was true even of those who had radical political backgrounds. We had many volunteers who were outside of their cultural experience being in a landscape like New Orleans. It was a shock to their systems to be immersed in a world that they may have only seen in a magazine or from the highway at sixty miles an hour.

I spent my little free time writing notes. For many of us, it was important that our organization be rooted in an antioppression analysis. l was desperate to establish a thoughtful culture. I wanted our growing forces to be conscious of the communities around us. We were there to support, defend, and build within these communities, but ultimately they would define their own destinies.

It was easier to communicate these ideas and values when our numbers were smaller. Constant informal conversations with a few core organizers, in addition to our daily activities, reinforced our commitments. Our growth was beginning to inhibit direct contact among all the volunteers. We needed to do more.

Well-intentioned and committed people were coming to aid others; they were also bringing their personal histories and their social and economic privilege, often without being aware of it. By "privilege," I mean the amorphous, institutionalized social, economic, and cultural constructs that grant rights and entitlement to certain social groups. More simply, privileges are advantages some of us have in our lives and social relations. They play out in various forms, such as being white, wealthy, male, able-bodied, or born in the U.S. People in privileged groups view their life experiences as "normal," as what everyone experiences. That imperceptible privilege affects our perceived status in the world, access to jobs and educational opportunities, what we think our entitlements are, and our self-perception.

Privilege has no hard-and-fast rules. Although there are some who will always benefit from it as long as the current social and economic and cultural systems are in place, for others it can be conditional. They may only have privilege and assimilation within certain social contexts; the privilege can be withdrawn in others.

I try to be conscious of the degree of privilege that I have. More importantly, I try to use it as a tool to access and share resources in support of disenfranchised communities. There is more strength in owning and using privilege for the common good than in denying it or feeling guilty about it. Our privilege is not something to be ashamed of. We were born into these systems; we didn't create them. It is what we do with our privilege that counts. Those with privilege can also be a force for collective liberation. There is a long history in this country of privileged people using it in solidarity to strengthen movements. Coming to New Orleans is my example. I tossed guilt for what I inherited to the curb years ago and rediscovered parts of my own roots that I had repressed. And as my engagements outside of white activist culture broadened, I learned it was all right to be who I am. I saw that it was more powerful to share my access to resources with other people than to deny I had any. This is not to say I have it all figured out. I still make mistakes. Oppression and privilege are complicated social constructs that impact individuals and communities profoundly. In some situations I can be ignorant of my privilege; but, when I discover it, I am that much more willing to own it, be forgiving to myself, and learn from it. Putting our privilege in perspective can be humbling.

Another complexity that we dealt with was the misconception shared by numerous volunteers that the predominantly black residents of New Orleans formed one homogeneous community. One of our practices at Common Ground to counter this was to ask questions of many different people in each neighborhood to find out who they were and what they needed. This community organizing approach, based on the Zapatista idea of "leading by obeying," was meant to allow us to see the complex relationships, socioeconomic subtleties, family dynamics, and subcultures that make up the many overlapping communities within any city. We didn't appeal only to self-described leaders, but to everyone who had a stake in the situation. Just as the volunteers probably already did in their own lives, if they thought about it!

When we are able to see the richness and depth of communities, we can build meaningful relationships and be good allies everywhere. Angela Davis once remarked:

> There is often as much heterogeneity within a black community, or more heterogeneity, than in cross-racial communities. An African-American woman might find it much easier to work together with a Xicana than with another black woman whose politics of race, class, gender, and sexuality would place her in an entirely different community. What is problematic is the degree to which nationalism has become a paradigm for our community-building processes. We need to move away from such arguments as "Well, she's not really black." "She comes from such-and-such a place." "Her hair is . . ." "She doesn't listen to 'our' music," and so forth. What counts as black is not so important as our political commitment to engage in anti-racist, antisexist, and antihomophobic work.[40]

So, in New Orleans, for example, any given community could have a combination of the working poor, LGBTQ, the elderly, families, immigrants, home and small business owners, kids, sex workers, students, and any number of religious affiliations. All of these people could be contained within a few square blocks. My hope is that we see these communities as complex and dynamic, composed of many divergent and overlapping parts. Such nuances can take years of engagement to recognize. In community organizing, we must begin by becoming aware of the differences within diverse communities. By not painting them in broad strokes, we allow ourselves to begin to understand our roles within them in moving toward collective liberation.

Culture of Respect

How could all of this knowledge be conveyed in the crisis we were facing? There were so many pressing concerns. We had committed ourselves to host collective liberation workshops, regular volunteer orientation introductions, and trainings at some time in the future. My first attempt at addressing the issues of privilege and oppression was to write out a pair of draft documents on two large sheets of butcher block paper late one night. The idea was to present the Common Ground Collective's mission and vision as well as our antioppression guidelines, or collective liberation guidelines as we called them, to incoming volunteers and local residents.

The first sheet was the mission and vision statements that I had drafted back in Austin. The second was a document titled Guidelines of Respect. They were organizational guidelines explaining how to interact with each other to counteract oppressive behaviors. The guidelines were adapted from people I had worked with. I have used variations of these guidelines over the years.

Common Ground Collective Guidelines of Respect Sept. 2005

- Everyone has a piece of the truth.
- Everyone can learn.
- Everyone can teach or share something. (We ALL have experiences & information to share.)
- Remember all of this a process. (What happens along the way is as important as the goals.)
- Respect the work and abilities of others.
- Create safe and inclusive environments for all participants.
- Take risks within yourself.
- Critique inappropriate behaviors, NOT the person.
- Be accountable to the people and communities we support and yourself.
- Speak only for yourself.
- Mistakes will be made by all of us. (None of us is perfect.)
- Be aware of the effects of your actions on the communities and others around you.
- Challenge oppressive behavior in a way that helps people grow.
- Take cues from people in the communities you are working with in the way you interact.
- Respect people's traditions, religions and cultures even if you don't agree with them.
- If you see a behavior that is inappropriate, intervene, don't wait for someone else to address it.
- Don't use alcohol, drugs or weapons in places where they can endanger people.

I presented them at our small coordinators' meeting, where we agreed to try them out. At the next morning's meeting they were presented with a small discussion. We posted them in common areas outside Malik's house to be reviewed and read by volunteers throughout the day. Posting these documents was a first step toward a liberatory culture at Common Ground. By following these guidelines, we could respect each other, check ourselves on behavioral patterns around privilege, and challenge ourselves to create a world of collective liberation. But given the fluidity of the people around us, I didn't know how to make the information stick or give it context. We were an open, constantly evolving collective. If we were not going to repeat the mistakes of the past, we would have to convey this information and be conscious of shaping our internal culture. But how to do it, in all this disaster, with just the few of us? I wished we had more time to develop.

Early Bridges into the Wards

A Food Not Bombs chapter from Hartford took the initial risk to get hot food in to people still stranded in the waters across the river in the Seventh and Ninth Wards. The Red Cross would not go there. We knew people on the other side needed water, food, and medical attention immediately.

Food Not Bombs is a decentralized network, influenced by anarchist ideas, of people who have organized to serve free food across the world for over thirty years. They feed people in public places such as parks. For many, working with Food Not Bombs is their first foray into anarchy in action. It helps people to interact outside their cultural experience. I see it as an important way to put ideas of cooperation and direct action into play. Many chapters commit civil disobedience in the face of resistance from law enforcement against feeding homeless people publicly.

Some in radical circles have dismissed the Food Not Bombs movement as reformist, but even if it is just service, does it really matter? Food Not Bombs is one of the only ongoing groups that involve youth working outside of the anarchist subculture. There is a long history of activists who have cut their teeth on deeper libertarian ideas through it.

When the first calls went out, Food Not Bombs members were some of the first responders, feeding hungry people before the water was gone. They brought mobile kitchens to the people where they were; they could go to a corner where people were gathered, serve, be harassed by the police, and come back an hour later and serve again. Food Not Bombs helped us to connect with Mama D (Diana French), a lifelong resident and firebrand community activist of the Seventh Ward. Malik had known her for many years. Unknown to us, she had also stayed through the storm and was now trying to keep herself and her neighbors alive without access to water, food, or electricity. She was fighting Homeland Security personnel that were trying to make them all leave, as well as the aid organizations that were doing nothing.

We created small teams to go into the Seventh and Ninth Wards. It was no small feat; each excursion took hours due to flooding, roadblocks, and the need to avoid the police, who were not only keeping people out, but trying to discourage those there from staying. We set up two gas-powered generators to power multiple homes simultaneously. We started to send Mama D supplies. Our support helped her group, the Soul Patrol, resist being forced from their homes. They didn't have the access to resources we did, and their fight was dangerous. We gave them sustenance and let the military know that outsiders were supporting them.

We defied the state by refusing to leave the areas we were told to, and by being in other areas that were off limits. The fact that our group was mostly white gave us some legitimacy in the eyes of the authorities. Many of us had a long history with civil disobedience as a tactic in social justice movements. Here, it was integral to survival. Civil disobedience underpinned almost everything Common Ground did. When someone said it couldn't be done, or we couldn't be here, we stayed; when they threatened to kill us, we stayed. We broke the law just by existing outside their reach. Our tactic of nonviolent civil disobedience was a major practice of solidarity in our operations as we developed.

On my earlier trips, I couldn't access many areas due to flooding and military blockades. Now, I finally got into the Ninth Ward to assess the situation there for myself. Standing in the Lower Ninth in a foot of water, I stared in disbelief at a rusted barge that had crashed through the levee wall into what was left of the neighborhood. I had seen the pictures in the news, but it was now in front of me. One house on the dead-end street nearest the levee hadn't been washed away in the flood currents; the mammoth barge had crushed the back of it and come to rest across empty lots and streets where other houses once stood. I could barely comprehend the force of the water that had carried it through the levee breach into the neighborhood.

Given the need for medical services and basic aid distribution, expeditions across the river became more frequent. They were difficult, showing us the severity of the devastation on that side of the river, as well as how far the state was willing to go to block aid to the residents.

Unfortunately, as September came to a close, Hurricane Rita was barreling down on the Gulf. More roadblocks came up as the state clamped down harder, creating blockades that once again cut off the residents completely. Martial law was in effect until the storm passed. Shoot-to-kill orders were still in effect.

Can You Relate? We're Livin' in a Police State

Incidents with the state's forces were happening frequently. Kevin, a black ex-prisoner from Angola State Penitentiary who had been volunteering with us since the beginning, had a run-in with the cops. They detained him, pushing his face down on the ground, accusing him of stealing and looting. He was let go, but tensions were mounting across Algiers.

One hot cloudless afternoon three weeks into our operations, the problematic white cop who seemed more out of control than most of the others arrived at our distribution center with two soldiers to "investigate us" again while a Danish TV crew filmed. This officer (while not alone by any means) led the charge in the continued, almost daily harassment of volunteers carrying out their rounds, using verbal threats and intimidation.

On his arrival, we followed our security protocol: most people stepped back and one or two people interacted with him, closing off access to Malik's yard. Against my better judgment, I attempted to use deescalating language and tried to defer to him when he approached. I was concerned that more serious violence was on the verge of exploding, so I tried to reassure him as he walked forward.

I wanted to negotiate a truce. I tried talking with him, treating him with some amount of respect. I was doing everything I could to calm two weeks of tensions, using the negotiating skills I had first learned navigating around my alcoholic father. He could win in his mind. It didn't matter to me. My goal was for him to leave. But it was useless. He was dead set on upholding his (the state's) agenda of law and order. To them, we had to either leave the region or stop what we were doing. As always, they were full of threats.

Immediately I felt I had betrayed my principles by trying to negotiate a truce. When he left, I felt like a fool. I didn't respect his authority or abilities, and so my attempt at deescalation had been abysmal (except that no one had been jailed or injured). We were on a mission that conflicted with theirs, and that was clear from their threats. The military were not there to protect and serve; they were there to do whatever they wanted with impunity. The more people that were gone, the fewer obstacles to controlling the area. They had followed orders all their lives. When their command structure broke down, they had a chance to do something different, to side with the people. They chose intimidation and brute force.

Two days later, the state's aggression culminated in an early evening raid on our distribution center. We were in the process of closing for the day when the military and state agencies arrived in Humvees and both unmarked and marked vehicles. As they came toward the open gate of the property they kept referring to it a "compound" and a "fortress." There was even a helicopter circling above, its light blinding us in the darkening sky.

Guns were drawn and there was lots of grandstanding by the forces of the state. We knew this wasn't a friendly visit.

Some of the soldiers and police officers entered the gate while the majority fanned across the street facing us. They searched through the relief supplies, which were mostly on pallets and covered with tarps. We informed them that we did not consent to them being on the property, but they didn't care. It was dusk, and volunteers, exhausted from the day, were caught off guard, producing great anxiety. The helicopter continued circling over us at low levels, blowing everything around. We had divided into two groups: the first tried to close the gates to keep them out; the second formed a human wall inside the distribution area to block off access. They got in anyway. Soldiers asked me questions while the cops were searching the front area.

Kevin was furious to see them and vocalized it when they barged in. Then, the racial epithets came spewing out from one of the white cops' mouths. That same problem cop we kept seeing said that "low-life niggers," "white trash," and "stupid hippies" was all we were. "You don't know shit," another added. We closed ranks and told them to leave. Finally they retreated, slowly, with one very adversarial white cop threatening to "get us" as they returned to their convoy. The dust storm and noise caused by the chopper faded.

What they didn't know was that, had they attacked us, we would have defended ourselves with arms. We were at the ready the moment they broke through the gate. They were confident they held the upper hand, but they would have met escalated resistance—we would not go quietly. They acted with no accountability to anyone. Who was going to stop them? This was not what we wanted, but how else could we have stopped them?

It was another night in Algiers, coming after days of crisis after crisis. Was there going to be a deadly confrontation with the police? The fact that it might happen was left unsaid, but it frightened our small crews, many of whom were not used to conflict of this scale. Not that I was used to it, either. But it had been going on so long that I expected it. I wondered whether I would be shot. Or was it going to be some random volunteer who didn't know better? These thoughts reverberated in my head. The cops were out of control and we didn't have enough resources to defend ourselves from their attacks. They wanted us to leave. We weren't leaving.

Rita

In the Gulf of Mexico, a Category 5 hurricane, Rita, was heading toward the coast at rapid speed. It was the largest tropical cyclone ever recorded in the Gulf and it was bearing down on the coast with ferocious power less than a month after Katrina. New Orleans was still underwater in most places. We knew the city could not survive another direct hit. We were a few days out from landfall when we started seeing the shift. The clouds along the skyline started moving rapidly from the south in waves, while stronger winds whipped around, threatening the tarps on rooftops around the neighborhood. It was an ominous time. In Algiers, we furiously battened down the hatches of the distro center and clinic. We didn't need to become part of the problem by not being safe.

We were struggling to secure ourselves while continuing to provide aid and shelter to at least some of the elderly, disabled, and most desperate. We were scared of what we were facing. With the storm approaching land, we had to climb roofs to secure tarps that weren't meant for hurricane winds. A few residents had returned to check on their homes or begin repairs, only to have to leave again; others were refused entry before they got close due to the storm. Hurricane Rita was a test of our resolve. We had barely gained any momentum.

At an emergency meeting, we decided to call off all but essential services. The clinic was to be staffed by only two people. Unequipped to handle a wide-scale evacuation, and after much discussion, we asked volunteers and neighbors with vehicles to leave for Baton Rouge and Slidell with the Veterans For Peace. It was painful. We couldn't support them and we were unsure of their safety. I was exhausted and getting feverish. I had a flu that had been going around the camp. Malik, Sharon, some of the neighbors, and I were showing signs of shock. After much debate, I came to the painful decision that I needed to leave as well. I waited until the last minute. I had not been home in a month. Meanwhile, a handful of people were going to stay at Malik's. If the water got too deep, they would break into a school nearby with a second story on it. The remaining generators and computers were put into an attic. Our little boat would be used to shuttle people to safety if necessary.

One of our initial programs had been to clean the street gutters block by block. We still had many to go if we were going to keep the flooding to a minimum in the immediate area. The storm clouds brought more rain, even while we could see the water lapping the levee half a block from us where the water still had not receded. Would it hold? Would the water breach it this time? We spent the last day clearing the gutters as the rain and wind intensified.

I loaded up with equipment that needed to be returned to people in Texas. I was shaking with sickness and fear. Saying goodbye to Malik, Sharon, and the others cut through us all. I felt that I was deserting everyone.

I hesitated. I did not want to walk away, not even for a day. Was I taking my privilege and leaving? Everyone who wanted to leave had done so. I had necessary skills and experience, but would I hinder everything by being a sick casualty? We all stood and cried. Then Malik and Sharon hugged me and said they loved me. Malik headed out to work with some volunteers on more street gutters. I headed to Texas on an eighteen-hour version of what would normally be an eight-hour trip. I was stuck in evacuation traffic, hallucinating from a 102-degree fever. Cars out of gas littered the highways, and no one was there to help as torrential rains poured down. Arriving home, I collapsed in bed. I slept for almost three days, having nightmares and crying about everyone who didn't leave. My heart and body ached as I drifted in and out of sleep.

With Thunder in Our Hearts

In this world, there is a kind of painful progress. Longing for what we've left behind, and dreaming ahead.

—Tony Kushner, *Angels in America, Part Two: Perestroika*

Gulf Tides and First Nations

Rita didn't strike New Orleans directly. It hit the coast at the Texas-Louisiana border, bringing a storm surge that breached the levees of the lower wards again, flooding them. Once more, the broader Gulf Coast area from Texas to Mississippi was under water.

Earlier, just after Katrina, we had learned by word of mouth of severe flooding in remote places along the coastal areas. Someone who had just returned from there described deep waters covering scattered trailer homes in out of the way towns and dead bodies abandoned on lonely roads. People had scrambled to the few dry places they could: rooftops, patches of dry land, various overcrowded churches, and a small recreation center. Longstanding environmental degradation of the Coastal wetlands in the name of commerce and progress had reduced the natural barrier protections from the tides to nothing.

People needed food and medical attention immediately. We had made initial scouting missions during mid to late September as far as we could reach into some outlying areas along the coast a week before Rita hit. With our limited capacity, we hadn't been able to get far into the heavily flooded areas of the small bayou communities so our focus had remained mostly within New Orleans. Tucked away in those bayous and coastal lowlands, there were many unseen yet vibrant communities, made up of small towns, villages, and sometimes just isolated houses. They were home to numerous small tribes of First Nations peoples, including the Biloxi Chitimacha, Houma, and Pointe-au-Chien, as well as Vietnamese fishing villages and small French Cajun and black communities. Thousands of people in these communities had lost their homes from Katrina. The succeeding hurricane water almost finished them off.

It was another hidden disaster, among many that the media ignored that fall. As in so many areas, the Red Cross, FEMA, and any number of agencies that should have been there to help, were absent. As with so many other historically forgotten rural and urban communities, those who assume Power didn't prioritize them.

While the worst of Rita's impact had lessened, the storm's rains were still beating down when we sent our van into flooded Lake Charles, west of New Orleans, to drop off supplies. The next day I returned to the region, still weak. but standing. We rented a truck and headed to Houma and Pointe-au-Chien to transport aid and medics near where people were gathered. We also sent a crew with our little boat to reach people stranded on the rooftops of their homes. It was beyond our scope, but we had to do something. The first scouting missions felt like my arrival to New Orleans after Katrina: destruction and sadness everywhere. The sixteen-foot box truck and the medical van set up in different communities daily, doing mobile distribution until the supplies were gone or no one else needed medical help.

Every time the back of the truck was opened in a parking lot surrounded by flooded streets, people flocked in to receive supplies and news from the outside. They were tired and hungry, like the people in New Orleans. Our supplies were usually gone within an hour, but we stayed to give people basic medical check-ups and to ask more questions to find out how we could help. The rural, isolated terrain hindered many of our rescue efforts; the crew in the boat could only go so far without great difficulty. Active power lines, downed trees, floating houses, and other detritus littered the water all around.

Over the next two weeks, while we were still heavily focused on New Orleans, overextending our services there, Common Ground also struggled to establish two new distro centers, one in Houma with representatives of various tribes and the other with church and community groups in Plaquemines Parish. Choosing these locations was difficult because there were so many areas hit hard by the flooding.

Not Leaving a Trail of Broken Promises

With help from Suncere, Naomi Archer[41] took the lead in establishing various tentative contacts with the leaders of the various tribes and communities throughout the coastal region.[42]

We had to be careful in our work with the United Houma Nation and Biloxi-Chitimacha Confederation of Muskogee because of their long history of experiencing broken promises and racism from outsiders. Like many officially designated tribes, these groups are made up of many smaller, different tribes who have come together under one larger banner, potentially making our engagement with them a disaster for those of us who knew little of their history. In the confusion of the moment, it was difficult to navigate those difficult histories (not to mention the factional relationships between the tribes). It was similar to what we faced in New Orleans, but with a different history of problems with outsiders. In the last two hundred years, the government had first tried to exterminate these tribes, then to assimilate them through aid programs.

We did not want to leave a trail of broken promises. They were wary but also grateful that someone came to help at all. Up front, we let them know that we were there to give support and aid, not to take charge. After consulting, we chose the areas where we knew the communities them-selves could serve the most people and continue the relief after we were gone if they had access to supplies coming in. The history of self-suffi-ciency within these small communities became evident when they quickly took the lead on many of the operations, delivering supplies and connect-ing our medical teams to those with the most pressing demands.

On October 8, Naomi left Common Ground to form Four Directions Network, working exclusively to restore the First Nations communities, continuing the work we had all begun.[43] We continued to supply them with materials as the communities rebuilt their lives. It would be weeks before the waters would recede and months before any normality could return. These communities rebuilt largely without outside assistance.

Too Little, Too Late: Red Cross and Red Faces

The Red Cross was not on our side of the river for almost four weeks. It was as if they had left people to die. Was it ineptitude, or was it planned? Algiers was one of the forgotten areas; because it was not underwater, it was as if it did not matter. Before Rita, we had begged them to go to the hard-hit coastal areas but there was no media to follow them there. It appeared to us that they had performed triage and left all of us as collateral damage.

The Red Cross, like the military, spread the word of their arrival far and wide for days beforehand. There was a big buzz in Algiers when we heard they were finally coming. Common Ground Relief had supplies, but we weren't the Red Cross! People built them up to be great saviors. They were bringing large tractor-trailers of supplies. No one would go without, so we thought. On the day of the delivery, the residents who could began to line up at a designated place in the early morning light. Their "heroes" had arrived.

Three large eighteen-wheel trailers pulled up as the cool morning air gave way to another hot day. Homeland Security was in full array to guard the Red Cross volunteers. (From what? We didn't know.) The anticipation grew as they prepared to open the trailers.

The Red Cross volunteers approached the first trailer, opening the back doors to reveal a full load of unmarked cardboard cases. People in the crowd murmured, assuming it was water. They climbed up to open the boxes, which contained individually wrapped utensil packs containing a plastic fork, spoon, and knife. They opened more of them to find the same. Next, the Red Cross volunteers went on to the second tractor-trailer and opened it, again exposing stacks of unmarked boxes. They unloaded them, and they were opened: this fifty-foot trailer was, floor to ceiling, full of napkins. People were starting to get agitated. The heat of day and the waiting were wearing on them. Flustered, the Red Cross volunteers came to the third trailer, which we all assumed would have the expected food and water. They pulled the doors open to reveal, again, cases of unmarked boxes. They turned out to contain "handi-wipes," little antiseptic cloths. The crowd murmured in disbelief and outrage. One woman shouted, "That is just wrong!" to no one in particular.

All of those resources, all of those volunteers, all of that money, and all they brought were napkins, plastic utensils, and baby-wipes! The crowd was insulted and angry, and the Red Cross volunteers were as surprised as anyone. They apologized profusely to everyone there. This made it perfectly clear how out of touch the Red Cross was with what was happening. Then, they had the gall to mention that they would be wrapping up their operations soon, leaving everything to FEMA. Most of the people left empty-handed and indignant.

A month into the largest manmade disaster in this country, this was the pathetic attempt to aid people they came up with. They unceremoniously informed the crowd that they would remain until midday, then leave. The government, once again, seemed to place no value on the lives of these communities.

Bill, an old hippie volunteer driver for Pastors for Peace, left to get the Pastors' bus from the distro center. Like the rest of the community, we didn't need much of what they had brought, but we could use baby wipes in our hygiene kits. He brought the brightly painted former school bus, which he had driven back and forth to Mexico for over ten years, and parked it on a side street near the Red Cross trailers.

Under the blazing sun, sweating from the heat and humidity, he and I carried the boxes down the block to the bus. We opened the back door and began to load the boxes. I was inside the bus, by the door, bending down and restacking them, while Bill had returned to the driver's seat and was pulling the bus closer toward the trailers, when suddenly I heard the words: "Freeze, motherfucker . . . put your fucking hands up, put your hands up now!" I turned to see two men in black T-shirts and ball caps that read ICE running with guns pointed at me. Bill, not seeing them, and being a little hard of hearing, continued to move the bus slowly forward. The cops split up, one still pointing his gun at me and yelling, "Make him stop or we'll shoot," the other one running to the front of the bus, pounding on the side as he ran. All of this seemed to happen in slow motion.

Once we had our hands on the back of our heads, they identified themselves as Homeland Security ICE (Immigration and Customs Enforcement) was the sleek new name for the old INS (Immigration and Naturalization Service). Immigration was now taking on the internal borders of our neighborhoods! The agents continued to bark at us, and asked many political questions. I explained who we were and what we were doing. This routine was common by now, and I wasn't afraid this time. We had lots of volunteers and witnesses nearby.

They accused us of stealing supplies from FEMA and Red Cross and selling them. I asked them if they had any proof. Of course, they had none. It was a pretext to engage and question us. We were outside of their jurisdiction and largely outside of their control. I told them to walk around the corner and talk to the Red Cross volunteers, who were giving us the mostly useless supplies. I then asked if we were being detained. I said that if not, we would like to continue our work. They made threatening comments under their breath and walked away. We continued loading in the heat. Interactions like that made me want to struggle harder against their repression. At any time, they could have put their weapons away and helped people instead of trying to choke off one of the only sources of support in these communities.

Witnessing the failure of both the government and the Red Cross on the same day would have been comedic if the circumstances were not so dire. Far from the realities of those left standing in the heat after surviving the storm, they forgot that they were supposed to work for the people. And they not only failed these people; they also insulted them. I couldn't figure out why we had let these people maintain power. I was angry!

A Right to Return

The arrival of the Red Cross had been a disaster, and FEMA had still not arrived. Meanwhile, in those same first few weeks of October, Common Ground took on the slow process of establishing broader mutual support among community leaders within the West Bank. With our expanding services, we were barely getting enough supplies to meet the demand, even in this small area of New Orleans with only a fraction of its former community remaining. But, at the same time, we were aware that residents were not returning as fast as we thought they might for many reasons. Some of them were still being denied reentry weeks after Katrina. Those weeks would turn into months. Word from the outside world spread among the largely isolated neighborhoods as to why their neighbors, their children, and their grandchildren could not return. It was another outrage, a constant topic of conversation.

Others were displaced to locations thousands of miles away by inefficient government evacuations. They had no real means to come home. Those in power had pushed tens of thousands of the most marginalized people, including the working class, the poor, and the elderly, out of the city to points unknown, scattering them across the country without any plans about how they would return. And, if they did, what were they returning to?

We had helped many individuals and families in the larger Algiers community; and, in turn, the people supported us too. After we helped them to become as stable as they could be given the situation, some of them in turn helped distribute aid to their neighbors and families, or helped us locate people in need. The outsiders who mainly made up Common Ground, whose hearts were in the right place, had earned the trust of the communities we served. The word about Common Ground's relief was slowly reaching more neighborhoods.

Constructing Relationships, Contravening Myths

Early October brought many growing pains for Common Ground. We redefined who were, solidifying our principles. We had struggled to build an internal culture based on the language of supporting the residents while moving toward collective liberation. It was becoming increasingly difficult to convey and maintain this culture, given the incoming and outgoing movement of volunteers amid crises.

Up to this time the organization had been built on relationships between an initial few: the people who had stayed or were left behind, and some other brave souls who had entered the aftermath. Small organizational fissures could become cracks that would affect our work if they were not addressed soon. There were too many details, problems, and tasks for our small group. The broad foundations Malik and I had cobbled together needed to be clarified, made sturdy, and expanded if we were going to develop any kind of horizontal organization to do what we set out to do.

Malik and Sharon, who both had lived in Algiers most of their lives, continued reaching out to, and strengthening relationships with community leaders and others in the neighborhood. I contacted other organizers across the country, people whose lives I had crossed in different struggles over the years. Many of them were unknown to Malik, but I had worked and learned from them, and trusted them under stressful situations before. Malik learned to trust them out of necessity, along with their commitments and actions. We needed them to grow.

Many of those who arrived first would probably have come to the Gulf whether an organization like Common Ground existed or not. It was clear that alternatives for direct aid and long-term rebuilding were needed in the face of the lack of government response. People from all over were waiting for a way to channel their energies of grief and rage. They wanted to come to the Gulf and needed ways to plug in without waiting on red tape. (The Red Cross was making volunteers attend a five-day orientation before they could come to the region. It was unnecessary; basic aid work is not rocket surgery!) From both of these networks, a chain reaction grew: from friends, to friends of friends, then to comrades in struggles, and eventually to people who had just heard about our efforts in the disaster areas. All of them came. We welcomed them all with open arms.

Movements like Shadows: Myth and History

As myths emerge, the subtleties of history are eroded away, among them the chorus of voices that create our movements. The voices of some who gave their blood, their sweat, and their lives are pushed into the shadows, while others are undeservingly exalted. Our culture, our media and textbook histories are fixated on the myth of the good hero, so they distort the contributions of the many people who created the movement. What is left is like a broken mirror: a fragmented reflection instead of a whole.

The myths around Common Ground, elevated Malik, Brandon, and me to a special status for our actions immediately following the storm. To destroy those myths, I want to emphasize that there were *many* pivotal people who participated in building our collective future in New Orleans. Malik, Sharon, Suncere, and I were joined by many organizers, among whom were Lisa Fithian, an organizer with many skills and tireless dedication, Kerul Dyer and Jenka Soderberg, two radical organizers who brought media and technical expertise, rounded out by Emily Posner, Tyler Norman, Soleil Rodriguez, Sean White, Brian Frank, and Carolina Reyes. They arrived at a critical juncture, helping to reimagine our work by adding their analysis, caring, and hard work. They deepened our vision and our commitment to an inclusive, horizontally organized project. With their arrival, the scope and depth of our projects rapidly expanded.

These organizers had many parallels in their principles and actions. I had only worked with some of them, and only some of their paths had ever crossed before the storms in the Gulf. Although there would be many who contributed immensely to the growth, development, and direction of Common Ground's collective efforts in the coming years and who deserve recognition for their commitments, this core group helped us to build the Common Ground Collective into a wider anarchist reality. They were all willing to use direct action to resist oblivion and dual-power frameworks to build the future. They helped us to reestablish the organization as something more than a quixotic endeavor in the chaotic, brutal, and desperate early days. With their arrival, we developed further Common Ground's internal culture while expanding our communications and building more relationships in New Orleans.

Having more strong women's voices added to our decision-making body began the process of balancing our male-dominated nucleus, opening more possibilities that many of us could not otherwise grasp. They confronted many faces of sexism and patriarchy, subtle and otherwise, but they never wavered in their resolve to continue to fight for justice for everyone in spite of the impediments thrown at them. They helped us to reexamine our internal communication culture and rethink the organizations' focus. This resulted, for example, in the creation of a women-only safe temporary shelter.

The voices of these women and men, like those of so many of the courageous residents and volunteers, have been largely left out of much of Common Ground's histories as written by others—and sometimes even by ourselves. My hope is that someday more of their stories will be told. Without their influence, strength, wisdom, and leadership, our original goals and the dreams of broader horizontal community engagement might have come apart at the seams within the first few weeks.

So, October was a rebirth in building a horizontal organization and a larger network based in anarchist practice that was for volunteers of all stripes, not just anarchists. Pressures from all sides only allowed us limited time to do any internal development. (In reality we needed years, not weeks, for the evolution of the stopgap and long term projects we were aiming for). Within the whirlwind first weeks we, the core coordinators, stole time for a few critical meetings to refine our mission: what we were, how we would continue to organize. This process also broadened our vision by multiplying the voices that would decide what steps to take next.

During this phase, we first improved our internal practices, developing decision-making processes, volunteer orientations, a volunteer manual, and the organization of committees (including communication, administration, security, and projects, etc.). Some aspects became more formal, while others remained informal. Much of the internal decision-making was spreading to a wider group of people, with continued consultation and leadership from the various communities we were working in. We now had more input and experience to guide us.

Shifting Narratives

There have been great societies that did not use the wheel, but there have been no societies that did not tell stories.

—Ursula K. Le Guin

Part of shifting culture is changing the stories we tell others and ourselves. To do this, we must develop our own narratives about our actions and what we imagine about the future. Communities and movements gain power in telling their own stories. If we tell our own stories we rebel against being defined by those who don't know us, such as the government, corporate media, or others with ideological axes to grind.

I have learned from many movements, including the Zapatistas and the Black Panthers, that there is power in telling their own stories to win the approval of civil society. The Zapatistas in particular have used narrative to resist annihilation while captivating the imagination of global civil society, showing a way to redescribe our social revolutions. A U.S. group called smartMeme has developed similar techniques. They call them story-based strategies that create "a framework to link movement building with an analysis of narrative power by placing storytelling at the center of social change strategy."[44] This is a way of understanding how the Panthers and Zapatistas turned on its head the old political language that has plagued movements for years. By consciously telling our stories we are able to reconnect with people in the real world, because it is language they can see themselves within.[45]

I used narrative strategies to get people to the Gulf from various radical subcultures. We had limited time to develop Common Ground's narrative, and even less to write it out, although I was able to issue a series of communiqués over the next two years. We needed to figure out our narratives both within and without the organization. Within the organization, we used our narratives to challenge the assumptions that privileged volunteers were bringing in. We wanted antiracist allies, not saviors to support these communities fighting for justice. We also used narrative strategies to counteract the myths that surrounded Common Ground's early days, demolishing the pedestals that people were on, to illustrate that we were all real people rising to extraordinary circumstances.

We wanted appeals for the Gulf that showed people having agency in their lives, not just as hapless victims. We believed our approach was different. Here is an example of one of my early communiqués from before we even had a name (the rest are in the appendix):

Date: September 10, 2005
Subject: Support in Algiers, New Orleans

To our anarchists, liberals, progressives, mothers, fathers, kids, grandparents, comrades, friends, sisters, brothers and people of concern,

Our story so far . . .

Imagine a community affected by disaster. The long slow disaster of neglect, the disaster of abandonment by most in civil society and government for 200 years. Now imagine the ravages of Mother Nature on this long disaster, we say a 'disaster within a disaster'.

A marginalized community made even more marginalized by nature and gov't.

What would you do?

Now picture the community deciding that it would not be broken down by this disaster. People in this community in Algiers New Orleans decided to rebuild itself, when society and government forgot them.

Some of the 4,0000 +/- citizens of Algiers who have remained, or were stranded due to lack of resources, since the hurricane have now organized themselves and appealed to the larger civil society for support in their effort to rebuild their lives.

This is not just relief, but the rebuilding of infrastructure within their means and ways . . .

But who will take out the garbage?

We will. The people of this community with the support and solidarity from the outside. We will deliver food, water and medical aid. We will watch and protect each other. We will secure, aid and reconnect the bonds the long history of disasters of neglect and abandonment have brought.

We have bicycles to transport us, deliver food, water and pick up garbage.

We have a first aid station set up.

We have communications with those outside of this community.

As the Black Panther Party used to say "We doin' for ourselves . . ." with the support of those on the outside.

We need supplies: gasoline, money, water, non-perishable foodstuff, medical items, tarps, power generators, boats and many other supplies NOW!!

We also need people to come. There is much to be done immediately!!

Please contact scott crow 512.###.###9 ####@####.net
Malik Rahim 504.###.6897

From the Gulf Coast Region
scott crow

Telling our own story was important to counteract misunderstandings about government failures and the criminalization of desperate people by the media and the state. Racial and class prejudices were common in mainstream media stories that portrayed people as helpless or criminal. In reality, there were people struggling to make their lives better. It was also important to counteract the media's reduction of complex social situations. Many stories focused on all the depressing details and suggested the hopelessness of trying to help. It was as if we all knew the ending before the curtain even closed in the first act of this unfolding drama. The Common Ground Collective's story, on the other hand, was that we all could make an immediate difference in people's lives. We didn't need governments or large aid agencies to save the people. We needed civil society to provide short-term relief and long-term support to establish healthier, safer, and more independent communities. Even if it is not the focus of movement work, telling our own stories is a critical component of an organizational framework.

Who's in Charge?

As an organization, we set out to develop an internal culture and practices that reflected our shared values. To do this we had to identify those shared values, then find ways to communicate them to the incoming volunteers, to the communities we served and to the media.

I wanted us to be as horizontal and democratic as possible. I reluctantly recognized that Common Ground Relief was probably going to be some sort of amalgam of a completely anarchist ideal, which in reality we needed years to build, and something more centralized. We were probably closer to the Zapatista model, with a base decision-making body that consulted and accepted some leadership from the various communities we were in. This challenged my dreams of having large, open assemblies.

In my experience of making decisions horizontally, especially in large groups, at least some of these factors must be present:

- Developed levels of trust or shared goals between those involved, usually built from personal relationships.
- Clearly defined and agreed upon group principles or values.
- Clear definitions of who is in the collective and what the collective effort is.
- Various means to communicate the information between all of those involved so people can make informed decisions.

We were missing several of those factors and could not bring them together even on our best days without jeopardizing other, seemingly more important, issues. We didn't have the luxury of lengthy meetings, a history of actions together, or longstanding community interactions to establish deeper relationships and consult with each other. It was not a secure foundation to build on.[46]

Many of our projects were initiated or directed by those directly affected and deeply committed volunteers. Nevertheless, some aspects of our internal organizing remained inaccessible. For example, decisions concerning financials and security had to be made by a smaller administrative collective. Even the directions of the long-term projects could not be made by all the residents or volunteers who passed through because it was impractical. We agreed to organize in the framework of a network of projects and programs under one umbrella.[47]

To minimize hierarchy we operated with group leadership instead of leaders. Leaders are those that try to exert power over a group without formal consent. Leadership happens when someone is given permission by the rest of the group to lead. Elizabeth "Betita" Martinez has written on this:

> As organizers, we need to reject the definition of leadership as domination, but without denying the existence and need for leadership. Denial can lead to a failure to demand accountability from our leaders. That demand must be embraced, along with anti-authoritarian methods, in leadership development. Accountability takes the measure of a person's responsibility; it means being accountable to one's fellow organizers, to the goals of one's collectivity and ultimately to the people one claims to serve.[48]

We attempted to keep people from being gatekeepers so that, when coordinators moved on, we would still have functioning programs. Ideally, once a project was started, it would be fairly autonomous, though still under the umbrella of the Common Ground Collective. Those who led it organized their groups and decision-making processes the way they needed to, with an emphasis on being participatory and accountable to those served as well as the collective. Some coordinators organized projects as affinity groups, some called them work groups or teams; it was up to them to decide. Some of the projects needed multiple coordinators who shared power, and some could have just one. Coordinators were removed for myriad reasons, including failing to meet these criteria or the goals of the project.[49] This structure was discussed in volunteer orientations when people arrived. It was one of the significant differences between the way Common Ground and other relief groups operated.

Imagine a web of interconnected projects (such as legal aid, eviction defense, house gutting, free school, aid distribution, medical, media, women's shelters) with a core of organizers that provided the logistical support (financial, technical and otherwise), but did not do all of the decision-making. This core focused on administrative work, long-term goals, internal organizing processes, legal issues, and responded to crises. Much of this went unseen to most people. The core collective fluctuated between four and twenty people. Meanwhile, the amount of coordinators eventually swelled to over forty.

Most projects retained a great amount of autonomy. This system had issues, but being bureaucratic was not among them. Even so, one of the problems was that the undercurrents of horizontalism were not clear to those who participated in it. We didn't have clear ways to support people in leadership positions, and in many cases acted according to social convention. Those who pushed their agenda vocally were acknowledged; those who quietly maintained their projects were sometimes undervalued. In some projects, the ends justified the means—sometimes detrimentally to those involved. In other projects, the process was consciously made as important as the mission it was trying to accomplish.

Paradoxically, though, at times Common Ground felt leaderless, as if no one, even those in the core, could sway what was happening. In these times it felt like a driverless bus careening down the road at top speed while the passengers argued about what color the bus should be. There were problems with direction: for example, we had no clear processes on how to start or stop projects, or how to get support for them, or where we were trying to go with any given project.

The word "collective" took on many connotations as more people came to join our efforts. In Malik's eyes (and those of some of the other coordinators) we were involved in a broad effort where many people worked for common goals, many provided input, while a few made decisions. To many antiauthoritarians, a collective meant a group of people organizing without any leadership where all voices are equal. These two ideas collided on many occasions. Some coordinators wanted to exert total control; others were angry because we were not "really anarchist" for not allowing every person who walked through the door to have equal say. Both of these unrealistic views created tensions that Common Ground would live with for years.

Kerul Dyer has summed it up this way: "Common Ground is a largely white activist organization, and most of the coordinators have come from an anti-authoritarian political culture. Malik and some of the core leadership in New Orleans, however, come from a radical black political culture with fundamentally different experiences and approaches. The organization incorporates many decentralized characteristics, but at base we are acting in solidarity with local black leadership, and Malik and a few others make many, but not all, of the final overall long term decisions."[50] She is right. Up to that point we were mostly outsiders who could leave at any time. We would probably only go so far in rebuilding New Orleans. Not so for people like Sharon, Malik, Rev. Powell, Rev. Brown, Mama D, or Reggie. Their communities were at stake. It would have been presumptuous, egotistical, and dare I say it, racist for us to tell them we knew better. We did not always grasp the complex relationships that existed before the storm, nor did we know firsthand the marginalization of these communities. We respected their cultures and history and they respected our ideals and practices. So our composite systems, including our decision-making processes, organizational structures, and principles, reflected this. It was not so much a compromise as a blending of different approaches in the struggle for balance between the individual and the collective, leaders and leadership.

Scratching Toward Collective Liberation

> Difference becomes so important, because you have to have struggles from people from different worlds, from different realities, yet we can figure out a way within the same space and push our commonalities forward but in a way that respects the individuality of the struggles.
> —Ashanti Alston

From the beginning many of us approached the Common Ground Collective from the point of view of a collective liberation analysis. That means a way of being deliberate in challenging oppression, creating dialogues for learning along the way. Building this analysis is difficult in the best of circumstances, such as within small groups. Our situation made it extremely difficult.

We were thrown together by circumstance from many political, social and cultural backgrounds. Most in our coordinator collective at this time had anarchist and antiauthoritarian influences, which were unheard of in this neighborhood. People there were used to "being organized" by old-school organizers or politicians, without having a say in how projects functioned. Many residents were very politicized, but they had not been shown tools to develop those thoughts into action under their own direction. Given time, we could have developed those things together. But we had to build on what we had.

Our interactions with people in the neighborhood could not be defined by political identity. Our actions and practices on individual projects were as varied as the people engaged in them. There were mixed levels of awareness. As an organization, we needed to recognize and navigate complexity, keeping our values while remaining respectful to local culture, social norms, and histories that many of us knew nothing about. This provided opportunities for radicals, and anarchists in particular, to put their best practices forward. We had a chance to challenge our movements' flaw of relegating ourselves to a subculture by working with communities outside of our own.

As I have mentioned before, we posted our important internal documents on large wall posters anywhere volunteers gathered. (They were also on our website.) Lisa Fithian and I started to work on the first volunteer handbook. It went through many incarnations over the next two years, becoming the most consistent tool with which to share information. Next, we established our first formal volunteer orientations to acquaint people with the urgency of the work and the long-term visions, and to counter the white privilege of many volunteers. We held the first ones in October for all of the volunteers: first at the distro center, then a second one at the clinic, where Malik and I gave presentations. They were awkward, but necessary.[51]

We were also striving to be consistent in our projects. Historically, many people with privilege have worked with communities only to leave when the funding ran out, or to go back to the rest of their comfortable lives leaving the project in a bad situation. It happened in the civil rights era; it still happens today. We were beginning to see volunteers come through Common Ground, proposing programs, starting them, then leaving us holding the bag. When they left, the collective was held responsible by the communities. It made us look bad.

Lastly, we made it a goal to establish antiracism or antioppression trainings for volunteers in the coming weeks. Lisa contacted the People's Institute for Survival and Beyond, the oldest antiracist training organization in the United States. Coincidentally, they were also in New Orleans, and we had some connections with their organizers within Common Ground. They could provide valuable insight, counsel, and tools; we would be supporting a local organization to get back on its feet. People's Institute had been flooded out of their space like most of the city, and were scattered across the country waiting to return. After a few false starts, their trainings began in December of 2005 and continued through the next year.[52]

Far Side of Certainty

Common Ground's appeal reached across many sectors of civil society. Our work was consistent and visible to people in neighborhood after neighborhood. To the outside world, we didn't look like an organization that was spending money sitting in offices and thinking about what to do next; we were on the ground, active and getting our hands dirty. This enthusiasm was bringing in many kinds of people.

We set out to be oriented toward social justice, but nonsectarian and nonpartisan. You didn't have to be an anarchist or a radical to work with us, just willing to help out, respectful and hardworking. We did not espouse any overt ideology (although many of us were clear about our anarchism with other volunteers, the media, and residents). This was done to include a wider group of people, to keep political infighting to a minimum, and to keep the state off our backs. We were fairly clear about our agendas of collective liberation without government interference. We knew we didn't want to lose ourselves in giant political coalitions or under some other group's authority. Even within the People's Hurricane Relief Fund coalition we maintained our autonomy.

One day in the early weeks, a truck from Islamic Relief showed up with supplies from Mormon and Catholic charities. It was unloaded by people from the neighborhood, anarchists, Communists, and hippies working together in solidarity. Sectarian ideologies were set aside not just on that day, but in the months and years to come. We were able to be who we were and didn't have to be something we were not.

There were rough patches, though. Throughout Common Ground's growth, individuals and groups tried to influence or even highjack our organization. They reminded me of sharks at a feeding, rabid and single-minded, with a focus on their agendas before the wishes of the populace. This included various Communist/socialist groups, black nationalists, anarchists, and radicals of different stripes. For example, members of the International Socialist Organization tried to come in and run the organization. A few of us on the security crew made them leave at gunpoint in the early days. They would not stop soliciting donations from people and trying to sell their damn newspapers in the middle of a disaster area. We, as an organization, were clear in our political principles and protective of our political space. They were usually given a choice to participate in an open democratic process just like the rest of us, or leave. One cool New Orleans night, we burned stacks of papers left behind by people from the Revolutionary Communist Party in our barrel stove for warmth.

Copwatch

> Every cop is a criminal and all the sinners saints
> —Rolling Stones, "Sympathy for the Devil"

We put our guns away as more members of civil society arrived, thinking that the media coverage, our relationships with community leaders, and our transparency about our work would provide us with enough protection. We were wrong.

We were under physical, photo, and video surveillance twenty-four hours a day. Detentions of locals, black and white, continued as more officers from other parts of the state streamed in. We struggled to find other ways to confront the escalating assaults.

One of the many hard-hit families in the neighborhood was large and poor. They were white folks that lived one street over from Malik. Two of the kids spent a lot of time hanging out, helping us, and getting fed. There were always some neighborhood kids underfoot, or riding their bikes around. It was nice to hear their laughter in the dead seriousness of the world around us. Josh was about ten, and his older brother Richard was eighteen. They had never learned to read. They didn't have much schooling before the storm and now had even less. Emily Posner spent time in between everything else teaching Josh to read.[53]

Richard was a big guy who had just gotten out of juvenile hall before Katrina (he had been in for theft). He made his way back to Algiers in the aftermath and began to volunteer. He was a misguided kid who could be really helpful and simultaneously steal from anyone, even his allies.

My radio crackled. Lisa Fithian was calling for back up around the corner from the distro center. A couple of us rushed down to find some policemen pummeling Richard into the ground in broad daylight. They held him down and beat him as stunned onlookers pleaded with them to stop. When the cops finished, they picked him up and told him to stop stealing or they would kill him. After everything that had happened in the previous weeks, we could do nothing. There were not enough of us to stop them; it was not safe to escalate the situation.

Due to ongoing police attacks like that one, Jenka Soderberg and Greg Griffith, along with other volunteers, tried another tactic by forming a Copwatch group. They intended to use video cameras to document law enforcement's constant stops of neighbors and volunteers, whether it was NOPD, state troopers, Homeland Security, or the military. They got cameras donated and developed a modified program. They documented prevalent abuses. They also spread the message about the abuse and illegal detentions that were happening in New Orleans through grassroots media.

Law enforcement officers did not like the light shining on their illegal and sometimes brutal behaviors; they started retaliating against the documenters. When Copwatch volunteers showed up to document a detention, the police would spew expletives and threaten them by name.

Two weeks into the program, a little after curfew, a young black man was being detained and harassed across the street from the clinic. Jenka and Greg jumped into action, filming from a safe distance. The white cop started with the usual threats: they had better "turn the fucking camera off or there is going to be trouble!" Greg continued filming, citing his rights to observe police activity from a distance. Two cops grabbed him, threw him against the car, and handcuffed him. The police officers told him he was "gonna get it." They let the detained man go, and took Greg in their cruiser, making threats on his life. We were angry and afraid as they whisked him away.

We had had guns drawn on us, endured constant hounding and the raid, but this was the first time a volunteer had been taken away. Greg later said that, as the police cruiser drove through dark and empty streets, they threatened to kill him numerous times. They said they would "drop him in the river" if Copwatch didn't stop videotaping. Then they pulled to the side of a street, uncuffed him and told him to walk back to Algiers in the dark. He was worried they would shoot him in the back as he walked away, but they just drove off into the night. He reached someone by phone and made it back safe but shaken.

Copwatch also uncovered that people were being locked up in a FEMA jail in a haphazardly converted Greyhound bus station near downtown. This place, full of forgotten prisoners, was dubbed Camp Greyhound. There were hundreds, if not thousands, of mostly black and Latino men locked behind rusting fencing in this hellhole, without access to water, food, or shelter from the elements, and limited access to bathroom facilities.

People were constantly piled in, some for petty crimes like jaywalking or being alone on a street at the wrong time. Many were locked away and forgotten for weeks. They were being held with no processing, without any documentation of their arrests, access to representation or means to communicate with anyone to where they were.[54]

With the assistance of Soleil Rodriguez and Bill Quigley (a New Orleans law professor), Greg and Jenka set up a wider legal aid project within Common Ground called NOLAW (New Orleans Legal Action Workers). They were a legal collective to counteract police oppression and address the legal concerns of New Orleans citizens.[55] They set up Know Your Rights workshops, offered free legal consultation on tenants' and homeowners' rights, housing, insurance, and other matters. NOLAW became another semiautonomous project in the Common Ground network.

Nothingman

> You hold onto what you have; you do not give it up easily, even when you know it is poisoning you.
>
> —Poppy Z. Brite

Brandon Darby returned to New Orleans in late October to an established and growing organization. In a chain reaction that had started immediately after the levees gave way, he went from being an activist with very little experience in social justice or even charity work to a coordinator with a lot of power.

Malik had never met Brandon before I brought him to his door in September. He ended up trusting Brandon because in the previous weeks the three of us had faced many dire situations together. This greatly affected Malik's perceptions, and the other volunteers' about him, as well as my own. Brandon benefited from his association with me, and my credibility within anarchist and radical circles. Coupled with Brandon's own blustering bravado, and the patriarchy and power dynamics within the organization, this led to assumptions that he was an anarchist revolutionary who had a lot of experience as a community organizer.

These factors allowed him to quickly gain more power within the organization than he deserved or could handle. This opened the doors to many private controversies and public fights about his role in the collective. I wasn't sorting out everything very well, and in the process I inadvertently became a shield for him.

Shortly after his arrival he was given the task of increasing our already small-scale clandestine operations across the river in the Ninth Ward. We were already making plans to wind down many of the larger operations on the West Bank in early 2006. Brandon didn't do it alone; many other people were instrumental in the endeavor.

I had shared my private objections and concerns with Malik about this decision. We had argued behind closed doors. Malik was adamant that he wanted Brandon to head it up. When Brandon first returned, I was glad to see him. He was one the few people who had lived through the early fucked-up situations. I didn't think, though, that he was the person to head this project. He had just arrived and was hardly plugged into anything yet. It entailed too much responsibility and power. He knew me, Malik, and Lisa Fithian; he didn't know how we were organized or who the coordinators or other volunteers were, much less the communities around us. He came back to an organization that was explicitly striving to be horizontal. He had no real experience, or any real agreement with those community-based organizing models. He had never organized anything even remotely close to this scale, and he was not good at working cooperatively with people. He had shown some capabilities that could be assets, I had to admit, but he was a mess! This set the stage for larger problems. I knew his past and his lack of experience was a concern. He could be charming on first encounters but troubling as the veneer peeled away. That day set into play unimaginable consequences.

Raising Common Ground

So raise your hands in the air like you're born again
But make a fist for the struggle we was born to win
                                        —The Coup, "Get Up"

From Point A to Somewhere

As summer's heat held on through mid-October, some semblance of normalcy was returning to the fortunate few west and north of New Orleans. In some of the outer suburbs, people were coming back; a few schools and businesses were open again. But even with some of the city infrastructure reappearing, New Orleans was a shadow of its former self. It was still largely empty, especially in the poorest neighborhoods. In the center of New Orleans, and in much of the Gulf Coast to the south and east (closer to ground zero of the storm and initial flooding), the situation was still bleak. Roadways were still buried under mud or water, while uprooted trees, downed power lines, and broken gas pipes littered the sides of the roads. Across most of the West Bank, electrical power was down, and telephone service was intermittent. A handful of working streetlights changed colors for no one while others lay half broken on the side of the street. Mountains of debris appeared across the cityscape as the contents of houses and some of their structures were pushed around by giant machines. For city officials, poor people were a low priority in terms of reconnecting services; but some of their homes were of the highest priority for the coming demolitions. New Orleans wasn't bouncing back for the majority. It was as if the city's heart had washed away in the tides and still had not returned.

Two corporate chain stores were the first to open near Algiers, as resources were prioritized for them before any of the nearby small businesses. Neither one was easy to get to: many of the main roads were obstructed by wreckage, construction or the military. For the first few weeks, there was no direct path. I stood in long lines for hours with contractors and other aid workers under a heavily armed military and police presence. Because of the hordes of other people looking for the same items, the shelves were often sparsely stocked or empty. We had the added issue of having to travel to the town of Gretna, a nearly all-white town. Its police force was racist and proud of it. They had revealed their racism after the storm, repelling hundreds of people who, out of desperation, walked to their town across a bridge looking for help. With gunfire and police lines, the City of Gretna police made the crowd turn back, refusing them entry or any help. By now, signs had been printed and placed in the yards of the white residents, thanking the police chief for his "heroism." The Gretna police were leery of our movement between Algiers and their city. They followed us regularly to the city line and occasionally stopped and questioned us.

In most areas of the city, New Orleans seemed to have more aid and contract workers than ordinary residents. The media was reporting that over 350,000 people of a population of around 500,000 still had not returned to their homes. Meanwhile, Halliburton subcontractors were getting jobs; their relationship with the Bush administration virtually guaranteed no-bid contracts. Contractors were hired to do clean-up and construction work that city, state and federal agencies would not do. It became a money-making opportunity for fly-by-night operators. There was no oversight. The subcontractors hired immigrant workers as day laborers. Small immigrant worker communities, including whole families, were cropping up in parks and other public spaces. The workers were not provided places to stay, and were not making enough money to afford the few hotel rooms available. As elsewhere in the U.S., they were hired to do arduous and dangerous work for near slave wages. Sometimes they did not get paid at all. Contractors were skipping town after getting paid, leaving the workers with less than nothing for their labor. Through Carolina Reyes, a labor organizer, Common Ground supported a campaign in defense of day laborers. We provided support services for the workers, feeding them and offering them medical attention with our mobile clinic. Eventually, we worked together to organize for the recuperation of lost wages and safer working conditions. Their stories remained largely invisible through the coverage of the entire calamity.[56]

The last of the floodwaters finally receded in many of the neighborhoods across the river from Algiers. They left mud-encrusted houses with watermarks and spray-paint marks left by the search and rescue teams of those who had died—reminders of the dead that now only haunted these empty houses. On windy days the drying mud created small dust storms that coated every surface, including our faces. Sometimes it looked like billowing smoke. New Orleans was becoming a breeding ground for respiratory illnesses and Common Ground a repository of coughs, fevers, and running noses, not to mention Staph infections. Immune systems were compromised by chronic stress, close quarters, mold, injuries, and unsanitary conditions as well as constant exposure to unknown chemicals in the water, soil, and air.

Our hub at Malik's house was overcrowded, buzzing with people in action and supplies in motion. We maintained a fairly consistent number of volunteers while our workload increased. Between the clinics and the distro center, we served hundreds of people a day. Pallets stacked high with cases of water bottles, cleaning supplies, canned foods, diapers, and hygiene kits continued to arrive. When we started, there were no more than five of us. By late September, over seventy volunteers were divided between the clinic and the distribution center, not counting the rotating cast of characters delivering supplies, coming and going through the military barricades, most of them staying only a day or two. It wasn't nearly enough. We were stretched desperately thin. Our calls to civil society were mostly for materials and money until we could figure out our next steps. The dangers around us included the nearby vigilantes and the police, who had only slightly been kept at bay by the presence of the media and the military. Now, deep into October, our headcount was over 120 people. This was thanks in part to the Veterans For Peace, who had set up an encampment in Slidell, north of New Orleans, from which busloads of people trekked in and out daily.

Common Ground was accomplishing most of its mission. Some of the projects were full scale, such as the clinic, distro and media centers in Algiers, and the distro and mobile clinic in the Houma Nation. Others were gaining priority, including prisoner advocacy, legal defense, and bioremediation. One of our greatest strengths was our flexibility. There was no command hierarchy that information had to go through, followed by useless paperwork and arbitrary rules. Often this meant that people would take up a project simply because they saw the need. Within a few weeks, as we moved from negotiating emergencies to other kinds of issues, a fragile sense of stability was emerging in the programs.

When we considered Common Ground's future, we realized we needed to find more spaces to operate from, warehouse supplies, and house volunteers. Finding spaces was not easy. In addition to the hurricane damage and floodwaters still standing in some areas, many property owners were having great difficulty returning due to the blockades. Also, city utilities remained in disarray. And the influx of aid and contract workers to the region added to the shortage of space. When Malik or I got a break from our daily tasks, we searched Algiers for more spaces: old schools, storefronts, churches, warehouses—any sound structure. I called numerous realtors to no avail. I finally reached one to talk about an empty space around the corner from us on General De Gaulle Street. The price, size, and condition were perfect for us. Malik and I thought we were going to make a deal. When the realtor showed up in his expensive car, we hesitated. He looked at us, a black man and a white man getting out of an old truck, and almost wouldn't show us the property. He stonewalled us all the way. He did not talk to Malik—he hardly even looked at him. I was dumbfounded at his barely concealed racism. Before we walked off the lot, Malik and I knew he was not going to rent it to us. We tried to call him back a few times, but he never returned our calls. For the time, we were out of options.

In all of this disaster, land and real estate speculation was spreading. Landlords started raising rents exorbitantly for current and future tenants. In some areas, residential rents went from $400 to $1200 overnight. Developers and landlords also started holding commercial property that they knew was going to become more valuable. Long-neglected or abandoned buildings became castles of gold in their eyes. Many of us had predicted it before the waters were gone, but it was coming to life faster than we had thought. It made it impossible for us to find more space. Funds were coming in, but we didn't want to spend all of our resources on warehousing supplies when they could go directly to aid.

We had begun all of this with fifty dollars. In the first few weeks, incoming money was sporadic. When the first donations of material aid began to arrive in September, there was around $200 available. The donated supplies covered most of what was required for distribution and medical concerns and fed the few of us. But even then, we needed money for items that were not coming in. It gave us a feeling of great insecurity: we knew we would need funds to purchase supplies and to reimburse people who had bought items on their way into the region. The PHRF coalition raised almost $200,000 in the first few weeks for future projects, while we were scraping by with no cash to continue our meager projects. Coalition member groups didn't have access to that money, though. At Common Ground, we sometimes wondered if money was going to come in at all. Then, somehow, people would get through the barricades, drop off supplies and money (five, ten, fifty dollars), and then leave.

By late September, this was changing. Small financial donations from people became a torrent of giving. We opened a bank account and a PO box in Gretna, the closest functioning post office. Every day, in amounts the Red Cross would scoff at, money arrived attached to wonderful heartfelt notes. Our appeals had always been to people of conscience in civil society. We were clear that we were working on our own terms, with all of the money going directly to aid and rebuilding, not bureaucracy or administra-tion. People were fed up with the waste and inefficiency of the Red Cross, which had reached epic proportions. Student groups from elementary schools, high schools, and colleges were raising money on their campuses and sending it to us with beautiful drawings and notes of support. Letters were also arriving from the elderly and people of modest incomes. There were thousands of them: people who could not come to the Gulf wanted to do something and were starting to find us. Every boxload of letters was a joyful confirmation. Sometimes, when I opened the envelopes, I would cry at the sincerity of people's words. It reinforced my view that people do care for each other when it matters. It was beyond politics, social status, or culture. Emergency hearts were in action everywhere. By the middle of October we had raised almost a hundred thousand dollars, ten and twenty dollars at a time.[57]

Pay No Attention to the Bureaucracy behind the Curtain

Shortly after the Red Cross fiasco in Algiers, FEMA finally came to town. Big trucks crawled up and down the blocks with pomp and fanfare, and, of course, the military and Homeland Security in tow. They took over an abandoned school on Atlantic Avenue, coincidentally one that we had tried to occupy as housing for displaced people, down the street from our distro center. They moved in massive loads of equipment and lots of personnel. Power must always seem large to feel important.

They spent days setting everything up, but they soon began to realize they could not help the majority of those who came to visit them. People needed medical assistance, food, and water; they needed to know when electricity was going to return and where their family members were. FEMA was set up to walk them through an intricate bureaucracy of federal services that would not be available to most people for months or years (if at all), leaving everyone to fend for themselves for anything else. Many of these people were going to need those services, but not as much as they needed debris removed, dogs rounded up, the leaking roofs of their houses patched, or even a basic medical checkup. FEMA only brought paperwork, legal books, computers, rules, regulations, and more paperwork. Through the brilliant puppetry of administration they were going to save the masses— but on the way to the coliseum they forgot to ask people what they needed.

The old school where they set up had more security than FEMA staff; it looked like a military compound. All of their personnel, and eventually anyone who represented the state in any way, would not go anywhere in New Orleans without armed Homeland Security bodyguards. It was comical. Children were playing in the streets every day, but an official had to have guards. It was another illustration of how out of touch they were with the population.

In Algiers, FEMA effectively became a giant referral service to Common Ground Relief and other aid agencies for everything that had to do with people's immediate concerns. We had a vague affiliation with FEMA. As an antiauthoritarian organization, we had been targeted and interfered with in our operations. But here they were, referring people to us. We kept our distance.

As I said, all that FEMA could really offer was the ability to sign up for federal financial aid and other long-term support services. Being as out of touch as they were, FEMA had made the service applications accessible over the Internet. They expected elderly and disadvantaged people, who had no access to computers in their homes much less Internet access even pre-Katrina, to know how to use a computer, access the Internet, and then figure out how to navigate their bureaucratic maze. FEMA ended up sending applicants to us at our media center, where we had people who could help them every step of the way. More importantly, many people stopped going to their heavily armored center. The guns and the staff made people apprehensive.

One day, the regional head of the FEMA office and her armed escort came to the door of our humble clinic on Teche St. She needed immediate minor medical attention, and she chose us over the Red Cross or the military's doctors. On the outside of our clinic, in large letters, a sign read NO FIREARMS ALLOWED INSIDE – NO EXCEPTIONS. This confused her bodyguard, who tried to enter but was rebuffed by volunteer staff. The FEMA director was given the same choice as all of us: either come in unarmed or go somewhere else. She acquiesced, coming in while the guard, agitated, waited outside. Upon leaving, she repeatedly remarked that it was the best medical service she had received or even seen in the region. Although it had been operating outside the rules of the state, the clinic soon gained legitimacy through its meticulous service. Not long after, the Center for Disease Control used the clinic's records to monitor the rise of epidemics in the region.

The military finally gave up their small, lonely clinic and cleared out debris in another building, which they offered to us for our use. We respectfully declined; we had two clinics running as well as our mobile clinics traveling into the bayous along the coast or across the river into the wards. Our hands were full and we wanted to continue to maintain our autonomy.

The state's inability to do anything of substance put us in the position of having to fill in large and overwhelming gaps. Their problem cases quickly became ours, as they left them at our doorstep with increasing frequency, especially the local police. Some of the issues were beyond our abilities, such as dealing with severe physical or psychological problems, or ex-prisoners without resources. We referred these people to other care providers. Mental health was not much of a priority to the establishment, creating a growing homeless street population with mental problems. Handling the people they dropped at our doorstep tested our resourcefulness and political will. It was as if the state wanted to create situations where we would implode from stress. At least we knew that we had to take people somewhere where there were more resources, not just drop them off randomly in the night. In some cases, we had to make hard choices, removing dangerous or damaging people by force. It was important for the health of the organization. It was a form of self-defense.

Nights Punctuate the Longer Days

> There isn't enough of anything
> as long as we live. But at intervals
> a sweetness appears and, given a chance,
> prevails.
>
> —Raymond Carver

The long days wore on in never-ending succession. My sleepless nights were often punctuated by events that had to be dealt with immediately. From dawn to late into the night, I felt like a firefighter, putting out fires of crisis, not an organizer. There were so many emergencies! It was almost impossible to prioritize. It was like having a top-ten list of things to do in which *everything* was number one. Every day, we were providing aid in difficult circumstances, strategizing for future projects, reaching out in new neighborhoods, following up on earlier projects, deflecting police harassment, dealing with the stress of being in close quarters with masses of people, and building internal infrastructure to feed, house, and provide sanitary conditions for incoming volunteers.

I was alternating between sleeping on the ground in a tent in Malik's yard with fifty other people, or on his floor in a maze of people, toe to head.

I could have taken a bed, but gave it up. Neither of my options were restful. Having lain down, I would sleep deeply for about four hours from complete exhaustion unless some calamitous noise or my thoughts of what we needed to do next brought me back to unwanted semiconsciousness. After those first few hours, the rest of my sleep was often troubled, as my mind raced with problem-solving and making lists for the next days.

In a city where food was already scarce, I maintained a vegan diet. This made for some really bad food choices, as well as days of hunger. My already-thin frame became almost fifteen pounds lighter. I was against trying to force people to eat vegan (which some wanted to do) in this situation; for myself, I was unwisely trying to hold on to some semblance of my former life. Water was only available in cases of little plastic bottles, but I could never seem to get enough water into my body out of those damn bottles on those long sweaty days. The one luxury I was able to maintain was brushing my teeth regularly when I woke up. I was glad for it. It was a small ritual I was able to maintain despite the uncertainty of most everything else.

The constant fatigue was wearing through my body and mind. It created surreal moments in which I could not separate days, nights, or weeks. It felt like the longest day of my life: the sun would not set, and my shadow never grew long. I was on high alert, living in the present, with future and past as vague blurs. I couldn't tell how long I had been in New Orleans. I would not give myself permission to relax or to rest. Not in this tragedy where my emergency heart was in overdrive! Sometimes, when I felt bad, I reminded myself that I had it easy, at least compared to those who had lost everything.

Every day, I met women who faced fear for themselves and their kids due to lack of shelter, food, or security; and young men who, in addition to those issues, had to face a police state where they were the targets. I had the privilege to exit the situation; most of them did not. I too had been a victim of unwarranted violence, but on most days my fatigue seemed somewhat trivial by comparison.

I was not alone in my hardship; I saw it all around me. Hundreds of other people were locked in similar tunnels, a sort of walking wounded suffering from traumatic stress due to constant fight or flight situations. Some of the other volunteers were struggling with the same discomforts and unhealthy comparisons I was making. Our souls were on the outside—bare. We were battered by despair over our surroundings and what needed to be done. But we maintained our resolve to continue. We worked endlessly and our hearts bled along with everyone else. How could we leave? We all needed each other. Even if what I contributed was only a small part, it was something. At the same time, though I did not want to think about leaving, I knew it would eventually kill me to stay in a situation like this—spiritually, if not physically.

Damn Everything but the Circus!

New Orleans has long been a home for disenfranchised traveling artists. Inventive dropouts go there to ply their crafts, or stop for a while to soak up the countercultural atmosphere before continuing on their merry traveling adventures. After the storm, this incoming tide accelerated. In part, it stemmed from the Common Ground Collective's calls out to radical communities. Our missives were bringing masses of volunteers into New Orleans. The networks we reached out to crossed other networks, with word spreading like wildfire across white radical subcultures, from train-hopping hobos, street and circus performers, DIY punks, to squatters, burners, and forest hippies. Most joined the efforts to relieve and rebuild the city, offering music and other creative endeavors as well as labor. But, disconcertingly, some within these subcultures came to live out a fantasy of living in a burned-out, postapocalyptic city. They gave little credence to the tragedies of the people who lived there, or to the ongoing relief work. Some of them were self-described anarchists, but they acted like assholes, giving anarchism and radical subculture a bad name. They were narcissists whose personal liberty meant more to them than being respectful or alleviating the suffering around them.

Although they were a minority even among all of these other groups, they took advantage of Common Ground's limited resources, using our food, water, and beds, and contributing nothing. Meanwhile, others squatted and wrote graffiti on abandoned houses and buildings near where we were working, which created difficulties between Common Ground and people in the communities who held us responsible for these actions. When we tried to hold these travelers accountable, they called us authoritarian. We shouldered this responsibility although it caused internal conflict; we had no control of who came and went.

This disrespect for surrounding communities and lack of accountability from people who should have been comrades was disappointing. Their refusal to reach outside of their small world revealed a deep cultural and political inexperience.

In a State of Contradictions

Various branches of the military, mostly made up of the National Guard, Army, and Marines established a series of large command centers and barracks in Algiers, increasing their visibility exponentially on our side of the river. Along the way, an unexpected thing happened. Compared to the ongoing hostilities we were having with the police, it was as though we had entered into an unspoken truce with them. This in spite of the fact that some commanders openly opposed Common Ground because we did not follow orders and leave the restricted areas we were in nor did we register with federal or local agencies to legitimize our presence in these areas.

In the odd dynamics of New Orleans, the military was one of the only buffers between the out-of-control police and everyone else. The police immediately reduced violent language and improved their demeanor toward detained people if the military arrived on the scene. Out of earshot of their commanders, a few soldiers acknowledged our observations. We started believing that the police would not kill anyone with the military presence in the area.

To be clear, the military units we encountered were not our friends (or even tactical allies) by any stretch of the imagination. In the complex dynamics of power, they were in a gray area: they had shifted from shaking down volunteers and residents in September to, at worst, treating us with indifference, and at best being cordial. Their actions at that later time contradicted my early experiences engaging with them immediately after the storm. I could see the humanity of many of these young soldiers, without having to fear them. But I always remembered that, like the police, given the order to shoot me they would. That is what they are trained to do. We maintained a questionable peace with the units that came and went.

Montgomery's Got the Answer

Around the time of the increase in military and media presence, the Algiers Point vigilantes receded back into the swampy waters of their lives. Their patrols were withering away while our projects flourished. They had been making themselves scarce in the previous weeks, but we would still see them occasionally. At first I did not know what to think when we didn't see them. I could not trust it. Our security people stayed on alert; Suncere speculated that they were regrouping. As the days passed, it became apparent that they were finally gone. Their patrols were becoming a series of bad memories. We still saw a few of them, individually armed, on foot within their own neighborhood of Algiers Point, but they did not leave those few blocks anymore.

It was truly strange to see these men who had terrorized the surrounding neighbors in armed groups now walking down the street by themselves, drinking at a bar or talking to their neighbors, white, black, or Latino, as if nothing had happened. Anger would well up when I came near them. My emotional wounds were still fresh. I could not forget, and neither could the people who had been terrorized by them. Is this how Klansmen acted in the not so distant past? Night riders under the cover of darkness, good citizens by daylight? I tried to channel my anger into the tasks at hand as we continued to protect communities against their remnants and the state.[58]

Tense Coalition

The relationships between the many groups in the PHRF coalition were beneficial but tenuous. The baggage of old personal and political relationships between locals, lack of clear channels of communication and transparency in the decisions about the allocations of resources, and the difficulties in coming up with strategies for the future were difficult for everyone. These issues, combined with the fact that Common Ground had a largely white base of volunteers with little exposure to the historical problems of oppression in New Orleans, led to disagreements over our place in the struggles. The Common Ground Collective was held (by some PHRF groups) to levels of accountability that were unattainable and damaging. It wasn't that, as an organization, we were oblivious to the questions of privilege, oppression, or our place in the struggles. But we were overwhelmed with overlapping priorities that we addressed as best as we could. We were in a double bind: lauded by the communities we served, but viewed as inauthentic by some local radicals.

PHRF effectively drew attention to the plights that New Orleanians were facing daily: police brutality, evictions, job losses, skyrocketing rent prices, demolitions, as well as empty government promises and outright lies. They organized demonstrations at government buildings. Common Ground helped coordinate and spoke at some of the events. Mostly, though, we gave PHRF logistical support. It was not uncommon for us to pull our work crews from other projects to attend rallies or other behind the scenes efforts. This gave a broader exposure to the intricacies of New Orleans politics to many young whites.[59]

PHRF and Common Ground needed each other, but we at the Common Ground Collective maintained our political autonomy due to our views on coalitions and united fronts. Broad coalitions are problematic in that groups are brought together in the name of noble ideals, but shared values and relationships between them are not concrete enough to flesh out the coalition's goals. The coalition we were part of was diverse and growing larger. We formed many lasting relationships, but there were also organizations fulfilling their own agendas along with coalition work.

One of the worst examples of a self-serving agenda in a PHRF organization was that of the New Black Panther Party, which constantly directed hostility toward us. The NBP is notorious for being a shortsighted, sexist, homophobic, and anti-Semitic organization that refuses to ally with white people. Common Ground volunteers had to face being chided as "crackers that needed to leave New Orleans and go work in our own cities" when NBP members spoke in public or at meetings. Remarks like these were due solely to the demographics of our organization, not to our politics or the work we were doing. At one event, I defiantly stated to NBP members from Chicago that Common Ground would leave any area they wanted if they would continue to organize and carry on the work we were already doing there. They refused the offer. As a group, they had yet to clean anything up, gut a house, or feed or provide medical aid to anyone. Yet they showed up at meetings and marches when the cameras were rolling, made their reactionary statements, and left. To longtime organizers (including former members of the original Panthers) who had been a part of multiracial coalitions, the NBP was just a disruptive force. To new volunteers who heard the NBP's words without context or history, however, they were intimidating and called into question Common Ground's legitimacy in New Orleans.

Generally, PHRF sometimes acted as an umbrella coalition representing many voices and, at other times as its own organization. This added to the confusion of navigating the spaces that Common Ground operated in. Despite the grievances between us, organizing in the coalition was important in shaping narratives to focus on local injustices. They addressed issues a majority of us in Common Ground didn't have the knowledge or history in the city to deal with.

The Hand of Maradona

The seven-day, sunup to late night workweek was burning everyone out. My soul was clamoring for play, something to break the stress. Amid all the turbulence, we decided to take our first afternoon off in mid-October to have a small neighborhood-wide block party where we could play anarchist soccer. Anarchist soccer is a friendly, noncompetitive, all-skill-level game that encourages teamwork. I think it is a great horizontal organizing tool, locally and internationally, because soccer is a game that transcends national borders.[60]

We hesitatingly closed the clinic and the distribution centers on a Sunday for the first time since our founding. We cleared a field as best we could on a vacant lot between two buildings. There were many deep holes; here and there, large rods of twisted rebar stuck out of the ground. We brought sheets of cardboard to cover a decaying dog carcass at the field's edge. Some neighbors put together a potluck cookout for everyone to enjoy.

Before the end of the day, a soccer game was organized. We separated into teams: the clinic vs. distro center—and the game was on! A sweaty mess of over forty people ran around furiously in the early evening. It was the first time we had taken a break, giving ourselves a chance to be ordinary humans bonding in fun. Nightfall came quickly, bringing our relief to an exhausted end. When the dawn returned the next day, we were in the thick of it again.

Urban Ecology

I think it is a travesty for families to live in contaminated areas with substandard housing and lack of access to fresh, healthy food. Many low-income New Orleans neighborhoods were near former dumpsites or shuttered industries that left their poisonous remnants near where people lived. Almost two months after the storm these issues came to the forefront.

The floodwaters had flowed through everything, including current and abandoned factories, commercial buildings, homes, and thousands of motor vehicles. All of the chemicals that make life as we know it were mixed in the water. Oil, gas, chemicals, paint, dirt, debris, decaying bodies—everything under the sun. Stagnant waters held on in some of the lowest-lying areas. In large areas of the city there was a thin, windswept film on everything from being under the toxic soup for weeks and then drying in the sun. No one knew for sure what was in the water, in the soil, or the occasional dust storms.

Refrigerators that had been abandoned were on the verge of being explosive due to rot. We had been moving them out since the first week, and we stepped it up as the weeks progressed. The boxes were clearly marked with hazard symbols in spray paint, sealed up tight with duct tape or rope, collected and piled high throughout the neighborhoods to be carted off at some unknown time. Occasionally a stray box would throw itself open with an undeniable, heavy stench that caused gag reflexes blocks away. We wore HAZMAT suits with heavy air filters when handling them.

Most residents still had not returned to their homes to check up on what damage they had incurred. Mold was filling houses, and putrid garbage had to be dealt with. The empty houses were becoming toxic tombs. The problem was compounded by state agencies that were still keeping people from returning to many areas. What would they return to? Some houses had been underwater for days or weeks. Others had been sealed tight against the stormy weather, only to have their rooftops damaged by wind or falling trees, allowing water to pour in. This scenario created an ideal combination of warmth and moisture for molds to grow unhampered.

Then, we began to hear rumors from local and federal agencies that, if owners did not come to take care of their homes, they would be torn down. Renters could be evicted for not returning. How could displaced people return without the means to do so? How could people come back to areas they were not allowed into?

Part of the Common Ground Collective's mission was to address immediate environmental impacts while helping to create long-term sustainability. So we decided to try gutting houses and removing debris after people approached us for help with wind and water damage. Polly from Veterans For Peace brought us mold remediation and equipment for the newly formed house gutting crews. Sean (a coordinator of the roof tarping projects), Malik, and I went to the first house to see what we could do. It belonged to a woman in her sixties whose roof had been torn off by severe winds. This left a gaping hole for the rain to come in. The house sat for weeks, leaving mold to grow.

On the outside, her house looked normal, except for the missing section of roofing shingles and wood. Inside black mold was creeping up the walls, the sheetrock turning to dust in places, while furniture, papers, and fabrics were all slowly disintegrating. Extreme humidity and heat had combined into a sort of pressure cooker. The smell set off my gag reflexes instantly. It is unforgettable, not like the smell of death and putrefaction, but rather a liquid decay of the organic and the chemical. The earth was reclaiming things and wiping remembrances, reducing everything to matted heaps: mementos of times past, photographs of loved ones through the decades, and family heirlooms, like her mother's shawl, were reduced to decaying detritus. It was a heartbreaking experience. My spirit swelled with sadness. Situations like this made me human; they made our large-scale operations personal. Every house we opened brought home how lives and memories were being consumed by decay.

We divided into two three-person crews, donning HAZMAT suits in the stifling heat. Before we started with heavy demolition, we experimented with some nonchemical enzyme cleaners to see if we could remediate the mold without creating more toxic problems. We eventually realized that we needed to remove almost everything, including the walls, down to the wooden studs, then spray bleach on the wood that was left. It was a primitive process. We sweated in the 95-degree heat, first carrying furniture and household items to the curb, then removing everything, including the sheetrock, to the bare wood with crowbars and hammers.

We only helped gut a few more houses. As the home demolitions loomed, though, especially in the Seventh and Ninth wards, we knew it was something we would need to do. Otherwise people were going to lose their homes. Our phones rang all day with calls for house gutting. It was sorely needed and in short supply.[61]

Despite the official word that New Orleans was environmentally safe, we wanted to find out for ourselves. My friend Lauren Ross, an environmental engineer and community organizer, came to New Orleans to do some testing. Shortly after her arrival came the Pagan Cluster.[62] Their goal was to gather toxicity information about the surrounding landscape, bioremediate neighborhood areas, and help create sustainable projects, such as community gardens, based on permaculture principles. Lauren, Lisa, and others gathered hundreds of samples for testing in a lab. In addition to the testing, volunteers set up barrels for rainwater harvesting and composting toilets at Malik's house. (The toilets were much-needed!). They reused materials from the debris that was everywhere.

Other volunteers set to work clearing the weeds, tall grasses, mud, and trash that lay in lots between buildings. They cleaned up gardens that had existed before the levees' failure, and dug a few new ones. They employed small-scale bioremediation techniques: cleaner soil was placed on top of some areas; plants that draw toxins out of the soil were planted in others. Some experimented with spraying microbes on soils to break down toxic chemicals.

The gardens were gathering places for conversation, beautifying unoccupied and derelict spaces that gathered garbage even before the storm. Eventually, they would provide food security to those around them. In the grueling circumstances we were in, it was a dream for the future to have a few small gardens dot the cityscape and to hear people talking about growing their own food. These projects helped me take notice of the wild sunflowers pushing through concrete in out-of-the-way places.

Homes Are More than Wood and Bricks

> Everybody needs to do what they need to do. But this is what I'm going to do. I'm going to fight for my community. I'm going to fight for my home. Because it's worth it and it means the world to me.
> —Pam Dashiell, Lower Ninth Ward Community Leader,
> Holy Cross Neighborhood Association

The fall was still hanging on to the summer heat when word started to spread that unscrupulous landlords had begun evicting people. The city government tacitly allowed them to do it, while setting ambiguous, unknown deadlines for people to return. Most of these evictions were illegal: landlords simply tossed belongings to the street. The rest were evictions with minimal notification. Developers and landlords were pushing government agencies for a veil of legitimacy to expand what they were doing illegally. Soon, city officials granted them that rubber stamp. If they got their way, they were going to start removing people from homes, whether or not they had been contacted or returned.

The first wave of illegal evictions affected people who had not been able to return for many reasons. It wasn't that people did not want to come back, even if only to get their things. Families had been evacuated by the state and did not have the money to return; jobs had evaporated due to the disaster. Large parts of the city still remained closed, and there was a lack of services (electricity, water, gas) except in the few neighborhoods that had not been affected so severely.

The landlords had ulterior motives. As I said, rental and housing prices in New Orleans were skyrocketing and the people who were pouring into the city were ready to pay the higher prices. These included both returning locals and recent arrivals such as aid, contract, and nonprofit workers. Landlords, developers, and real estate agents wanted to cash in on the new money.

It was imperative to stop landlords from forcing people from their homes. There were some Common Ground volunteers who had experience as housing advocates: Jeremy, Jenka, Bork, and others quickly mobilized to form Common Ground Eviction Defense using direct-action strategies. The homeless population from the disaster was already on the rise. Groups of volunteers were dedicated to un-evicting people from their homes. When landlords removed belongings, the eviction defense team returned them to their homes and set everything back up. In a number of cases, the landlords did not check back to see if the housing had been reoccupied, and families were able to stay in their places longer. In the cases of unoccupied homes, the belongings were returned instead of being ruined on the streets. It was a short-term tactic, part of a strategy of giving people a chance while bringing larger housing issues to light.

Our eviction defense teams were part of a larger antieviction coalition that Common Ground cofounded with residents from Forest Park Tenants Association, Hands Off Iberville Coalition, and volunteers from PHRF called NOHEAT (New Orleans Housing Emergency Action Team). This small, raucous coalition, made up of pre- and post-Katrina groups, began working together on eviction defense strategies. Through our own eviction defense teams and NOHEAT, we were working to stop a good number of evictions. We also protested against city and federal housing authorities, using public events to shame them into stopping displacement. Common Ground volunteers used their privilege to directly alleviate the problem and challenge the landlords and the state, risking arrest, while NOHEAT's community organizing efforts used media events and legal maneuvers to expose unscrupulous landlords.

Their first effort was at Forest Park Public Housing in Algiers, not far from the distro center. It was a typical public housing complex in New Orleans. It had not been maintained properly, but was still livable. HUD (U.S. Department of Housing and Urban Development) wanted to shut it down and remove all of the tenants without giving them any place to go. The tenants quickly formed a group to counter it and reached out to a volunteer at Common Ground. When local police showed up to remove the first tenants, NOHEAT was there, stopping the evictions and forcing these issues into the media. In a few days, HUD acquiesced and people were given a reprieve. No one was going to be put out onto the streets anytime soon. It seemed like a big win for all of us on the ground, to push back and hold those important spaces. Eventually, such actions led to calls for moratoriums on evictions across the city. The direct-action and mobilizing skills used in eviction defense were soon incorporated into stopping large-scale home demolitions. Entire neighborhoods that had been heavily flooded and almost all public housing across the city were in danger.

Neighborhoods were on the cusp of being erased, house by house, apartment by apartment, from working-class areas to the poorest, hardest-hit communities. The Common Ground Collective was just beginning to use its potential as a grassroots political force to accomplish more than aid and service work. The struggles for self-determination around housing issues became critical, from the bayous to the Seventh Ward and especially the Ninth Ward. People deserved to be able to come back to their homes.[63]

A Sort of Homecoming

Common Ground was distributing thousands of pounds of aid across the region. Our mobile medical clinics were setting up all over the parishes to give people who hadn't received any medical attention after Katrina initial consultations. When our mobile teams, showed up, lines of people formed. We had been successful in getting the word out. November was around the corner when Kerul, Emily, Lisa, and Malik started developing the idea of bringing college students from all over the country to New Orleans to spend their holiday there. It was a way to harness the energy of college students, based on the Freedom Riders of the 1960s. The first event was to be called Roadtrip for Relief.[64] We were going to sponsor it over the Thanksgiving holiday. The hope was that it was going to bring over a thousand college students to volunteer for a week in New Orleans.

On many fronts, all of the grassroots organizations fighting for justice and providing aid were beginning to hold critical physical and psychological spaces for people to come back. Some were just beginning to make the journey back home. We were fighting for a better New Orleans for them, one where they could work for a living wage, have access to healthy food, decent housing, and quality education for their children, and be treated with respect.[65]

We had established the largest functioning organization based on anarchist ideals in the United States since the IWW of the 1920s. We were participating in direct democracy at every turn with local residents, community leaders, and volunteers through neighborhood assemblies. Our general meetings were swelling with people, and our coordinators' meetings were growing as well. Everyone was in the streets. Community-organized revolution was in the air—not for a seizure of state power, but a revolution of a different kind, the revolution of exercising grassroots power to make the changes we all wanted to see. Our revolution challenged the standard pessimism about people's limited agency in their own lives. We were making some difference for today and for tomorrow. It was a Battle for New Orleans with the people whose lives depended on it.

Common Ground was far from being a well-oiled machine, but that is the beauty of living revolutions: even with the best of plans, they are open-ended, like watching your dreams play out in waking life. Differing levels of commitment, knowledge, skills, and abilities were interweaving to make these dreams a reality. People with compassion and a desire to improve the world were willing to give up their lives and privilege, in the name of hope, for the lives of people they had never met. Why? For the simple reason that it was the right thing to do.

But I was headed elsewhere. As hard as it was, from the first day, at the kitchen table, I repeatedly expressed to Malik, Sharon and others that I could not be there forever. I would help build and stabilize the project, but ultimately they would decide its future. When I would remind Malik that at some point I would have to leave the day-to-day operations to return to my other life, he would look at me and say, "Aw, you just sayin' that, bro!" Then we would share an uncomfortable laugh and try to forget about it.

Now, as October was drawing to a close, the moment was here. I needed to leave. Between long, hot days of work and all of the confrontations with the police and military, I was a mess. (Malik was too. However, he had left the region on many occasions to raise funds and had gotten some regular sleep along the way.) Although I had gained strength from what we were accomplishing, my heart was broken. I had continued to eat badly, sleeping on the ground in what felt like a war zone of gunfire and sirens, while having to use every ounce of my energy at every minute. I had lost weight, my adrenal glands were spent, and I was getting sick again. I was suffering from undiagnosed shell shock. I couldn't see straight. The other parts of my life were severely strained by my absence. I had originally intended to be there for a few days, which became weeks—and now it had been two months. It was time for me to go home. While I had been in New Orleans, everything outside of this had become an abstraction. I wanted the joy of returning to my normal life, to see my partner and my home, and to sleep in my own bed.

But I didn't want to leave. There was so much more to do! I wanted to continue to be on the ground. It was my revolutionary vision to be a part of something like this. It was the chance of a lifetime to do something that could offer profound change in people's lives, including my own. Everything in my life had brought me here. We were on the cusp of something that was having a larger impact, something that would reverberate for years to come. And there was still so much reimagining to do for a better New Orleans. I had been there almost continuously through the most chaotic, transformative, tragic, and critical times.

I felt that I was leaving people in dangerous situations. My guiding principle in actions has always been never to leave anyone behind, and yet here I was, possibly leaving thousands of people in need behind. We had become an extended family, integral parts of each others' lives with deep love for each other.

Yes, I had deeply contradictory feelings about leaving. I was tied to this place and the people. Sadness, guilt, fear, and joy moved in waves, rising and falling through my soul. I could not put it into words. I was concerned that we were not doing enough to support and protect these still vulnerable communities, though I didn't know how we could do more. I didn't want Common Ground to lose momentum, or, worse, attract more repression as we expanded our operations into the neighborhoods across the river. I was sure the organization would continue without me. I wondered, however, if people would step in as we had if faced with continued adversity. Given Common Ground's direct-action tactics and dual-power strategy, we were already breaking unjust and immoral laws for the sake of people. We would need to continue this to build a strong political will to defend ourselves as well as the neighborhoods from further attacks by the state or other interests. I didn't know if I would be able to defend a community as we had done in September without relief from my present responsibilities. I tried to remember that I was just one person in a swirl of thousands fighting of justice. It was one of the few thoughts that gave me comfort.

Given the rapid pace of change, leaving meant that, when I came back, small things would always be different. Houses would still be vacant and lots would still be full of debris, but the heightened social connections built on daily interaction would fade. Neighborhood people would be meeting continuous flows of new faces. Even if we held a special place in each other's hearts, it would be blurred by time and circumstance. Although there were many scenes and events that I wanted to leave behind, there are some faces and words exchanged while working together that I will never forget. I value the solidarity, the beauty of deep convictions, and the love of humanity of the many good people who rose up together.

These were some of the most difficult, engaging, and beautiful months of my life. The Common Ground Collective was far from over. I had given everything I had to help establish it. I was not leaving the collective, but I wasn't going to be there on a daily basis anymore. I would only see it when I returned for meetings or events. I wouldn't see its daily ebb and flow first-hand anymore, but I would carry it with me from afar. The organization continued to do amazing things under adverse conditions while I continued my involvement from behind the scenes in Texas.

An important part of the swirling emotions was a reserved joy. We had created a crack in history. We had revealed the lies, corruption, and failures of the state, and, without hesitating, we had done something about it. I had seen a transition from hopelessness to hope as thousands of people answered the call to come to the Gulf. We were part of a grassroots struggle to rebuild the city from below. We were fighting for the right of return for residents who were scattered into a diaspora by incompetence and corruption. Through the projects of the Common Ground Collective we were providing ongoing basic health care, legal aid, and safe shelter for women while forcing police accountability, supporting prisoners' rights, defending housing from being demolished, stopping evictions, gutting houses, working with neighborhood councils, and creating food security for the future. All of our efforts would continue to be based in solidarity and eventually in mutual aid.

In spite of the constant attacks, and our illegitimacy in the clouded eyes of the state, we had successfully established a foothold for ourselves. We had gathered together in areas to which it was said no one would return. We were helping them to return. The clinics, both in Algiers and the mobile unit, were running smoothly, seeing over a hundred patients per day. People answered our calls with material aid and smiling, determined faces.

Our organization was stabilized, and we had strength in numbers, creativity, determination, and local support. We were not afraid of the indifference, corruption, or violence of the state. We would not let them bulldoze homes, evict families or deny city services to starve people out. They would not be able make it impossible for people to return. We would not let Power deny dignity and self-determination to anyone.

The ideas and actions had come at the right time, in the right place and taken root. While we were in the thick of it, a few cynics said that our dream of revolution would amount to nothing. I say: bullshit! Our critics tried to belittle our ideas and all that we had done by saying that we were white kids trying to relive the dreams of the 1960s, or that we were looking for activist cred. As if all we were engaged in was some protest to make ourselves feel better! Common Ground was in the midst of a revolution. We were, as June Jordan once put it, naming our destiny. We ignored the cynics. Our dreams of justice and self-determination had helped thousands of people in direct and meaningful ways. It was painful and difficult, but it was also remarkable. No one can take that away from us. Was it idealistic? Hell yes! When anyone said that what we were attempting was impossible. I would respond that I would rather die a dreamer than live as a cynic. Dreaming the impossible had gotten us this far!

We had not waited for them before and we were not going to wait now. Those who assumed Power could not break the spirits, love, or commitment of the dispossessed. My part of this story was ending, but the future of New Orleans remained unwritten. With emergency hearts, we stood with the people of New Orleans, resisting and rebuilding on common ground.

An Ending and a Beginning

> History is hard to know, because of all the hired bullshit, but even without being sure of "history" it seems entirely reasonable to think that every now and then the energy of a whole generation comes to a head in a long fine flash, for reasons that nobody really understands at the time—and which never explain, in retrospect, what actually happened.
>
> —Hunter S. Thompson, *Fear and Loathing in Las Vegas*

Ghost in the Machine

After I made my way back to Texas to pick up the pieces of my life, I struggled to adapt to being out of the region. Physically and emotionally, I was still in emergency mode. I couldn't let my guard down, and so much needed to be done. In 2006 I frequented New Orleans every few weeks, but as the years passed and the organization stabilized I came back less often. I became a ghost in the machine, filling several nearly invisible roles. I focused on handling the chronic internal struggles of organizing horizontally, wrote communiqués and letters documenting some of those struggles, and provided guidance to coordinators under constant pressure. Such support roles were important to me and to the organization. They allowed me to be actively involved from home without having to give everything else up as I struggled to put my life back together. I was able to provide somewhat removed perspective to people in daily crisis.

For a long time, I continued to live between two worlds. New Orleans continued to occupy much of my life, even from hundreds of miles away. My life had changed and I was grappling with what it all meant. Acts of violence haunted my psyche. I slept with a loaded .45 pistol under my pillow the first year I was back. It wasn't rational, but it helped me to feel safe. Once I began to emerge from the darkness in my own soul, my emergency heart kicked in. I wanted to continue to build collective futures where I lived as we had been doing in New Orleans, not in the traditional activist paths. Our work in the Gulf showed me that movements need infrastructure and counter-institutions if we want people to stay engaged. If we want people to leave the destructive capitalist system, we have to create something better.

In Austin, I set out to build self-sufficient businesses based on cooperation and mutual aid. Our network of businesses consists of worker-owned, worker-run, or collectively volunteer-run projects. It is a framework for us to create economic self-sufficiency with liberatory aspirations and to fund projects and programs with minimum reliance on traditional fundraising models if possible.

It began with cofounding a thrift store called Treasure City Thrift in late 2006, an idea I had kicked around since leaving the antiques co-op. Treasure City diverts useable items from the landfill, sells items at affordable prices, and provides economic support to underfunded local projects like the anarchist collective Inside Books Project, which provides free books and support to Texas prisoners. TCT employs four full-time staff on a living wage, diverts surplus material aid (clothes, art supplies, medical equipment, bikes, etc.) and money every month to groups, and is a good neighbor to the surrounding communities. It has also supported others trying to incubate similar projects across the United States.

For six years, I also worked at an anarchist, horizontally structured worker cooperative recycling center called Ecology Action. It focuses on recycling and commercial composting while also providing education on environmental stewardship and consultation to diverse communities in support of creating emerging worker co-ops and horizontal organizations. Because both of these projects are housed in downtown Austin, which has sizable houseless and sex worker populations, over the years we have also supported other service projects on our lots, such as a needle exchange program, which is illegal in Texas; ongoing AIDS outreach and education; and the self-organization for those who slept on our lots at night. This is an important intersectionality to us, a way to connect with struggles and services that were supposedly outside of our scope as "businesses." These projects are intentionally horizontally run organizations and businesses that maintain multiple bottom lines, both internal in power sharing and externally in how we engage. Are these projects liberatory? That remains to be seen, but they are steps in better directions. They are open-ended and allow us to develop ways to move beyond just protesting the ills of the world. We are creating practices that open other possibilities for the future.

Paper Tigers

While rebuilding my life after Katrina there were other unsettling developments that began to take shape. In late 2008, two friends of mine, Brad Crowder and David McKay, were arrested and eventually convicted of felonies for making Molotov cocktails during the Republican National Convention in Minnesota. In the media coverage that followed, it was revealed that there had been an informant in the small group of anarchists and radicals who had gone to the convention from Texas with Brad and David. This was unbelievable information because we all knew all the people who had travelled from Texas. Within a few weeks of the informant stories floating in Austin, we received leaked unredacted FBI files detailing reports from the informant. A number of the people named in the documents, including me, had nothing to do with the RNC protests. We noticed that there was one name glaringly conspicuously absent from all the documents (which included private conversations and small meetings where there were only three people present). That name was Brandon Darby.

Before the RNC, back in 2006 (while still part of the Common Ground Collective but unbeknownst to us) Brandon had surreptitiously begun to supply the FBI with information on people around him. During this time he reported on people in New Orleans, Austin, and eventually Minneapolis over the next three years. Due to his actions and choices, two people ended up going to prison, and a third man, longtime Austin peace activist Riad Hamad, took his own life from the stress of FBI harassment brought on by Brandon's involvement in his life.[66]

These revelations and a plethora of others were finally revealed more completely in 2010, when I received over six hundred pages of mostly redacted FBI documents through the federal Freedom of Information Act due to the diligent work of Karly Dixon and James Clark of the Austin Peoples Legal Collective on behalf of many Austin activists and organizations.[67] It turns out that I had been listed on the FBI's NCIC (National Crime Information Center) Violent Gang and Terrorist Organization Index and under investigation by thirteen FBI field offices in nine states since the late 1990s. I had gone from being a civil activist to a terrorist by federal definition, although I have never been convicted of anything more than low-level misdemeanors for civil disobedience related to political protests. In the documents, I was labeled an "environmental terrorist," "environmental extremist," "animal rights extremist," and "domestic terrorist."

From 2001 onward, I had been secretly placed under multi-agency, long-term physical surveillance and pursued by the IRS for tax evasion while my utility, mortgage, bank, and credit card companies were subpoenaed. My trash was repeatedly searched, my phones and Internet were tapped (just the meta data!), and closed-circuit cameras were pointed at the exteriors of my home. Dossiers were gathered on my known associates. I was flagged on the no-fly list as early as 2003. I couldn't get a boarding pass early and airline agents were often flustered when they ran my name, needing to call in security. I stopped flying from 2006 until 2011 due to numerous occasions where I couldn't fly without two-hour interrogations, which caused me to miss flights. Later, when it became more obvious I was under surveillance, I was threatened with grand juries and subpoenas, and agents continued to visit my work and home.

In all of the investigations, over forty people and twenty organizations were listed in my FBI documents, including some with whom I had no association with or even knowledge of who they were. The narratives told by the FBI were so ludicrous and far removed from reality that it would have been macabre funny had the endgame not been about putting me in prison for decades. I can't tell if the agents and informants didn't actually believe what they wrote or were just stupid. Either way, it was scary stuff. I often had to pause for moment to remember I wasn't alone in this. They had cast a wide net, often with more dire consequences on others than myself; I had it comparatively easy. I also remembered that I had a lot of experienced support that most others don't. Even as I was walking free, it was hard to comprehend. Questions of the unknown abounded: would they snatch me off the street, raid my house? Their investigations and harassment reeked of counterinsurgency by the book, an attempt to neutralize a political activist.

The FBI's overarching myopic investigations were for three possible crimes that fit the standard rulebook. The first was the allegation I was part of a *nexus of terrorism*, which meant that I was investigated for funneling money from international sources into U.S. terrorist organizations or vice versa. I had worked with relief groups against the sanctions in Iraq in the '90s and Palestinian solidarity groups, but it was humanitarian aid. A cursory look at my bank account would also prove otherwise, but this accusation is a common pretext to extend weak investigations. The same pretext was used to open a massive investigation against some of my comrades at the Holy Land Foundation, who were eventually railroaded by it.[68] Secondly, they alleged I was *stockpiling weapons*. I do live in Texas and own guns, which is not uncommon—lots of people have guns. The two firearms I own could not be called a stockpile, even if one of them is an AK-47. But the FBI was insistent that there were more and apparently obsessed with this point. Remember when the Bush administration was "sure" Iraq was stockpiling weapons of mass destruction? On several occasions when I tried to purchase a legal firearm, the FBI intervened by visiting the dealer immediately, alarming them, and making it very difficult for me to legally purchase a gun. Third was the all-encompassing attempt to pin unsolved Earth or Animal Liberation Front acts of property destruction across the country on me. These *crimes*, which they desperately wanted to solve, varied from spray painted walls to arson. I cannot remember if I was in those places or not, but in some cases, I would most certainly have had to be in two places at the same time.

What Me Worry?

My life had turned into a surreal, Kafkaesque tale. The FBI engaged in a whisper campaign of lies and distortions aimed at me, but brought no actual criminal charges. If they had, I could have at least fought them in court. This was more insidious because there was no way for me to counter the lies. Between 2004 and 2008, the FBI and JTTF's operations escalated both nationally and in my life. Shortly after almost being killed by law enforcement and Homeland Security in New Orleans on separate occasions in 2005, and while deep in the throes of PTSD, I was unceremoniously removed from the prison visiting list of the Angola 3's Herman Wallace "due to information received from outside law enforcement." This was in 2006, after five years of visits, and was decided in a secret hearing I could not appeal. I was heartbroken and angry because I could do nothing about it. My partner and I visited often. It was some of the only human contact Herman got in solitary. I was standing in the middle of a giant box store lumber isle, buying lumber, when the accusations of *eco-terrorist* were relayed from the other end of the phone. I looked around thinking, if only they could have seen the irony. This information confirmed what I had suspected for years. The cars in front of my house weren't a figment of my imagination or friendly visitors. They meant harm. A few months later, during Herman's first court appeal hearing in Louisiana in three decades, a SWAT team showed in full force on intel that I was going to attend.[69] I wasn't. Afterwards, the Baton Rouge District Attorney apprised Angola 3's lawyer Nick Trennicosta of the SWAT's presence. They feared that I would try to help Herman escape from court. Did they really believe that or was it a charade to bolster their case against Herman? Did FBI informant Brandon Darby, who was present, lead to the SWAT? Herman remained in prison.

At the height of their paranoia, the FBI and the ATF repeatedly threatened to send a SWAT team to kick my doors at my home to serve a subpoena compelling me to answer questions. It was blatant retaliation for refusing to submit. Though afraid of this happening, I had nothing to say, and no lawyers.

The whisper campaign alarmed local law enforcement everywhere I traveled, including my hometown, Austin. My face appeared on an FBI issued regional BOLO (Be on the Lookout) poster (much like a wanted poster) around city municipal offices for a year. According to several anonymous tipsters who saw the posters, it listed all of my private information and stated that I could "commit injury to police officers," "destroy police cars," and "incite riots." All of these were unsubstantiated allegations. Additionally, the police were instructed to avoid apprehension, and inform the FBI of my presence, as I was "armed and dangerous" with a "predicate for violence." This was a fabricated pretext they would use for years and it appeared repeatedly in my FBI documents. "Predicate for violence" was supposed to mean that I had been convicted of a violent act previously. Since I have never been charged with a violent crime, political or otherwise, it was of course made up and intended to make me sound like a madman. Fortunately I never got shot by a fearful cop. Legal recourse to stop the campaign was not available to me since I wasn't actually charged with anything, though this attempt went beyond passive surveillance to overt intimidation, harassment and covert surveillance, COINTELPRO-style. The only part that wasn't surprising to me was why it was happening. These attacks didn't come out of the blue; I knew those bullshit *gang stalking* conspiracies didn't exist, but the ferocity of it was startling. The long histories of power to combat social movements had come to my doorstep. During all of this, friends and comrades around the country were being called to grand juries, or worse, going to prison for political activities. The FBI had a war on terror and we were top domestic priority.

Fear Is Our Enemy

Many of our worst fears about surveillance and government repression have happened to me since 1999. In the extreme circumstances of New Orleans in particular, there were numerous chances for the state to kill me after drawing guns on me and threatening to shoot me repeatedly. There were times I thought I was going to die but didn't. Despite best efforts, I am not imprisoned. Along the way, hundreds of thousands of dollars have been spent on investigating me. Three secret grand juries have been convened without being able to return one indictment for any crime, much less terrorism. I have had some privileges that have kept me free and alive, unlike others who have struggled for liberation. I am keenly aware of this.

Had I been black in New Orleans, I would be dead today; if I were Muslim, my religious beliefs could have put me in prison after 2001. I am grateful and privileged to be able to talk about this openly.

Was I targeted because I was some exceptionally effective, badass organizer? I wish! Unfortunately the truth is that, like many others, I fit the skewed and distorted profile of a domestic terrorist who justifies their bloated budgets and mega-bureaucracies. To have an unending and undefined war on terror, there have to be some terrorists. In this country, they have been scant so far, especially since the FBI historically and continuously largely ignores right-wing, fascistic violence that includes murders of judges, of doctors who perform abortions, and bombings of clinics and synagogues. Those acts rarely count. The war on terror is undeniably politically motivated.

The widening surveillance state is all about money, power, and social control rooted in fear. Do not be afraid! We cannot allow Power to rule over us with fear. If we are afraid, we will give up our liberties and ultimately our freedom. If we give in to fear, then they have already won. We will have given up before we have started. I have been terrified and felt really vulnerable at points. So have my comrades and loved ones in their situations. It *is* scary when grand juries are convened, visits happen, or friends and comrades are imprisoned, but in our day-to-day lives, and as connected powerful movements, we must refuse to live in fear. Revolutionary struggles for justice are long and winding paths we cannot always see around the bend or over the hill. Some of us may not make it, but that is part of the process of life.

Fear can also be decisive in our lives. It's hard to build relationships if fear is sewn into the fabric. At the end of the day, despite the surveillance, the informants and the injustices, it's imperative that we all continue to trust each other and to create bonds that cannot be broken by fear if we are to be free. These bonds we create are stronger than any state intervention. Trusting ourselves and each other can be the glue that binds our connections, networks, and communities. Trust involves being open and taking emotional risks that are far more rewarding than isolation. With all that has happened to me and those around me—the betrayals, lying, and dysfunctionality—I still basically trust people until their actions or words deem I should do otherwise. One of the best tools for fighting back in my life has been a great community of friends ready to support each other through grand juries, infiltration, and repression. My heart is still open. I have learned that to depend on dependable people gets us through a lot more than being afraid of everything.

Tomorrow, Tomorrow, Tomorrow

The Common Ground Collective's history from September 2005 until early 2008 showed that anarchist practices were useful for supporting communities to organize themselves. It was an anarchism based on idealism, history, and common sense. Although we had a transparently revolutionary agenda, some of our programs and projects were just humanitarian services. I think there is great value in that. During it all, countless variations of horizontal and liberatory organizing models were adapted, experimented with, or developed within Common Ground Relief. There were always active internal debates over the meaning of anarchist principles, their applications and sometimes the language of organizing or not itself.

Common Ground Relief drew from contemporary anarchist political movements that had been reborn in small corners across the United States in the late 1960s and then rapidly accelerated in the early part of the millennium after the Seattle World Trade Organization protest in 1999. Since this anarchist renaissance has been newly emerging, most individuals and collectives involved did not have decades developed practices or even modern histories to draw on. Common Ground was another step in that development that challenged all of us on what anarchist engagement and principles mean.

By 2008, the organization stabilized, evolving into a traditional nonprofit with strong roots in New Orleans. I do not interpret this as a result of inherent flaws in anarchist ideas. For three years, anarchist practice achieved incredible things there. But there were more entrenched forces with greater resources beyond us. Thom Pepper stepped in as director and into the difficult role of reigning in the finances, programs, communications, and roles of CGC within various communities. An ever-changing, all-volunteer force had left many loose ends within the organization that sorely needed to be sorted out. Thom brought excellent skills to the table that kept the organization and network functioning and evolving. Given the changing circumstances all around, it was almost inevitable that our more radical elements would be co-opted, crushing the openings that we had created, or that they would wither as the masses of volunteers moved on. Over a few years, Thom was able to maintain the balance in the transition as the rebuilding phases became the priority and it all changed.

Common Ground's scale and scope have grown smaller, but more manageable. It operates from the heart of the Ninth Ward out of a two-story house restored by volunteers about fifty feet from where the barge had crashed through the levee wall. It continues with a fair amount of autonomy to support rebuilding and resists the criminal corruption of local politics that never ceases. Its active long-term programs include:

- *Anita Roddick Advocacy Center*: a community resource, much like our earlier media center, for residents returning to rebuild their homes, provides access to the Internet, fax machines, telephone, and a support staff.
- *Free Legal Aid*: provides legal resources and information.
- *Meg Perry Healthy Soil*: Initiative focuses on increasing food security and sustainability efforts in the Lower Ninth Ward by supporting local urban agriculture initiatives and community gardens.
- *Wetlands Restoration Project*: focuses on advocacy and direct action in actively replanting the diminishing wetlands of the Gulf Coast due to erosion.
- *CG Job Training and Worker Cooperative*: provides on-the-job skills training and living-wage work to local residents. Former trainees have gone on to form small worker cooperative construction companies.
- *Garden of Eatin'*: is a project that teaches kids to grow their own food.
- *Volunteer Rebuilding*: is a cornerstone project of volunteers providing skills and labor to people in rebuilding their homes.

Additionally, over the years the Common Ground Collective has incubated a network of service providers, cooperatives and organizations that began as major programs within the organization and later became successful autonomous entities. These include the Common Ground Health Clinic (Algiers), New Orleans Women's Shelter, Four Directions, the Lower 9th Ward Health Clinic, and the RUBARB Bike Collective. Although they are not all horizontally organized, these projects are rooted in many of Common Ground's original ideals of cooperation, mutual aid, and solidarity.[70]

If Not Us, Then Who? A Few Thoughts on Security, Accountability, and Violence

From the beginning of CGC's formation, we had to messily resolve issues like violence, sexual assault and rape on our own without state intervention. The corrupt local police, the ineffective governments and our principles brought us to our choices of actions. We had internal security teams of women and men who would step into to take appropriate actions to protect those around us to the best of our abilities. We used many tools available, from conflict de-escalation and threat of use of force to use of force—yes, violence. This is the hard dirty part of anarchy or revolutionary movements that often remain unwritten: how to deal with people who cannot or will not abide by community guidelines or are endangering others around them. These are conversations without easy answers that have gone on since I have been engaged in political discourse. The list of alternatives was long: banishment, our own forms of jails, accountability processes, restorative justice, sweeping it under the rug, and violence in self-defense. In our situations—facing the crushing failure of the state and without the luxury of time—we acted. We minimized violence, but it was necessary to protect those around us and ourselves. It is something some of us still to this day carry with us. It was never a question of whether the actions were right, but whether they were effective in creating safer places. What is the difference between revolutionary and vigilante violence? Those are some questions I will carry for the rest of my life.

Only Time, Reflection, and Healing Fix Broken Hearts

Common Ground as a set of ideas, as an organization, and as a network was often like a speeding train that had left the station at full throttle, rattling down the trembling tracks on the verge of derailing at every new turn as it barrelled onward barely able to contain its own unknown trajectory. Occasionally, it would all derail, scattered about in a giant mess from some crisis or event, and all of our projects, programs, or people would collide and explode. When the smoke settled, we would dust ourselves off, pick up the pieces, and place it all back on the tracks to start again. It was far from intentional or rational, it was just the unsaid mode of operations that added to great internal difficulties. As a microcosm of larger civil society, even as we consciously strove to transcend the baggage, we were still occasionally afflicted by many of the same problems.

Ideals of independence sometimes collided with our actual abilities to cope with serious issues such as sexual assault, violence, or rape that happened, or with people that had addiction problems or mental health issues—challenges we were largely ineffective in handling. With all our ideals and our dreams, these realities could crush them in an instant. Sometimes it was like a war on multiple fronts; fighting the state, the militias, developers, other organizations, and among ourselves. It was often easy for people to forgive our shortcomings in dealing with outside forces because we had obvious limits in our resources and the deck was stacked against all of us. Internally and in wider activist communities, though, we could be brutally harsh and unforgiving to each other and ourselves when some "ideal" was not attained or more often just convoluted in meaning.

Too often a malice born of hurt and moral judgements poured out at meetings and online from frustrations, missteps, miscommunications, and assumptions, sometimes cripplingly so. Anarchy and the radical steps we were taking presented many openings, but also a myriad of interpretations of what it means to be free and how we might live it daily. There were those who left Common Ground with bitterness and broken hearts along with some for whom it was the most rewarding challenge in their lives. To all of us, it was a transformative set of experiences that we will take with us for the rest of our lives.

To Occupy, Decolonize, and Intersect
Once the anarchist heyday at Common Ground receded, it wasn't really over, it just looked different. Many original outside core organizers and volunteers went their separate ways back to their communities to heal to reclaim their lives and participate in other movements. In the immediate years after the disaster, the revolutionary fervor waned, the victories seemed more muddled, and the futures of many of those most impacted in the Gulf still seemed wrecked. For those who have never looked to past movements, forget that revolutionary ruptures are always fraught with strife, disappointments, setbacks, and shortcomings within them. Those narratives get left out in the retellings. All movements look better in the rear-view mirror after we have left them, after the pain recedes and when time and distance have opened that space for deeper reflection and healing. Only then are we are able to see the impacts and contributions we made and have some meaningful assessments of them. Once we do, though, a kind of obscured beauty emerges even when there aren't clear delineations of what was or was not accomplished. In all people's movements, the heartaches and needs often remain less fulfilled from long term exploitative systems. That is not failure of an organization or movements; it's just another set of realities of small ruptures. In New Orleans and in the Gulf Coast, communities haven't come back like they were before. Some are far better off, while others still struggle along. One organization, one network, one revolutionary movement cannot upright that rudderless ship. We can only steer what we can.

As climate change and unfettered capitalism continue, the coastlines in the Gulf will disappear before the sun sets too many more times. The economic and living situations of the 99% will continue to deteriorate. The challenges created by ecological destruction like the BP oil spill, the ongoing ecological crisis of climate change, and domination by corporations and bad governments are formidable. These socioeconomic systems that took hundreds of years to create will take serious time to dismantle and confront while creating alternatives to them.

These crises expose, like nothing else, raw exploitation and injustice, and reveal the house of cards of our vulnerable biosphere and economic systems that can crumble with one unknown touch. In response, another beautiful and flourishing tendency has been revealed: the efforts of decentralized responses to disasters, both ecological and economic, rooted in anarchist-inspired solidarity, direct action, and mutual aid. These emerging tendencies are offering rudimentary, but viable alternatives to the continuing crisis wrought by climate change and capitalism's effects on communities in direct response and in rebuilding pieces from below.

Mutual aid, as anarchists have defined it since Peter Kropotkin's seminal book, has been used to respond to disasters for more than a hundred years. It just began to look different after the rocky first decade at the turn of the twenty-first century. The fusion of ideas, praxis, and programs of the Common Ground Collective had positive unintended reverberating impacts far outside of the Gulf Coast in reviving these traditions due to a confluence of factors. These disasters are quickening and requiring the immediate actions for the need for those most vulnerable to them. In addition to the vulnerability of our systems, they expose the false veneer of safety that governments cannot or will not provide in daily life, and especially within disasters. Common Ground was more than a relief organization or network, it was part of larger grassroots movements for justice in the Gulf Coast. Our efforts were just another rupture of ordinary people rising up in the face of injustices. Tens of thousands of people came to participate in the project over the years and went on to organize in other communities afterward, carrying the seeds of praxis that continued through the stories of the organization through radical circles just like raindrops causing overlapping ripples in water.

When a massive earthquake destroyed the worlds and lives of Haitians in 2008, people from Common Ground's medical and construction networks that had been strengthened after Katrina became the first responders in two delegations using similar skillsets and autonomous models in aid and rebuilding.[71]

As the turbulent decade waned, the Wall Street banksters' financial Ponzi schemes created a financial meltdown that ended in an economic disaster causing massive job losses, collapsed businesses, and evaporated life savings, leading to large scale home foreclosures and evictions. Spontaneously, thousands rose up to retake public spaces by reclaiming the commons, gathering together in mutual aid in city after city. Millions of disaffected people supported the various movements under the umbrella name Occupy beginning in September 2011. These uprisings were inspiring to see in cities large and small. I had the good fortune to be on the road for book tours that fall and spring. I visited over twenty-five camps on both coasts, in Canada, in the Midwest and the South. I saw forty years of anarchist inspired organizing and practices in a direct lineage from the alternative globalization movement to Common Ground clearly take root from the beginning in the nascent Occupy camps. People coming in participated in general assemblies, affinity groups, spokes councils, with medical tents, legal and eviction defense teams, all being fed by Food Not Bombs and food groups like them. Hundreds if not thousands of organizers and volunteers who had been active within Common Ground were part of these decentralized Occupy camps and networks, building further on the ideas of mutual aid and solidarity with direct and indirect influence. In some places, they were key organizers. This is not to say that it was all born of Common Ground, but that the influences from that rupture continued to have unintended reverberations that were clearer as time moved forward.

Superstorm Hurricane Sandy struck the East Coast in October 2012 with devastating effect in numerous states. Much like Katrina, once the storm passed, the government and Red Cross response was abysmal in more marginalized communities. The momentum from people within the Occupy movements morphed into the decentralized efforts called Occupy Sandy, taking cues from the Common Ground and other radical movements' models and ideals, as embodied in the slogan "Mutual Aid Not Charity." Volunteers became first responders in ignored communities, helping to set up programs and projects or supporting ongoing efforts. Former key Common Ground coordinators consulted and support behind the scenes or were frontline organizers in some of the projects. After the immediate crisis abated, many Occupy Sandy projects have continued to support communities in their rebuilding efforts for self-determination. Due to their continuity of having evolved largely from Occupy Wall St., Occupy Sandy organizers got to avoid mistakes and shortfalls that Common Ground had from the beginning. It was nice to see the ideas expand and take uncharted directions.[72]

Another instance occurred in May 2013, when a massive tornado devastated rural parts of Central Oklahoma. People from the Occupy movements and former Common Grounders, anarchists and other radicals from COBRA (Central Oklahoma Red and Black Alliance) once again set up decentralized mutual aid support for immediate relief and longer term rebuilding under the banner of OpOk, drawing from the established networks of health care, responders, food distribution, open source web and media support, and the more recent Internet activism of Anonymous. People were able to mobilize quickly and more effectively to the events and disseminate information broadly though social media.

The ideas and practices of mutual aid are alive and well in the twenty-first century. Our capacity to put our emergency hearts into action, together, will continue to propel us forward at mass mobilizations, in parking lots, prisons, community centers, and future disasters. Humans are wired for it, and it's critical to maintain in our atomized and often destructive society. Disasters, especially, will be the forefront in some communities; being able to respond with decentralized direct action and mutual aid is central when they strike. These outpourings now have connected networks and communication channels to rely on quick responses; histories to build from; and people who bring experience in dealing with crises and power-sharing skills. Sadly, these disasters often affect communities more than any single issue. But they also open a crack for people to see themselves and their own power by rebuilding small pieces of their communities differently than before through mutual aid and direct action. In direct and meaningful ways, people learn that they do not have to wait on those in power to make their lives better. They begin to realize that they *can* do it for themselves, with support, even in the worst times. These concepts, which are as old as life on this planet and which anarchists have politically named mutual aid, will continue to be needed for the survival and health of all of us in our day-to-day lives as we face uncertain futures, whether it's disasters, crises, or just living. Common Ground didn't invent them, we just put them into practice in a different way that showed it could be done. It was a small opening, with lots of accidental outcomes. For those of us engaged in anarchist organizing, the long histories of mutual aid, direct action, and solidarity around disasters should consciously be added to how we view collective liberation.

Hello. Farewell.

> I wanted you to see what real courage is, instead of getting the idea that courage is a man with a gun in his hand. It's when you know you're licked before you begin but you begin anyway and you see it through no matter what. You rarely win, but sometimes you do.
>
> —Harper Lee, *To Kill a Mockingbird*

From far-reaching places, I have seen glimpses of better futures. All that I have seen and participated in has transformed me. Anarchy, thought of as a living and dynamic set of ideas and philosophies, turns out to also offer some guideposts for ways out of the political, philosophical, economic, and social traps we have been stuck in for a long time under capitalism. Its foundations don't provide the answers, as much as they challenge us to look at different questions and thinking of possible outcomes. If past ideologies have failed, why should we continue to cling to them? Why not try something different?

Participating in Common Ground showed me and thousands of others some of these other possibilities, even when it was a struggle to remain engaged. I saw more than the fleeting opening of possibilities that happen during protests that fade quickly. We achieved quite a bit for a small organization, especially for our scale. Sure, Power still rules, we weren't superhuman, and it was far from perfect, but we were able to exercise power from below with thousands of people with some lasting impacts. From supporting and aiding over 250,000 people on shoestring budgets since its inception to the wider movements for shared liberation across the country, Common Ground revealed that anarchy is more than impractical idealism; it opens a politics of possibilities to create impossible communities. Climate change, capitalism, and Power will continue to affect everything including the pockets of hope and resistance that refuse to give in, but these openings, small or large, that we can all make, are important to crack open substantial reverberating shifts in ourselves and for those around us. We can do this together, locally, in decentralized ways that share power, resist exploitation and oppression, but more importantly challenge us to imagine our futures differently if we choose to do so. The future is open. We're standing on the edge of our potential, so how's it going to look?

Do not be afraid.

Do not be cynical.

Continue to trust yourself and others.

Continue to dream of collective liberation.

Dream the future

Know your history

Organize your people

Fight to win

Apr 28 06 10:04a   FBI-Austin RA JTTF

b2
b6
b7C

To: San Antonio   From: San Antonio
Re: 266I-SA-57180-ELA,   04/28/2006

        Scott Crow is a professional protestor who is known to work
for the Ruckus Society and is involved in direct action campaigns
as one who incites action. He has traveled to Portland, Oregon;
Houston, Texas; Dallas; Texas; and Detroit, Michigan. He has
been observed and/or arrested at a variety of different events,
e.g, oil conferences, furrier conventions, animal rights
gatherings, and high-tech events. He has been involved in Direct
Action camps learning ho to break police lines, how to counter
gas and other chemical agents. He is involved in aggressive and
proactive civil disobedience skills. Crow is involved in direct
action and goes to events to instigate trouble; he is the one who
will throw the rocks as opposed to the person who holds the
poster.

2006 FBI memo that says I use direct action to go to events to cause trouble.

Treasure City Thrift, an anarchist worker
co-op I cofounded in Austin, TX, 2006.
PHOTO CREDIT: ANN HARKNESS

With Rebecca Solnit, talking about the
aftermath of disasters.
PHOTO CREDIT: LIZ HIGHLEYMAN

In Austin with Ann Harkness and Robert King, 2009.

Left to right: Jeff Luers, Ryan Shapiro, Will Potter, scott crow.

Original Common Ground Collective cofounders: (left to right) Malik Rahim, Sharon Johnson, scott crow. PHOTO CREDIT: TODD SANCHIONI

Unidentified, bullet-riddled dead black male. When I first arrived in Algiers in September 2005, we put the metal on him to cover him up. Who killed him—the police or the white militia?
PHOTO CREDIT: JAKE APPLEBAUM

Common Ground cofounder Sharon Johnson and volunteer Hali Stone.
PHOTO CREDIT: DAVID AMPERSAND

First distribution center in Algiers neighborhood, 2005.
PHOTO CREDIT: JACKIE SUMELL

PHOTO CREDIT: CGSTORIES.ORG

Common Ground general assembly, 2006. PHOTO CREDIT: CGSTORIES.ORG

"House of Excellence," one of the many community Internet/phone access sites set up by Common Ground. PHOTO CREDIT: CGSTORIES.ORG

Signs that were all too common across New Orleans in white areas.
PHOTO CREDIT: JACKIE SUMELL

A sign with relevance before and after the disaster.
PHOTO CREDIT: JACKIE SUMELL

Soldiers in front of Common Ground's little blue house in the Ninth Ward, 2006.
PHOTO CREDIT: CGSTORIES.ORG

MLK school where volunteers using civil disobedience cut the locks and cleaned out the school, 2006. PHOTO CREDIT: CGSTORIES.ORG

Speaking to a crowd in New Orleans: (left to right) Kerul Dyer, Lisa Fithian, Malik Rahim, and Sakura Kone, 2006.
PHOTO CREDIT: CGSTORIES.ORG

Meg Perry, young tireless organizer from Maine who was tragically killed while working for Common Ground.
PHOTO CREDIT: CGSTORIES.ORG

Shifting Culture without Government

DJ Pangburn

I recently spoke to noted anarchist community organizer scott crow about how average people—people with dreams, vision, grit, and motivation—can affect change in a very real and quantifiable way after the vote. This isn't a playbook for smashing some McDonald's or Starbucks windows but for taking the fight to communities.

A tired cycle exists in American electoral culture. Every two years we vote for federal representatives and senators, and every four years we vote in the presidential election. Each election cycle builds to a critical mass of ideological recriminations that crescendo on election day. Americans then rather sadly wash their hands of the mess and resolve to do little or nothing to actively make democracy work. There is a relinquishing of the responsibility of democracy to representatives. And as we've seen in the last twelve years of bitter partisan divide, it has produced paralysis instead of results. It has popularized politicians who behave more like actors or programmed holograms than actual problem solvers.

Mr. crow has had a roughly two-decade-long résumé of working in community organizing circles, most notably as one of the founders of the Common Ground Collective, one of the largest and most-organized volunteer forces in the post-Katrina wasteland. When W's buddy "Brownie" (Michael Brown) was botching the FEMA response, and the National Guard was enforcing martial law on New Orleans streets, CGC was busy cleaning out destroyed homes, mobilizing free healthcare, clothing, and food, and otherwise delivering mutual aid to a grateful New Orleans population. Much of crow's current work involves helping communities build worker cooperatives and local economies horizontally, which is explained in more detail below.

We Are More than Just Voters and Consumers

The voter, says crow, must pass into oblivion. In his or her place must arise the doer, the creator—that person who sees all potential and jumps into action.

Ancient Rome suffered a political paralysis similar to contemporary America. In Rome, voters were mostly irrelevant. Into this political void came the Roman emperors who, while bringing some domestic stability, only hastened Rome's fall. Whereas the great American political paralysis might be a melancholic moment for this country's patriots, scott crow sees vast opportunities to do great things. "There are a set of paths in the middle that we haven't even explored to a great extent in this country," he says. "The dominant paradigm tells us that we are just voters and consumers with a void of other alternatives. Life—politics, culture, and economies—[involves] more complicated social relationships in this country." The trick is to be a creator, someone who sees new paths and pursues them energetically. "The [new paths] aren't always going to be easy," he says. "But we will be doing them together; block by block and community by community, as needed."

Asked if voting has any real redeeming value, crow is mostly pessimistic. "Voting is a lot like recycling: if you're so damned lazy that you can't do anything else, then at least do that," he says. "It's the least you can do. Pulling the lever or throwing something in the correct bin; neither require great effort or thinking, but neither have real impact either."

Community organizers like crow have no time for political saviors. They are individuals who eschew antiquated democratic politics. Dreamers and doers who depart the political reservation for more unknown trajectories.

"We've had this mythology of the Great White Hope, that some great leader who will take us from our chains into the future," notes crow, a little astonished that so many still buy into the collective democratic hallucination. "When 'he' fails—as they always do—we blame the person and not the systems that got us there. We need to look anew at our world and think of the different ways we can engage with the world, our city, our neighborhoods, and ourselves."

"We have other choices," he adds. "Why is that we demand choices in MP3 players, sodas, or schools, for example, but not in our economic, cultural, or political systems that affect everything about us and our world?"

Issues Do Not Exist in Isolation

Americans have the tendency to engage issues in isolation. For the extreme (and even the mainstream) conservatives, "socialism," "immigrants" or "gays" are the viruses corrupting the system—other domestic and international considerations be damned. A matrix of interrelated issues work at one another like a neural network. One cause may have several effects. And that cause may itself be the byproduct of other variables.

"If you want to stop hunger, you can't just go, Well, I'll just feed somebody and it's over," crow argues. "You start with that and then ask, Why are they hungry? Did they not have access to good schooling? So then we need to fix the schools or create new ones. Did they not have good access to jobs? Then we need to create good jobs with a living wage, dignity, and respect. Or did they have healthcare issues that aren't being addressed, even just basic stuff? Well then we need to get community clinics in every community so that people can have their basic needs looked at before they become major issues like cancer or diabetes."

For this sort of education, crow had to look toward more revolutionary movements for this sort of education. "I had to look at what the Black Panthers and the Zapatistas did for their communities," he says. "I had to look at what the Spanish anarchists did when fascism was taking over. They were inspiring in that they helped their people and rebuilt their world. Those are just political references. In every subculture, whether it's religious groups, charities, or hip-hop communities, there are examples of people doing things themselves without waiting for government or other people to do it."

"In what I like to call anarchism with a little 'a,' we need to explore ideas of direct action so that we're not waiting on others to fix the problems," he adds. "We will do it ourselves. Mutual aid, cooperation, collective liberation—the idea that we're all in this together. But there also needs to be an awareness that you are in this yourself." He points out the unvarnished political reality: no leader, party or group is going to do this for Americans. But there is a more salient point. Even if a single leader or political party had this sort of desire, the country is far too big and complex for such national policymaking. They are mere band-aids on gushing wounds. "We need to decentralize and localize to solve the problems around us, while looking to support other communities doing the similar things and connect on larger issues," he says. "And to do this we have to first look at history."

Create Localized Economies

"It's absolutely cliché to say we need to think globally and act locally," says crow. "But that's exactly what we need to do while we are creating localized economies (gift, barter, or local currencies), opening the common spaces from the holds of corporate private property (like shopping malls) and becoming neighbors again."

"We need to know what is happening around the world and share the information, successes and challenges that we face in our communities to help each other," adds crow. "What happens to a rice farmer in India or a landless peasant in Brazil or a family in Appalachia is of utmost importance to me in thinking of supporting each other." The internet and social media in particular will help in this flow of information.

Perhaps the most important lesson in the recent trend of localization is that scaling down just might be what saves us. It doesn't require a singular savior but hundreds of millions, indeed billions of them. Centralized government and corporations haven't worked for humanity, argues crow. And who would disagree in this second decade of the twenty-first century?

"Centralizing corporations—these giant pyramids with elites at the top—aren't working out for the rest of us," adds crow. "And it's not just the 99%—it's not working out for any of us, not even some of the elites."

Government and industry aren't the only institutions ripe for a downsizing, according to crow—the world's social movements could use it as well. "Instead of having one big movement, what if we have thousands of decentralized movements that are working toward common ideals?" suggests crow. "We need to value difference."

In crow's practical wisdom this means not one ideological boat but many boats full of a multitude of dreams and ideas. "We start to move at our own pace, and we help each other along but maintain our autonomy and differences as individuals, neighborhoods, communities, etc., at the same time cooperating when necessary to reach the goals."

Organizers like crow have noticed that even corporations are starting to see things this way. "Instead of trying to centralize, they're breaking it down," he says. "They see networks having advantages over their traditional hierarchies. Advertising is doing this in the corporate world in what they call micro-marketing." He also wants people to stop confusing convenience and choices with democracy. This is a difficult proposition in America, a country that has trained its citizens from an early age to expect convenience. And what is voting if not the culmination of convenience culture and democracy?

"A choice of fifty different soft drinks doesn't make us any more democratic than any other country," says crow. "Especially when those fifty soft drinks are made by five or ten companies. The same could be extrapolated to political parties. There's a perception of choice, but its not meaningful or real and definitely not democratic."

Build Horizontally

The worker cooperative has certainly entered the popular American lexicon, but it wasn't always so. Intrigued early on by the co-op's possibilities, crow says resources and literature on the subject were sparse. So he and other Austin organizers educated themselves and just started building their own. Eventually it led to horizontalization: the process of co-ops and other services overlapping in communities. He has spent the last several years building horizontal worker cooperatives and consulting when he can.

"There's no boss and everyone involved makes the same wage and has the same amount of say in their futures," he says. "I'm interested in creating localized jobs for people with dignity, respect and a living wage. These businesses have the potential to be small scale economic engines for localized economies, where we start to close the loop in taking care of our own transportation, health care, cultural, and educational centers in neighborhoods and communities." He envisions a community in which these services would be offered to anybody who needs them. "These services would be offered in various neighborhoods and they would start to overlap," says crow, with enthusiasm that is contagious. "Imagine instead of big box stores taking up acres of land, there were farm stands, free health clinics, or small functioning schools on every corner. Community members of all stripes could actually benefit instead of corporations and governments sucking the resources away."

Empower the Disempowered

A certain percentage of the U.S. population believes that the poor and disempowered can only be lifted up through tax breaks and the good auspices of job creators. While job creation has its economic and political benefits (cynically, employed populations are much more passive than its opposite), it often doesn't empower any individuals in the labor force. There is the perception of power: a wage pays the rent and all of life's necessities. Beyond that, is there any substantial and meaningful empowerment?

"At Ecology Action [a recycling co-op] we often supported the homeless people that surrounded us," says crow. "First by not criminalizing them but treating them with dignity and respect, then by allowing other service organizations to provide services live HIV information and testing, a needle exchange (which is illegal in Austin). Third we also provided a downtown space where people could sleep after hours as long as they followed guidelines we set up with them."

Ecology Action, as crow notes, also held meetings with the transient population and made them reinforce the guidelines amongst themselves. "We never called the cops unless severe violence was taking place," says crow.

He remembers one man's empowerment in particular. "There was this one guy who just had a streak of bad luck, who didn't have a drug or alcohol problem, and he lived on our lot for a year and volunteered. We ended up hiring him in and he worked for Ecology Action for almost three and a half years. His experience as a fifty-five year-old black man, who had never heard of horizontal organizing but worked at a job where his voice counted, was an eye-opening, transformational experience for all of us. When he left he said it was the best job he had ever had. It didn't make us saints or saviors, but it was a small piece of what we could do. And it's not the only example."

When speaking of power-sharing, crow points to the Occupy movement. "It was the first grassroots movement of movements in this country, very decentralized," he says. "I went to twenty-four different Occupy camps across the country last year and all of them looked very different. But there were very similar elements to them: the ideas of participatory democracy, power sharing amongst the people, the use of affinity groups, mic checks, general assemblies and spokes council models, etc. All of those things came out of at least twenty years of anarchism and decentralized organizing in this country."

Community organizers like crow also see small businesses as integral to real empowerment. "The real engines of this country are small business," he says. "Corporations have more concentrated wealth, but there are still more small businesses employing more people everywhere. Some small businesses are starting to make themselves more egalitarian." crow sees a trend of sharing power and resources because it makes sense, and he's quick to point out that this is not just his myopic view. "It's happening all over the world," he says, thrilled by this subtle cultural revolution, "and it's happening not because of one voice but many voices. There's more worker cooperatives, more intentional communities, consumer cooperatives, agricultural cooperatives than ever before. They're on the rise. And what's beautiful about it is that nothing is driving it but need and necessity."

Shift Culture, Be an Innovator

Boring, informational leaflets aren't just going to cut it any longer, says crow. Not when corporate media can tailor its advertising message to individual subcultures in communities.

"If we don't create our own counter-advertising, we're just shooting ourselves in the foot. Living in this present political and economic system, we must use its tools. Creating beautiful posters, books, social/web media, and videos."

There is no better advertising than creating something better. People often need "to be shown by example what it can look like," he says. "Make it appeal it to people. Traditional advertising is part of that. CrimethInc. has been doing it for ten years. Justseeds Artists' Cooperative and Little Black Cart press are some other groups that have developed aesthetics with knowledge."

"Our roles as radicals of all kinds, activists and organizers is to move ideas from the margin to the mainstream—that's really what we do," says crow, who reminds us that slavery was at one point culturally and economically embedded in America's DNA. "We would not have built this country the way we did without slavery. Working to abolish slavery was an act of sedition—a crazy, radical idea." This type of cultural shift, he says, is what is needed in America. "We need to stop protesting and think of other ways of doing things like creative interventions and valuing aesthetics along the way."

No Government Required

It's almost a cliché to say that it only takes a small group of people to make change in this world. But it is a cliché that crow believes in wholeheartedly.

"After Hurricane Katrina, Common Ground Collective (CGC) was one organization of many that were doing things. At the most, we had 28,000 people involved from 2005 to 2008," says crow. "In that time we served over 150,000 families. It had a huge political, social and cultural impact not only on New Orleans but on grassroots organizations around the United States." The life-transforming experiences of so many CGC volunteers reverberated. "Many Occupy participants and organizers came through it. CGC volunteers also went to Haiti as first responders. On the East Coast, Occupy Sandy and other decentralized grassroots efforts have taken CGC's models in new directions. Occupy Sandy organizers reached out directly to some of the core CGC organizers who either went and put boots on the ground or consulted." crow believes that people have more power than they can imagine.

"Change is scalable," he says. "It doesn't take much for ideas to spread. Look at all the bad ideas governments and corporations have spread over the decades. Remember Crystal Pepsi or the war on Iraq?"

Experience More and Be Content Not Knowing the Answers

Not knowing all of the answers doesn't bother crow at all. He believes as an anarchist, community organizer or cultural innovator should be prepared to learn. Lack of answers can function as the seeds for new ideas.

"I learned from the Zapatista Revolution that as revolutionaries you don't have to have the answers just be willing to look at and be open to possibilities," says crow, who believes the old days of "1–2–3 steps to revolution" have failed and are now dead.

"My other role as an organizer—and part time futurist—is to be an innovator to challenge our own radical assumptions and ways of engaging as well as envisioning and spreading new ideas or ways to engage," he adds. "I do this because I love people and have seen for decades that we have the creativity—once we add the determination and willingness to make substantial and powerful changes, we do," concludes crow, ever hopeful against the prospect of the unknown.

"We are always standing on the edge of potential—so how is it going to look?"

Originally published in a slightly different version on the website Medium, February 22, 2013, https://medium.com/american-dreamers/b0b346416485.

DJ Pangburn is an editor and contributor for culture magazines and websites including *VICE*, Boing Boing, Medium, *OMNI Reboot*, *Death and Taxes*, and *Makeshift*. He is also a filmmaker and Pataphysician.

Black Flags and Radical Relief Efforts in New Orleans: An Interview with scott crow

Stevie Peace and Kevin Van Meter of Team Colors

Team Colors: Can you speak to the writing process behind *Black Flags and Windmills* and describe the process of shifting roles from an organizer to an author?

One word: difficult. I haven't considered myself a writer. I have written a few pieces over the years mostly out of necessity. From the first time I went to New Orleans and every back and forth to Algiers, I was taking notes as I was driving in the car because I'm a big note-taker. Sometimes it helps me think. At Common Ground from the very get-go, I took copious notes every time I would get moments to get away. It was almost like a diary, but they weren't that detailed. I have a lot of notes about organizational structure and the ideas of what it could look like. Some of those became communiqués. I wrote my first longer essay about the first traumatic experience going to New Orleans in 2006 from some of those notes and communiqués. From that it all kind of snowballed.

In early 2007, I got this idea to do an anthology book of collective voices about Common Ground that would include core organizers on the ground and some outside voices. The unfortunate thing is that I wanted to do it too early when the wounds were still fresh. People were still dealing with lots of trauma from Common Ground and New Orleans in general. I'm speaking about the organizers specifically. I submitted my essay and a couple of others from the anthology to PM Press, who were just getting started in 2008. They turned down the anthology, but said, "We'd like you to do a book." I was one of the first people that signed on. I also sent them a rough manuscript from Robert King of the Angola 3, who got a book deal at the same time. I am still going to do that Common Ground anthology because I think there are more voices that need to be heard. The timeline is just longer now.

What the writing became I was compelled to do. As I mentioned, I had written communiqués since September 5. I call them communiqués because they were public writings that I sent out on the internet to different lists, to INFOSHOP and the Indymedia websites. I issued communiqués for almost three years from Common Ground when I was there and when I was away, analyzing and clarifying the constantly changing situations on the ground because there were so many questions, assumptions, and bad information about how or what Common Ground was doing and the situation on the Gulf Coast in general. I went back to all of those writings using them as foundations to build longer stories, analysis, reflections, or chapters.

On a personal level, it was really healing to write, I came back with post-traumatic stress. I wasn't doing very well functioning in society from all the violence. I felt like the ghost in the machine a lot—I write about that a little bit. The writing actually helped me to relive those traumas in a different way. I really dissected them in a lot of ways and through the process, it was almost a five-year process, I feel so much better now than I did when I started the book. There is plenty of time when writing that I thought that I wasn't going to do it, it was too painful, in talking about certain painful events that I couldn't or hadn't talk about. That's not to say that it's a sorrow-filled book. I want to be clear that are lots of beautiful stories along the way and lots of really engaging organizing that went on, but these are some of my processes of thoughts and feelings I had in doing this.

Shifting from being mostly an organizer to writer has been unsettling [laughs]. I am used to being on the front lines in the streets, but as the years passed I saw other needs to transmit information and change my role.

Would you talk a little more about the nitty-grittiness? Did you go back and interview folks, speak to friends? What other kind of processes did you do to kind of remind yourself of these stories? Did you do outside research, and how did that look?
I did some outside research. I also revisited with people because memory is a tricky thing as we all know. I informally talked to key organizers or to residents we worked alongside and asked questions like, "Do you remember

when this happened?" or, "Do you remember how it felt?" Sometimes it was completely different from how I remembered it, so it was really good to get clarifications or other perspectives. Also, as the events got further away, I went back to some news articles and pieces from corporate, independent, and grassroots media—like Indymedia reports, as well as people's blogs—to look at specific events, dates, or the way things unfolded. There were so many voices and lots of documentation. We had 35,000 people come through in the first five or six years. Of those people, there were hundreds of key organizers. I couldn't remember everybody, so I would track somebody down and ask, "Do you remember this person?" and "Who was there as this particular time?" They would say, "Oh that's this person," and I would go find them to talk and ask them questions. These interactions kind of reinforced or changed some of the ideas. I didn't set out for this book as an absolute historical document. I state at the beginning that I say this is my interpretation of what happened. It is factual, but it also is a personal narrative with whatever colorations that brings. I don't claim to speak as the voice of Common Ground. I think that would do a disservice of the thousands of people who participated and the hundreds of key organizers that were there.

It was refreshing that you choose to paint a narrative that was not completely linear, choosing at times to bring in certain contexts and histories of other radical movements that informed the work of Common Ground, combined with your own personal biographical history. Were there were particular ways / reasons you chose to structure the book with this jumping around approach? And have you given any thought to the parts you chose to focus on content-wise?

Thanks. The structure was a collaborative editorial decision. For example, to have a really blast-off narrative at the beginning of the book came from Andrea Gibbons, my editor from PM Press. She thought we should have a story that hooks people in. She handled a lot of the macro-organizing. Alejandro de Acosta, who also edited the book, really made me think about and develop content and ideas. The jumping around is also because of the way my brain works. When I tell a story, I want people to understand it, so I feel that they have to have context for that. It creates common bonds for telling the story and gives people of all persuasions perspective on where or why events unfold as they do. I wrote this book to be accessible for people who might not have any understanding about some of these concepts, and I wanted to bring them along for the ride. One of the things I always ask myself is, Would someone like my mom relate to this? My target audience were those who were coming into political movements who might be inspired in what we did and what we were building on so they could continue to build further than that. I didn't set out to write the most concise histories of social movements and I didn't try to tell the deepest philosophical, theoretical background of anarchist ideas or practice. I just wanted to give a primer to those histories and let others dig deeper.

As for telling my own personal narrative, I think its important to realize that I tell my story not because I think my story is important but to show that I am a regular person and that all of us were regular people caught up in extraordinary circumstances. That any of us could do this and that anarchy was a good guiding framework to do it. That anarchy could be practical on larger scales. Also that I am a real person and it wasn't all heroics. History has a tendency to create myths around people, and I know that there are myths created around me. I think it's important to dispel these. All of us just did what most rational people would have done with the resources and privilege they had. So I wanted to write that. I didn't want a pedestal; this is real people doing real things.

Let's switch gears from book process back to the organization itself. Post-Katrina New Orleans has been described as a "disaster within a disaster." How do we address current and less spectacular disasters with an eye to preparing for future large-scale relief efforts and organizing?
I think that preparing for the future is the answer. We don't need to look for the next disaster or the next crisis to organize. We cannot afford to be short-sighted when it comes to practical applications of long-term vision. We need to develop dual power philosophies and practices where we resist on one hand while building and creating on the other hand. What I would like to do is get people to really think about twenty-year, thirty-year, and fifty-year futures. If we protest day in and day out, we squander our energy and limited resources to build long-term capacity and power. Climate change, capitalism are dramatically changing our landscapes of all types. I am proposing that we build our own power all the time, and that we save resistance for when it's really, really important and has dramatic, incredible, and far-reaching effects. Additionally, we should look at movements as having multiple points of intersection. It takes all kinds of things to make changes happen, and people come into movements for all different reasons. We need to make our mirror reflection bigger than ourselves, and we have to meet people where they are. This is obviously a much longer conversation that we are not going to

wrap up in this one question, but I think these are key pieces. As I often put it, "Dream the future. Know our history. Organize ourselves. Fight to win."

This is an excerpt of a longer interview that originally appeared in *Left Eye on Books* in November 2011.

Stevie Peace and **Kevin Van Meter** coedited, with Team Colors Collective, *Uses of a Whirlwind: Movement, Movements and Contemporary Radical Currents in the United States* (AK Press, 2010) and coauthored the short book *Wind(s) from Below: Radical Community Organizing to Make a Revolution Possible* (Team Colors & Eberhardt Press, 2010). Both have been involved in various organizing efforts together for over a decade. Peace worked in various organizing and administrative roles at the Common Ground Health Clinic in New Orleans following Hurricane Katrina for fifteen months, and Van Meter spent a few weeks volunteering at the clinic in the winter of 2005.

Common Ground Communiqués (2005–2009)

This chapter is a record of events as they unfolded. It shows my development as I struggled to find words to convey the situations we faced; many of the communiqués are personal, almost like public journals. Essentially these are historical documents. They have been reproduced almost exactly as they were sent to give a better feel for the urgency and stress of the time, although some of the content has also been reworked into the main body of the book. It is subdivided into the following three sections:

1. Early Communiqués

In the first section are the messages written in the early days after the levee failures. I was trying to keep people updated and draw attention to what was developing outside of the corporate media's hype. We had many comrades and friends who were waiting on word of what happened to Robert King.

They were written in haste, but the messages are honest and show the first developments of what was to be the Common Ground Collective. My lone tired voice documents how we discussed who and what we were as we occupied space and defended our lives and those of people around us. They were sent to a few friends on small list, and (I believe) Houston Indymedia as updates.

The last message in September was the first to go to public lists and groups around the country. My intent was to draw people and attention to the region. It was composed when I was home gathering supplies for my third return to New Orleans within just over a week, when Common Ground was going to begin our first wide-scale aid work.

2. Soapbox

The second section consists of a series of communiqués written to address concerns as well as unfounded rumors. They showed what was happening internally within Common Ground. At the time, I was moving between New Orleans and my home and had more time to reflect and write on the many issues we were facing from growing too fast. It was a way to respond to many criticisms from people who were not there.

They were directed at radicals, anarchists, and antiauthoritarians who were flooding into New Orleans and Common Ground. It was my attempt to show people that we were practicing anarchism within devastated surroundings, and that we were self-reflective, trying to further develop horizontal principles.

They were also to serve as a challenge to activists to ask themselves why they wanted to come to New Orleans, if that was how they could be the most useful in supporting these communities. I wanted people to know that we were not some monolithic entity, that we were different people struggling to achieve our visions of better worlds while dealing with true internal contradictions.

The later reflections are anniversary letters or communiqués to remind civil society to keep the dreams alive, to remember what we were trying to achieve with the people of New Orleans.

3. Allied Voices

The third section is two communiqués I wrote and published widely in 2006–2007 within mostly radical circles to bolster support for other grassroots projects led by people of color directly affected in the region whose work was being overshadowed by Common Ground because we had more access to grassroots media.

These groups were engaged in hard work, but historical marginalization and systemic racism continued to present itself after the storm, even among those on the Left. During this period Common Ground greatly needed resources—but so did these groups. My aim was to use my words to get these posted through every outlet we had access to. Common Ground supported and worked in coalition with many of the groups in New Orleans, sharing material aid, volunteers, and sometimes funding, but I felt it was the least I could do to support them in the outside world.

The words still draw to the surface some of the feelings I carried as I put them down to paper or onto a screen.

My only regret was that I didn't write more.

1. Early Communiqués

Date: Sep 3, 2005
Subject: In the water in New Orleans

I just returned from New Orleans. We are safe. I am in Houston, We may organize another rescue party.

I have limited email access right now. I can be reached by phone 512.29#.###9 for emergencies or interest in going. If you are interested you must have your own supplies. EVERYTHING.

Please email first if you are interested in the possibility of going, before calling.

Call only if you need specific info about something else. I have limited battery on my phone.

scott

Date: Sep 7, 2005
Subject: Robert King is ALIVE/ New Orleans Updates

Quick update

I went back in. This time to the Algiers neighborhood to work with our comrade Malik Rahim and the neighbors in Algiers.

We rescued KING from his house. Brandon made it to the inner city, crossed water (and debris) and flagged a boat to go get King. They (Homeland Security) found him on his porch with his dog in great shape.

They dropped King with Brandon at his truck and they came back to Algiers with us.

We left quite a bit of supplies for the neighbors there. They are self organizing to aid their communities. They need more support.

More updates to follow.

Exhausted, but standing
scott crow

Date: September 9, 2005
Subject: Re: Money Raised/needed in Algiers

We could use the money for the *Algiers Community Project* with Malik and the people of Algiers.

Algiers Community Project:
This is a brief introduction to what is happening in southern New Orleans.

We really need money as well as material aid. This is a project for the people and by the people.

The people in Algiers have decided to take the project on to take care of themselves in this disaster. There is about 4,000 residents in a five square mile radius that are being minimally cared for by an indifferent military.

These people didn't have their houses destroyed or under water. Most have running water and some have gas or phone. There is no electricity, services or open businesses.

They are receiving MRE's (meals ready to eat) if they can leave their homes to travel 10–20 miles to get them. Occasionally the military trucks will quickly drive by to throw some food (MRE's) out.

There is barely any water being distributed at all. Residents are encouraged to boil the water from the tap. The water besides potential bacteria etc, could also contain chemicals or other harmful components.

We are setting up:
- First Aid stations through out the community
- Food stations through out the community
- Schools
- Garbage pick up
- Water/ hot food delivery by bicycle
- Free bicycles for transportation for the residents (as there is no gas)
- Communications Center
- Media Center
- Security detail
- Volunteer encampment

This is being organized with help from groups around the country. What makes this effort different is that 'the people' in the community told us what they needed and we are organizing it. We will set up relief in the short term and empower them to continue with the projects after we are gone.

Imagine for a minute . . . a scene like Chiapas, Mexico Jan 1, 1994. We are coming out of the jungle . . . not to fight, but to build power and support for our affected people without government help, indifference or interference.

Imagine those that have been made seemingly powerless by this disaster and the history of the disasters on their communities before that, now are taking their power back!!!

We will have volunteers on the ground to support and help people help themselves. We want to make our word deed.

I work for the people of Algiers.

From the gulf coast basin
"Everything for everyone and Nothing for ourselves"
–Zapatistas

subcomandante ;)
scott crow
_____

[**September 10, 2005**, see page 135]

2. Soapbox

Date: March 13, 2006
Subject: Anarchy and the Common Ground Collective

Intro

This piece is born out a misconception (presumptions?) about the Common Ground Collective and it's overarching philosophies and organizing in New Orleans. This is an excerpt of a larger piece I am working about the work we have done there, are doing now and where we might head in the future.

These are my thoughts and opinions of the work I helped lay down and think about daily—they do not necessarily reflect Common Ground Collective as 'official' statements. This is a rough draft, so apologies for some of the disjointedness to it.

One critique that we at Common Ground Collective have had from some volunteers within 'anarchist'/'anti-authoritarian' communities is that we are 'authoritarian' or 'hierarchical.'

Privilege and Assumptions

I would propose that ALL volunteers that come to Common Ground Collective and NOLA (short for New Orleans) in general; check themselves before they come down. Why are you coming to New Orleans? We must remember that we ALL bring our ideas, privilege as well as ASSUMPTIONS about the way things SHOULD be. A number of people, when they show up bring some sense of 'entitlement' around a few issues: that they should be in power, or in decision making roles simply because they are anarchist and propose to know better. This view in many ways is unrealistic and unhealthy to them, to us as an organization and to the people we serve in the communities. The picture in NOLA is large, complex and Common Ground Collective is one piece in that whole puzzle. Even though our organization has grown large we have many autonomous projects going on simultaneously within a larger framework of many organizations (like the People's Hurricane Relief Fund Coalition) working on similar as well as separate goals. This is a real life situation, not a theoretical abstract with many varied actors and participants from all political ideologies and disciplines. Mass mobilization organizing, 'free states', temporary autonomous zones and regional gatherings were but brief trial runs for what is going on in NOLA right now. If you have concerns or questions ASK, don't assume you know the ins and outs of the political climate in this region. There are longstanding political feuds, historical oppression, ongoing state repression and plain differences of opinion within the context of rebuilding NOLA.

Leadership within CGC

There are leadership positions within Common Ground Collective (CGC) that are necessary and which we work to be as transparent about as possible.

People have been put into positions of responsibility through commitment and dedication to the ongoing work. Many of our projects constantly evolve from new input and the fact that we maintain flexibility in what we do.

A misconception about CGC for example is: that when someone shows up for a few days (which is a righteous thing to do) we are going to automatically let them start deciding what to do with our programs, finances or structures. This has happened often, especially from people that have no track record with us, and are not known to us or to anyone in NOLA. Again I hope they would ask "Why have I come to NOLA?"

But once people establish commitment, a work record and some ACCOUNTABILITY to CGC and the residents then they are welcomed openly to more decision making processes and responsibility. People have been put into positions of responsibility through their commitment and dedication to the ongoing work, not because of cronyism or political maneuvering. Many of our projects and leadership constantly evolve from new input and the fact that we maintain flexibility in what we do. Malik has often said: "it's what you do, not what you say you will do that matters here."

Organizing Structures

In brief, the way Common Ground Collective strives to organize is: once a project is started it is autonomous under the umbrella of CGC. The people who 'bottom line it' (leadership) can organize their teams and decision making processes the way they need to. They are accountable to their project, CGC and to the people they serve (this is discussed in volunteer orientation on the ground). Some call them 'affinity groups' some call them 'work groups/teams', that is up to them to decide. Some projects have multiple coordinators and some have just one. Coordinators can and have been removed for a myriad of reasons. They must be accountable on many levels.

That said we don't have a centralized body that micro manages every detail either. The central collective body works on long term goals, strategies, internal organizing processes and finances with each project maintaining a great amount of autonomy. Is it bureaucratic? Not even close, but it is getting more tightly organized. We are setting up guidelines and processes for the way we function so that we can continue to do so. We don't set up arbitrary rules that exist for themselves. We set up blueprints to make everything move forward as democratically as possible.

The word 'collective' should not imply that everyone who shows up automatically is part of it. Our collective is in transition and growing. We are using that term in it's broadest sense at this point. The people who are our core organizers (about 40 people +/-) are more or less the amorphous 'collective'. This is a piece that internally we are working on and developing. We are also working on the transparency around what 'collective' means in our work.

The clinics are the one exception; they have more hierarchical elements to them at this point due to their intense scrutiny by the state in just keeping the doors open. The clinics must work with bureaucratic institutions like Center for Disease Control and Health and Human Services (whether they want to or not) to maintain the quality of free services we offers opposed to many of our other programs which are out of sight from state control. See their site (http://cghc.org/) for more info on this. Still with that, the clinics have many open processes in keeping with our principles and beliefs.

Consistency

One VERY critical component in working with low income or ANY traditionally marginalized communities (devastated or not) is consistency in the work that we do. If we start programs and drop them then we are not doing our jobs. We, with privilege and relative power in society must recognize this. Historically 'white middle class' or 'folx with privilege' and many good intentions have aligned themselves in good faith to work in communities such as these, only to co-opt the work, abandon the issues when it wasn't a 'hot' anymore or take over the work being done for their own gains. These concerns are some of the 'baggage' that we ALL bring to the table in working in NOLA.

Many well intentioned folx have come through CGC with great ideas, propose programs, start them, then have left us holding the bag. When that volunteer leaves: we as a collective entity are held to it by the communities we serve. Good intentions do not rebuild what 400 years of abandonment and neglect have done.

So we at CGC strive to overcome this by a strong self critique in all the work we potentially engage in which means that every well intentioned person with a 'great idea' does not get to automatically start making decisions or have input. We also ask of our volunteers that they set their preconceived ideas aside and be open to a different experience. But what sometimes happens is that those with privilege and entitlement assume they know better what to do than those who have lived their whole lives there, or have been working there for months through all the conflict, repression, neglect and hard work. So I would ask of these people: Did you come for 'activist points'? To push your ideology? Or to do the arduous hard work of building power with and for people in NOLA without personal glory?

We at CGC walk the tenuous tightrope of "equilibrio" (from the Mondragon Cooperatives in Spain) between horizontal and more centralized organizing, personal experience in balance with the goals and needs of the communities we serve.

As one of our core organizers Kerul Dyer succinctly put it "Common Ground is a largely white activist organization, and most of the coordinators come from an anti-authoritarian political culture. Malik Rahim and some of the core leadership in NOLA, however, come from a radical black political culture with fundamentally different experiences and approaches. The organization incorporates many decentralized characteristics, but at base we are acting in solidarity with local black leadership, and Malik makes many of the final overall long term decisions."

This is where much of our 'solidarity' comes from. Long term and difficult commitments in complex political/socio-economic landscapes within NOLA. We are blending decision making processes and coordinator structures as we go.

Many times I have challenged my beliefs about the way it 'should be' and the practicalities of 'what is' on the ground while still keeping my principles and the working principles of the organization.

Conclusions?

Anarchism is not rigid, it is flexible and fluid so cast aside your thoughts about the way it 'should' be and help make it what it 'could be'.

CGC doesn't have the answers; actually in many ways we have more questions as we go. Like the Zapatistas (who have informed some of the basic underlying group philosophy) we 'Lead by asking' as much as possible. It doesn't mean that we have it figured out or that we know the answers. What it means is that we are struggling along to make a better world for all of us. Our slice of putting principles into action is through our work in NOLA.

Another critique we have heard about CGC volunteers being only 'jocks', 'christians' etc.; we have cast a wide open net to anyone with honorable intentions to come and do hard work. We don't need just radical subcultures to change society we need people from all walks of life. What if 'radical' people had conversations with these folks and introduced them to alternative perspectives? What if we shifted the thinking in American political culture through this shared experience rather than looking down on them? Kwame Ture once said "White people need to organize in their own communities." What if this was an opportunity?

One of the most beautiful scenes in the early days was when a truck from Islamic Relief showed up with supplies from the Mormons and Catholic charities; which was all unloaded by people from the neighborhood, anarchist, communist and socialist working together in solidarity for a common good. Sectarian ideologies were set aside for the common good.

This doesn't make CGC "feel-good" charity, we have radical analysis of our work but we do mix service programs with our challenges to the oppressive systems. The Black Panther Party used to have "survival programs pending revolution" We are mixing those concepts with modern anarchist interpretation of 'dual power' models ('resisting while building counter institutions'). People need service and even our most benign programs still get heat from many sectors of 'the state'. Homeland Security has been no friend to volunteers or organizers within CGC. We give people HOPE for a better future in which communities have control over what happens in their lives. This fundamentally flies in the face of what many sectors of the corporate-state want. We know who we are politically and where we fit into the complicated structures both historically and presently. There are many reasons to stand up to white militia, defend houses from being bulldozed as well as cleaning up a neighborhood, sharing kind words or any of the less visible things that support people putting their lives back together.

We invite AND encourage those that have issues with the structures, programs or concepts within Common Ground to take direct action and start their own projects. This is not flippant, there is SO much work that needs to be done and there are autonomous groups needed to fulfill this, otherwise it is left to developers, the state and corporations to decides the fate of historically marginalized people in the Gulf Coast region.

We are standing on the edge of potential . . . so how is it going to look?

From the Gulf Coast Basin
scott crow
co-founder Common Ground Collective

Date: April 2006
Subject: A moment in time that changed the fabric of what we thought we knew.

This was written to a large group of comrades that were co-founding a group based on the "Sixth Declaration of the Lacandon Jungle" from the Zapatistas in Texas.

Hello Comrades, Friends and Allies

I must offer many apologies for not being able to meet with you today. I really wish to be back in Austin walking towards a better future with all of you. I feel if I am missing on some crucial shifts in our movements within our local communities that may lead us on paths that we haven't traveled for a long time.

I always feel that I am late to the game and that I must catch up with all of you, so please forgive my tardiness. I will be back soon and look forward to seeing you. Also many apologies for my writing—I am not a writer—so please bear with me.

All of that that said, I would like briefly to share with many of you how Zapatismo has influenced my ideas and work with building the Common Ground Collective in New Orleans.

First and foremost the EZLN and Zapatismo provided for me the first postmodern blueprint for revolution. That is a revolution that didn't look like the old stale ones from the past. They have, in my mind, created a living revolution that breathes, moves and changes.

In many ways they don't have the answers, but are willing to stumble along. How freeing is that to think we can try this and if it doesn't work try something else?

The many words they have shared with the world over the years give hope to change and challenge realities as we see them now.

Marcos once said a few years ago:

"We are united by the imagination, by creativity, by tomorrow . . . We left skepticism hanging on the hook of big capital and discovered that we could believe, and it was worth believing, that we should believe—in ourselves"

And the Zapatistas say often, "We have not come to take power but to exercise it."

Just those two ideas, that took root in me while New Orleans was underwater, lead me to cast aside my skepticism and replace it with big hopes and big dreams of change. Not just a campaign or an action but society.

OUR dreams—that took form were that we would aid people in the short term, and those of us from the outside would work with those historically marginalized people in the gulf to build their power for the long term.

New Orleans was a level playing field in many ways the old order was in crisis. We saw—we dreamed—of people doing for themselves even in the face of devastation—the face of indignity—we built Common Ground Collective with the face of hope and dignity, and together we have built power within the shell of what used to be New Orleans.

We didn't need the permission of the state, we didn't need their resources, we didn't need them at all. We only needed our dreams and the willingness to do it all for ourselves—affected communities and those from the outside.

We cast doubt aside and said we can—and will do this.

It became a reality. We started with three people, now 10,000 volunteers have come through and the residents have begun to come back, because we all dared to care and dream the biggest dreams.

The state wanted us to believe the story that it was over, things would never be the same—and they were partially right—it is not the same. The residents are returning—and their power grows day by day but their stories are unwritten.

Together we have built women's shelters, medical clinics, opened schools, provided legal assistance, stopped home demolitions, cleaned neighborhoods that have never been cleaned, restored hope and civic pride.

We have begun to change the long history of disasters on these communities.

the slow disasters of neglect and abandonment.

Our work at Common Ground is no where near perfect, but Zapatismo opened that space inside me and others, when the levees broke, to see it as an opportunity to build the changes we couldn't see under our own doubt in our daily lives.

There are bumps in the road and as we build power the state sees it as a challenge, but we continue in the face of it.

We are learning as we go and leading by obeying.

We are a thread in the history of struggles within New Orleans, the U.S. and the world. I am grateful to the Zapatistas for bringing an open ended revolution to all of our collective consciousness. It provides a framework to which we can all envision our futures to build from. I am excited and grateful to all of you for coming together to weave a new fabric in thinking of how we can all live in more just, democratic and sustainable ways.

Please Remember:
"Dream the future
Know your history
Organize your people
Fight to win"

From the Gulf Coast Basin and a concrete jungle
scott crow

Date: September 2006
Subject: It's been a year already? My brief subjective reflection on Katrina

---

I have avoided much of the media and the media hype around Katrina, the levee failure and the aftermath. I didn't need to see it again I, like many others feel it almost everyday.

I woke up this morning and all my feelings came back hard like the storm from which they were born. The fear, anger, frustration, inadequacy and compassion that drove me, and countless others into the flood waters and into a people's nightmare.

The scenes play out like broken movies and shattered images in mind at every turn. The devastation, the debris, the bodies the bureaucracy of the state who were blind (by choice and by habit) to move into action. When the scenes in my head start I just let them go (they would play out anyway). The smells of chemicals and sewage, the quiet on the water, the noises of gunshots, screams for help in the distance, and the constant helicopters overhead.

These are the reminders to me of why we went in the first place and why we should always go to places that need support. These historically marginalized communities deserve our support from the long, slow history of disasters wrought on them of neglect and abandonment.

My hurt is a small reminder to me to continue to use my access to privilege in our civil society to stop the levees from breaking in all traditionally neglected communities. When the scenes play out in my head and I feel the fear, the anger and the love I remember that it was worth it and will be worth it to do the same in the future.

Common Ground Collective and the many other grassroots organizations on the ground have given people a fighting chance, as well as returned their hope and faith in those outside their families, neighborhoods and cities that people do care and are willing to fight to do what is right no matter what the state says or does.

I have deep admiration and respect for those residents who are fighting for their self determination and to all the comrades and allies who have come to aid them and work with them in that struggle. From the short term relief to the long road of rebuilding, many dedicated people have given up a lot to be good allies. Hopefully we can continue to learn from that in all our radical movements. Despite some of Common Ground Relief's short comings and missteps over this time we have been part of a making something different and creating a fighting chance for all of us. For a time we really reached for the dry land and achieved common ground for the good of many. I have tears as I write this and the scenes play out, but I also have deep love and faith in what we can accomplish.

From where I humbly sit in, awe at the devastation we can wreak and the compassion within us.

Form the concrete jungle in the gulf coast basin
scott crow

Date: May 2007
Subject: Common Ground Collective: Black Flags and Windmills

The conversations about Common Ground Collective/Relief in New Orleans are always interesting. When I meet people who came to CG I never know if I am going to hear about the worst—or the best—time of their lives. I think it depended on when, where, or how you came in as well as what your expectations were.

But one thing is clearly emerging it has had a deep effect on many grassroots movements and groups within the U.S. in it's brief history. What will this look like in the future? How can we take these lessons and actions to apply them in future organizing?

Common Ground was an experience within the devastation of the gulf that will take years to sort out internally as well as publicly by many. I wanted to add some small fragmented perspective from my point of view to the dialog.

A Rough House Is Built

Common Ground IS NOT the same organization we co-founded at the kitchen table in 2005 after the levees gave away. I look at the 'heyday' of that phase to have ended within the first year, and then it moved towards a service organization only model—with less radical analysis and more 'non-profit' type work and structures. That is not to say that 'anarchist' or anti-authoritarian elements didn't still exist or weren't dreamed of, but they were not as valued or supported by the open door white volunteer base that was coming through.

The original framework in the formation of the organization that was discussed, written, and eventually faded from memory was simple and to the point—I know because I wrote it. Those of us from the outside would bring our access to resources (material aid, money and volunteers) into the region to work/stand in solidarity WITH the residents NOT for the residents in getting their lives back together, then move into supporting them in rebuilding infrastructure that was lost or that never existed. And lastly we would all recede in steps from the areas as people came back or had enough stability to carry it all.

We wrote that on Sept. 8th while fending off armed white men who thought they were the 'law' and wanted black people dead or in submission. There were no heroics—it was our moral imperative to do because we were asked by community members to come and do it. It seemed so basic and right—support impacted communities—anyway we could. We went into the communities and asked the people what they needed or wanted and built programs or work based on that. We never came in to tell people how it was going to be —we asked questions and built from that. I and others who worked on the early foundations—including Malik—didn't say we had the answers. We just knew were going to do the best we could without state support or interference.

In the early part this kept us from 'Mcdonald-izing' our support work. In some neighborhoods we had armed patrols, some we had the clinics, others it was tarping, gutting and clean out.—

But a strange thing happened on the way—we grew too big too fast—and being mostly outsiders as well as an organization started from scratch we didn't have the deep roots we needed to keep our paths and visions clear. We went from a handful of rebels to thousands of volunteers in months. And many of our old habits from society—baggage if you will—began to surface in some ways.

Internally, Common Ground, strove to be a hybrid between old school top down organizing and newer horizontal structures. Think of blending the Black Panther Party (survival programs pending revolution) and the Zapatista concepts (E.Z.L.N.) of autonomy and leading by obeying. There was always internal conflict and struggles between the two models even from day one—and eventually over time the old school models 'won' out. These contradictions were hurtful and confusing to many who came into contact with CG either as volunteers with radical leanings or to other groups we worked with. Many volunteers brought their assumptions of what they thought anarchist or horizontal organizing should look like as well as lots of privilege—that they couldn't even see. (see the article on Infoshop 'Anarchy and Common Ground').

Could We See These Things?

Some of the mistakes we made were: never formalizing the culture in our decision making processes and roles, allowing a constant influx of new volunteers (without limits or screening), defining and keeping our political space in the context of our broader work in communities (i.e. removing the 'wingnuts' or people who were harmful), and instilling that culture of humbleness and respect—the leading by asking—we began with.

By never formalizing our internal culture and processes—hell we didn't have time when it was critical to do so—we were not able to pass these along very well as more people came. So when many volunteers came they brought with them our societies baggage. We didn't get them to challenge why they were there or how they could support the impacted people—the solidarity not charity part

By not screening volunteers and having an open door policy we flooded some communities with sincere but misguided 'kids' who perpetuated ideas we were trying to dismantle (racism, privilege etc.) and we never had a clear exit strategy of how they would leave. This lead to people staying who shouldn't have; and New Orleans groups being angered at CG for not being clear about how we would turn over projects back to community control.

By not instilling that culture of humbleness and to 'lead by asking' we became the victims of our own internal CG culture and for periods during the first two years— we became disconnected from those we were supposed to serve.

We consciously sought out organizations like the People's Institute (from New Orleans) and Catalyst Project (Oakland) who provided invaluable internal work around issues of racism and class as well as mediating conflict between different groups in NOLA. Over 2,000 of our volunteers participated in the People's Institute Undoing Racism training and the Catalyst Project helped us to form anti-oppression working groups as well as ally mentoring.

But while we focused on those forms of oppression some in the organization played down or ignored our own subtle forms of internal sexism. I don't mean the overt 'hey baby' type, but the deeper more systemic type where women's voices—especially radical—didn't carry as much weight with some in 'leadership' as they should. That is not to say we didn't have BADASS women coordinators that lead or did amazing things—we did and many examples come to my mind—but many times women in leadership had to 'act like a man' to argue their points, to get funding, or the way a project or the organization was run. We didn't provide enough space for that and open dialog about it.

Our Narratives

From the beginnings our group narrative—the stories we would tell about Common Ground—was to be important—that is we weren't going to rely on anyone else to do it. And it is amazing how stories took on lives of their own.

We never had a public relations machine—just many people passionate and willing to get the word out about the work.

As in all of history with so many stories though many important ones are forgotten—along with the people who participated in them. Not because they we not valuable—but our collective memories erased or forgot along the way.

No one person built, maintained or made that organization happen—and hopefully in the future a larger picture will emerge.

The flipside are the myths that have built around 'the beginnings' of for example:

Malik, Sharon and I at the kitchen table or *Mayday DC* opening the first aid station or Brandon Darby and I looking for our friend Robert King in a boat or sitting with guns on the front porch.

All of these things happened—but these events have become 'heroic' stories that mythologize the real intent, purpose and work that real people did in turbulent times. How could we retell these events so people can see they might have done the same thing In the circumstances?

So on one hand we did well in bringing attention and resources through getting the word out—but we were also victims of that. Eventually our story eclipsed smaller or longer standing groups from the region.

When asked by a member of *INCITE* and *Critical Resistance* to give them support in spreading their message —as well as other local groups too—I felt we didn't give them enough of that and have felt regret about it since.

We never set out to tell our story and have NEVER told our story only to raise money for ANYBODY in the organization.

But even with our relative success in telling our own stories they still have been distorted and we have been the subjects of endless speculations, rumors, innuendos and conjecture. Media corporate and independent have also done their share to warp the realities of how CG fit into the bigger picture. They wanted heroes, backdrops, easy answers and solutions. So that is the framework of the stories they have told. They often ignored the subtleties of the political or radical nature that ran through the first two years.

We Built the Road as We Traveled

My work within and from the outside has been has been some of the most traumatic, most heart breaking and the most inspiring movement I have ever been a part of.

We had no blueprints, no models, no roots as an organization only motivation and history laid before us to build upon. We have been held to incredible and sometimes unrealistic scrutiny by 'the left', by 'leaders' in NOLA and even by ourselves. The bar for our successes and our failures have been really high—some would say too high. This organization was built, run and will die by ordinary people who were doing the best they could with what they had.

This doesn't excuse or sweep under the rug the issues—but I hope it opens a space for recognizing that. Most who came and participated came with sincere—even if misguided—and honorable intentions. The experiences that any one person who interacted with CG was life changing—sometimes for the better and sometimes not. That was life when civilization as we know it collapsed in the gulf coast region.

I now look at the early days—say the first year and some change—as the time when we had the largest anarchist influence and the spaces to experience what our lives could be like and how we might be part our self determination and that of others self determination. It doesn't mean it all worked—but it was a crack in history to peek inside. For this we had backlash from the state at all levels.

Now that the organization has transformed into a more traditional 'non-profit' doesn't negate the still important work that CG does. It just looks—and is—different.

People going to NOLA now should carry the spirit of 'solidarity not charity' but recognize it is not as it once was or strove to be. This doesn't mean we should all pack up and hold a funeral—but that we should just recognize that it is what it is.

There are many amazing radical homegrown grassroots groups In NOLA that are doing good deep long term work.

Our Place Within the Picture

Common Ground was never the answer to the history of exploitation and oppression—and we never said we were the saviors. We just wanted to do what we could in our part WITH residents to reclaim their lives. We put anarchy into action. Mutual aid, direct action, self defense, sharing power—these were real—even of they were brief.

My hopes are that we—as individuals—will be able to heal from these experiences in our lives and be forgiving of ourselves and each other and that we—as movements—will be able to draw on the experiences of CG to better as part of transforming societies that are just, sustainable and truly democratic.

From the concrete jungle
scott crow

Date: October 03 2007
Subject: Response to White Vigilante Justice

I, as well as others, can also testify that there WERE white vigilantes in at least two area of NOLA. In Algiers Point, where we formed Common Ground, there was the Algiers Point Militia and near Center City (by . . .).

The militias were interesting in that their make up was of mostly white men from various socio-economic backgrounds. But ultimately in their actions and words they acted like Klansmen straight out of the deep south from some long ago era. The way they paraded around in their trucks they looked like something from a bygone era without the Klan hoods.

I have said this numerous times that they were more interested in 'their' private property and 'security' than the well being of anyone who wasn't white. They were also chickenshits who ONLY acted, talked tough when they outnumbered anyone on the street.

I have reasons to believe they did shoot people, or how else could we explain the bullet riddled body that was left rotting or the people in the neighborhood who were shot at or had guns drawn on them by these yahoos. They threatened to kill Malik from the get go.

When Brandon Darby and I went for the second time—on Sept. 5th—we came to give support to Malik and the people in Algiers from these vigilantes.

Support you say? What do you mean?

We stood watch on Malik's porch and began safety patrols over the next few weeks in armed self defense. This wasn't two white guys taking it on themselves this was WITH people from the neighborhoods affected by the very real threats on their lives. When the vigilantes drew guns on us—or really threatened too while the stood their armed—we held our ground from Malik's porch. We knew we were not there to strike out but to hold the space. It was the one of the scariest—to say the least—times of my life. We made our presence known.

We continued to be open that we were armed—hell many people were at that time. But an interesting thing happened after incidents like that. The vigilantes began to subside from the picture. We always asked ourselves was it due to meeting armed opposition? or was it fear of the National Guard who began to show up?

This wasn't some heroic machismo or savior mentality. This—in my analysis—was anti racist work at its core. This was what was asked of us and this is why we did it. We were not trained as soldiers—we were community organizers. Calls of support were sent and answered.

To give context—as many have heard or seen—there were no *laws* at the time. Even forces of the state acted 'lawlessly' and often in their own interest. Needless to say our tactics, politics and developing survival programs— Common Ground—caused the state to come down on us. But many of us feel that our stance and practice of armed self defense protected us and kept us from being 'dropped in the river' as we were threatened with often by elements of the state.

The state?? who? what?
At this time it was made up of local, regional and national 'officials' from every acronym of a department you could think of. All operating under 'their' interpretation of the law with no command structures or accountability—dare I say like the wild, wild west?

The worst of those times were over in the first few weeks as Common Ground became more established and the vigilantes—'lawful and unlawful'— began to subside.

Many lessons were learned and more to be learned as the stories and tragedy continued to unfold.

The surface is just being scratched to reveal the crack in those histories. My admiration goes out to others from the Algiers neighborhoods and volunteers from CG who are nameless that put their lives on the line— literally—to stop the white supremacist vigilantes.

You can see a trailer to a film by a Danish filmmaker that has footage of the deep racism of these people. Some of these are the ones we drove back.

http://www.welcometoneworleans.dk/

To be continued . . .

From the concrete jungle
scott crow

Date: August 29, 2008
Subject: On Remembrances and Anniversaries: Tears for the Gulf Coast and
               Immediate Concerns, Katrina and Gustav

Hello comrades, friends, family, allies and strangers

I am writing on this day of remembrance and tears, struggle and concerns of the disaster from Katrina in the Gulf Coast of three years ago in 2005.

We cannot let history as told by those who assume Power forget. Forget today, forget 2005 or forget the 500 years of neglect, abandonment and indifference that lead to the slow disasters on communities like those in the Gulf or anywhere in our world.

New Orleans today is still dichotomies on the ground; hope and sadness, emptiness and return—beauty and distress. Lives still need to be rebuilt but hope still resides in many areas.

I had just been learning to sleep better again since 2005, but with Gustav approaching I—like many of you—have been watching and thinking of the past and of today. I still carry that time and Gustav becomes the reminder of the fragility of it all.

Some of you may be aware there is a hurricane named Gustav that is working its way into the Gulf Of Mexico as we speak. It has already left devastation in its wake upon small Caribbean countries whose people have suffered under Power and now natural disaster.

It is predicted to become a category 3 by landfall in the u.s. It is also has indications of heading for the New Orleans area—at this point most likely Morgan City west of NOLA. Of course these are only predictions. But with predictions and memory come concerns.

Why would I care you may ask?

Good question. A couple of reasons, remember Katrina and the levee failure in NOLA? Besides the travesty of indifference and arrogance from the government and the Red Cross that we remember, there were many other places along the Gulf Coast that suffered in silence. Now on the third anniversary many of these communities are under direct threat from the storm as well as indirect threat of being ignored and forgotten again.

Vigilance and deeds

We of Common Ground Relief are asking that you all remain aware. Aware that the potential for history to repeat in response to disaster or really to anything. Also not forget during this time of remembrances. New Orleans has still not been rebuilt, and the progress is slow. The levees are only 20% completed and millions of dollars over budget. The coastal areas which include First Nation and other small towns and Vietnamese and Cajun fishing villages; these people are still in disrepair and vulnerable due to major wetlands loss of human cause.

We at Common Ground are making preparations to again be first responders through out most any region in the Gulf. We will need people, material aid and ways to keep the story visible. We have supplies and coordination to mobilize quickly and efficiently but we also need you. We are monitoring the situation, preparing ourselves and others to be ready to act should it be necessary.

Stay alert and prepared to support those in the Gulf Coast if necessary. It is we—in civil society—and those affected directly who will face the real needs head on. Governments and large bureaucratic agencies will raise money, will do little and often will not do it well.

There are many small grassroots groups throughout the region that will need support. Find them, and do what you can from your home with what you have access to. Don't let corporate media and complacency forget. Don't let the pageantry and fireworks of systemic corrupted Power distract us from immediate needs. All empires fall and theirs despite pomp and circumstance will be no different. On this third anniversary of remembrances tell and retell the stories to move us all into actions again.

We are the ones we have been waiting on. With Hope and determination

From the concrete jungle in the Gulf Coast Basin
scott crow
Co-Founder of Common Ground Collective
(On behalf of Common Ground Relief)
08.29.08

For more information please see the site: http://www.commongroundrelief.org or find other grassroots group in the Gulf that could use your support.

Date: September 04 2008
Subject: Report back from Common Ground Relief

Hello friends, comrades and allies

We, from Common Ground Relief, have just returned from the Louisiana Gulf Coast from delivering supplies, as well as assessing the situation within the region to the best of limited our abilities. Common Grounders based in New Orleans evacuated to Hattiesburg, Mississippi where they remained safe until we all could gather information and respond. while I and a contingent from Austin, Texas traveled in to deliver much needed supplies.

A group of first responders traveled to some areas and were blocked from others. The situation in the outlying areas along the coast as many of you know were harder hit with minimal flooding and wind damage to NOLA itself.

In comparison to Katrina's aftermath, the damages and neglect from the government and Red Cross, the situations from this storm were not nearly as dire or severe.

The state and the large bureaucratic NGO's could not let the response of 2005 happen again, not because they care, but because populations of people held them more accountable. Their strategies were again to first control the situation with direct force and control of the affected areas, then second to supply aid. They controlled access and aid points throughout, but we were able to maneuver through them into affected areas.

Majority of the populations in all of the areas were truly gone, It was deserted mostly with few hold outs as well as those who couldn't leave. This was true in all the areas we visited. The presence of the state in the form of FEMA, military and law enforcement agencies were often times the only population in areas.

Flooding due to storm surges were minimal and affected people in lower lying as well as remote areas. There was wind damage with what you would expect downed power lines and trees. There were not many roofs blown off and small amounts of mudslides across roadways.

Around Houma, Dulac and areas along the coast there was mostly wind damage but little flooding of what you would expect with rising tides, rains and Hurricane waters.

Roads were cleared in New Orleans and outlying areas with great speed within the first 48 hours even in residential areas.

The greatest damage to the area in my opinion is the long slow disaster still enacted on these communities. The disasters of neglect, abandonment and forgetting. Neglect in that rebuilding and return into the most marginalized communities by the most vulnerable people is still minimal or non-existent.

Abandonment in that many non-profits, foundations and us in civil society have given attention to other matters while New Orleans and the Gulf Coast region still needs our ideas, imagination and support to rebuild. Forgetting, that we forget the impact the small things can have on peoples lives in what we can do. Those of us with access to resources to still aid the region and the groups doing the work.

Katrina and the levee failures were the last disaster in the long slow history of disasters on these historically communities and Gustav was the reminder of the vulnerability of them.

New Orleans and the region, to me, are just unwitting canaries in the coal mine, and reminders of how vulnerable many communities throughout this country are.

In the coming days, Common Ground will be re-establishing a distribution center for basic aid supplies for residents as they return and for those who didn't or couldn't leave. We are already providing basic food, water and hygiene kits in the 7th and Lower 9th Wards.

We cleared debris and trees from the streets of NOLA into Dulac on the coast.

We are working with Four Directions to provide support the Native and coastal communities. We will have legal aid and communications up ASAP. Please see our site for more updated information. www.commongroundrelief.org

We need long-term SKILLED volunteers to help in continued rebuilding, Gustav served as the reminder, that more and safer housing is still needed.

We need carpenters, plumbers, electricians and other skilled trades to continue our rebuilding efforts. We will need some medical personnel in the short term to make sure there are no crises as residents return to NOLA and to the coastal area. But mostly we need you, in civil society, to not forget. Remember why you gave support in the first place, why it is important for us to build bridges across differences that matter and strengthen communities even ones we do not know. Tell the stories, don't let your communities forget, keep rebuilding the Gulf Coast region alive in the minds and hearts of caring people. Your words and actions from afar have impact, they have meaning even if you cannot feel it directly. Don't let history told by those who assume Power to say its ok. To return to your home is a right not a privilege from Palestine to New Orleans.

Towards Collective Liberation for all of us!

From the concrete jungle in Gulf Coast Basin
scott crow

Date: August 29, 2009
Subject: Anniversaries so we don't forget: Katrina, Common Ground and
             New Orleans four years on.

Hello comrades, friends, companera's and allies

It is that annual time of the year when in the South the heat is oppressive, summer lingers and storms grow off shores in the distances.

While August holds on, I can never see this month the same as I had all my life.

My heart and mind are forever moved by the levees failure and in turn the governments in the fall of 2005 and the spontaneous uprisings that grew from those failures.

The historically marginalized residents from neighborhood to neighborhood resisted oblivion, they resisted invisibility and they did what they could to save their own lives—because no one else was going to.

And when they resisted others came from coast to coast to support them, join the struggles and try to set right the painful wrongs that had been perpetrated on people who were left or couldn't leave. Together movements were born from the travesty to build and rebuild necessary infrastructure and services that were neglected way before the levees every collapsed.

Anniversaries of the cracks in history that were created and still live
It wasn't governments, who operated in fear, loathing and failure, that set things right. It was civil society, it was you, me and thousands we don't know. It was people who were motivated by love, by moral imperatives despite governments and large professional relief agencies. We didn't need road maps, rules and regulations to tell us to do the right thing. We just needed

each other and the belief that everyone deserves health care, dignity, shelter, support and safety.

The Common Ground Collective was one of the organizations born of that movement and now four years on we still exist, and we still support the struggles of the people of New Orleans for justice and memory.

Anniversaries so we continue our actions

Even as media and civil society forgets. We must remember and never forget. Not for morbidity, not for statistics, not for spectacle, but to keep the dreams and the struggles for better worlds alive. It can be a living memory for all of us, not of ghosts and failures, but a living memory of resistance and building.

There is much support, healing and work to be done yet. The stories of New Orleans and the Gulf Coast are not closed. Corruption, ineptitude, racism, blindness and bureaucracy of the state and big business will always stop them from being able to solve the deep rooted problems. Small grassroots work of the many organizations and neighborhood groups with continued outside support from the bottom up will grow the seeds of better Gulf Coast. Even if we falter along the way, we have walked the paths for something far better than if we did nothing. The solidarity of support, not charity of grief and guilt, of all our struggles for survival are intertwined and can overcome many obstacles. We must continue to support the communities in creating the worlds the way they imagine it; where their voices count, where it is just and sustainable.

The beauty and the tragedies are still alive for many. Anniversaries are reminders that we must never give up, give in or forget.

Still dreaming of collective liberation for everyone four years on.

From a historic drought in the concrete jungle of
the great wide Gulf Coast Basin
scott crow
Co-Founder Common Ground Collective
08.29.09

3. Allied Voices

Date: March 29, 2006
Subject: Support people of color/low income communities working in the
              Gulf

Support grassroots groups lead by people of color/low income communities working on the destruction in the Gulf Coast Region.

As a 'white allied' organizer working in NOLA it is important to support grassroots groups lead by people of color/low income communities working on the destruction in the Gulf Coast Region. Some of the groups are national, with local NOLA chapters. Many of these groups were doing work in the region before Katrina struck or the levees broke.

As mostly 'white allied' groups we are asking that groups with access to networks of people/resources please use this to get information out about these groups who could use support in their continued critical work.

Common Ground Collective has benefited from our privilege of access to many resources and want to make sure other groups are not overlooked in this process. Our work in the region is linked to many of these groups; we need to mutually support each other for the rights of dignity and self determination for many historically marginalized communities.

Please forward to any appropriate lists of people that may be interested.

NOTE: The list of organizations has been redacted due to space considerations.

Still dreaming from the Gulf Coast Region
scott crow
Co-Founder Common Ground Collective

Date: Dec. 2007
Subject: New Orleans Women's Health & Justice Initiative

Comrades, Friends, Allies and Concerned People

Below is a call out for an amazing and important health project that hasn't gotten the exposure that Common Ground's clinics have but deserves recognition and support for their mission and work.

Their analysis of intersecting wider reproductive and women's rights issues has largely been missing from many conversations and defense work within and without New Orleans.

Please support their work AND spread the word. All the health care we can be a part of supporting in NOLA helps to create autonomy and self-determination in the face of forgetting by bad governments, the corporate media and larger society.

Their letter is below.

Towards Liberation
scott crow
Co-Founder Common Ground Collective

New Orleans Women's Health & Justice Initiative
December 2007
"Moving from the margins to the center is vital for the health and well being of women of color and poor women. To do so, we must address the control and exploitation of our bodies and the regulation of our reproduction. We must center our needs and experiences by designing a table without restrictions or exploitation, dictating who can sit where and

when . . . creating a location which we feel is ours to sit at and be heard . . .
The New Orleans Women's Health Clinic is that table."
–Shana griffin

Dear Supporters of the New Orleans Women's Health Clinic:
Even before Hurricane Katrina, women of color and low income women
in New Orleans lacked access to basic health care. Today, twenty-eight
months after the storm, the limited health care resources that existed
before the storm for low income and uninsured individuals have yet to be
replaced, despite repeated commitments by public officials to create a
"better system." In reality, this "better system" includes plans to shift from
public services to subsidized private health insurance, leaving over 60
percent of Louisiana's most vulnerable residents without health insurance
or a safety net.

Combined with the loss of needed public resources and the
continuation of economic isolation, gender inequality, environmental
hazards, limited housing affordability, and racial discrimination, this lack
of services and access to safe, affordable preventative care is equal to a
public health disaster that directly impacts women of color and low-income
women—particularly those who are young, uninsured, immigrant, elders,
head of households, HIV/AIDS positive, homeless, sex workers, queer,
disabled/differently-abled, incarcerated and formerly incarcerated, and
living in public housing—as they face increased barriers to health care.

The need to organize to address this public health crisis in New Orleans
is clear, but the specific needs of women and the issues of sexual and
reproductive oppression have not been prioritized in the rebuilding of the
city. The manifestations of ill-health, lack of preventative care, inadequate
medical resources, and the absence of a comprehensive health policy paint
an unpromising picture as the voices of low income and uninsured women
of color are largely silenced. Despite this harsh reality, the New Orleans
Women's Health Clinic (NOWHC), a women of color-led project, has
become a CRITICAL resource with vast potential for comprehensive health
education and grassroots organizing activities.

The mission of the New Orleans Women's Health Clinic is to equip
marginalized and underserved women with the means to control and
care for their own bodies, sexuality, and reproduction through a holistic,
community-centered well women approach to health care which integrates
sexual health and reproductive justice. Through the organizing and health
advocacy work of INCITE! Women of Color Against Violence, the New
Orleans Women's Health Clinic was conceived to combine health services
with a political analysis of the oppression that prevents low income,
uninsured, immigrant, disabled/differently-abled, formerly incarcerated, and
LBTQ women of color from receiving comprehensive health care.

NOWHC not only provides health care services, but also addresses
the social invisibility of low-income women of color that allows their needs

to be chronically ignored and unmet. As corporate healthcare programs attempt to fill the gaps in health care existing for low-income women in New Orleans, NOWHC stands out as a clinic that is grassroots in origin and support, and that incorporates an analysis of the root causes of the current health care crisis into the services it provides.

Since the New Orleans Women's Health Clinic opened in May of this year, the demand for our services has steadily increased month by month. We currently provide a range of gynecological care and preliminary obstetrical visits including pregnancy testing and counseling; pap smears; pelvic exams; diagnosis and treatment of irregular menstruation, vaginal, urinary tract, and sexually transmitted infections; comprehensive sex education and access to safe and effective contraceptives; and prenatal care and education. The low cost sliding fee scale rates of the Clinic are possible due to the support we've received this year, most of which has come from individuals like you.

Most recently, we established a Women's Healthcare Fund, designed to ensure that uninsured women who cannot afford the cost of care or medications can receive care at NOWHC. In the coming year, NOWHC plans to begin providing midwifery care, expand our services to gender variant people, conduct educational workshops at the Clinic space and in community settings throughout the city, and engage in base building activities to build support and awareness of the Clinic locally and nationally.

At NOWHC, we are working to build the "table," as we continue to assist women access safe, affordable, and quality health services and resources they need to take care of their over health, bodies, sexuality, and reproductive. To continue this, we are asking you to support the New Orleans Women's Health Clinic in the following ways:

* Make a financial contribution to the New Orleans Women's Health Clinic. We rely primarily on donations from individuals such as you to provide sliding scale medical services to local women, and organize to build our long-term capacity. Donations help NOWHC to pay living wage salaries, rent and maintain our space, and cover the cost of laboratory services for uninsured women. A financial contribution of $50 will provide an annual exam for a woman who otherwise could not afford one, through our Women's Health Care Fund. Hosting a benefit house party will raise enough for a supplies order or a piece of medical equipment, as well as spread the word about NOWHC. In addition to financial donations, we are also accepting gift cards from Office Depot, and prepaid medical supply orders through PSS Medical Supplies. Financial contributions should be made out to our fiscal sponsor: Women With A Vision, with NOWHC listed in the memo line of check. Checks and gift cards should be mailed to:

New Orleans Women's Health Clinic
1406 Esplanade Ave.
New Orleans, LA 70116

Spread the word about the New Orleans Women's Health Clinic. Publicity in local, national, and international press helps NOWHC spread the word about our services, connects us with people engaged in similar work, provides publicity, and generates support. But, it's something we often don't have time to coordinate ourselves. If you have an idea for an article, please contact us at 504.524.8255 or at nowhc_info [at] yahoo.com for an interview and press points. Alternately, reach people directly by spreading the word about NOWHC to five potential donors. Your direct appeal saves us time and administrative costs!

Donate needed supplies to the New Orleans Women's Health Clinic. The supplies that NOWHC uses daily really add up. Additionally, there are several pieces of medical equipment that we still need. If you would like to sponsor a supply order, or have supplies or equipment to donate, please contact Cassandra Burrows at nowhc_info [at] yahoo.com to determine if NOWHC can use them, or to get a list of needed supplies. Please don't send unsolicited material.

The New Orleans Women's Health Clinic warmly thanks our network of donors and volunteers for your continued generous support. You are needed now more than ever. Our ability to provide needed services, maintain autonomy, and participate in grassroots organizing is made possible through the support of individuals and organizations in our community and nationwide.

Sincerely,

Shana M. Griffin, Interim Director
Isabel Barrios, Board Member
Rosana Cruz, Board Member
Monique Harden, Board Member
Deon Haywood, Board Member
Mayaba Liebenthal, Board Member
Thea Patterson, Board Member

Common Ground Documents

Vision/Mission
October 2005

VISION
We are a community-initiated volunteer organization offering assistance, mutual aid and support to communities that are neglected and traditionally marginalized. The work gives hope to communities by working with them, providing for their immediate needs and emphasizing people working together to rebuild their lives in sustainable ways.

MISSION
Common Ground's mission is to provide short-term relief for victims of hurricane disasters in the Gulf Coast region, and long-term support in rebuilding the communities affected in the New Orleans area.

Working with Respect
October 2005
Some elements of this document were originally adapted from SOUL (school of unity and liberation), the Ruckus Society and People's Institute for Survival and Beyond. I began adapting and using these elements with many organizations over the years since 2000.

Our backgrounds have not given many of us the tools to build just and sustainable society, so we have to recognize, learn from, and work with each other to build these visions and practices.

These points provide us a starting place to work from, learning respect and trust to build stronger relationships and organization.
- Everyone has a piece of the truth
- Everyone can learn

- Everyone can teach or share something.
- Remember all of this is a process. What happens along the way is as important as the goals.
- Respect the work and abilities of others
- Create safe and inclusive environments for all.
- Take risks within yourself: Participate, give it a chance; have some trust to try on new ideas.
- Critique inappropriate behaviors NOT the person. Remember, we are ALL still learning.
- Actively listen to each other: listen to what others are saying, before speaking.
- Be accountable to the people and communities we support and yourself.
- Speak only for yourself. Remember we all have different experiences and values to share.
- Step up, Step back: Give space for MANY voices to be heard.
- Avoid defensiveness: Be open to legitimate critique or challenges of ideas, patterns or behaviors.
- Mistakes will be made by all of us. None of us is perfect.
- Be aware of the effects of your actions on the communities and others around you.
- Challenge oppressive behavior in a way that helps people grow
- Take cues from people in the communities you are working with in the way you interact
- If you see a behavior that is inappropriate intervene, don't wait for someone else to address it.
- Don't use alcohol or drugs in places where they can endanger people. (These have been historical problems).
- Don't use acronyms: It can make people to feel left out.

Sexual Harassment Prevention Guidelines
November 2005

Common Ground believes that all people have a right to be free of any form of harassment and oppression, and in particular, sexual harassment. No volunteer is to threaten or insinuate, either explicitly or implicitly, that another volunteer or community members' refusal or willingness to submit to sexual advances will affect their participation in Common Ground.

All sexual contact between volunteers/community members be consented to prior to contact.

Other sexually harassing or offensive conduct is not welcome at Common Ground.

This conduct may include:

- Unwanted physical contact or conduct of any kind, including sexual flirtations, touching, advances, or propositions;
- Verbal harassment of a sexual nature, such as lewd comments, sexual jokes or references, and offensive personal references;
- Demeaning, insulting, intimidating, or sexually suggestive comments about an individual's personal appearance;
- The display of demeaning, insulting, intimidating or sexually suggestive objects, pictures or photographs;
- Demeaning, insulting, intimidating, or sexually suggestive written, recorded, or electronically transmitted messages

Anyone who believes that another person's actions or words constitute unwelcome harassment, should address that person directly as well as let one of the coordinators know as soon as possible. All complaints of harassment will be investigated promptly and in as impartial and confidential a manner as possible. Volunteers are asked to cooperate in any investigation. A timely resolution of each complaint should be reached and communicated to the parties involved. Common Ground treats false accusations, which can be incredibly destructive, equally seriously.

Any volunteer who is found to have violated the harassment policy may be asked to leave. Proven sexual assault may be subject to legal action.

Outline of Common Ground Activities and Programs

OVERVIEW

Common Ground Relief has provided direct or indirect services to over 500,000 people since its founding on September 5, 2005.

SEPTEMBER–DECEMBER 2005

Common Ground was founded on September 5; the distribution center opened its doors on September 13. In the first week of October, Common Ground had a second founding and stabilization with an influx of organizers. We began with three people; by the end of the year ended, there were hundreds. That fall, Common Ground was incorporated as a nonprofit in Louisiana.

Material Aid

- Begin implementing and building Common Ground relief programs: roof tarping, search and rescue, distribution of two hundred free bicycles, large scale debris and dead animal removal, tree trimming, street/gutter clean out, assisting residents with FEMA, Red Cross and family searches for family by Internet or phone.
- First experiments with house gutting and house debris removal occur at two locations in Algiers and Seventh Ward.
- Established mobile aid distribution and mobile health clinics in coastal areas of Houma, and Plaquemines Parish; eventually, permanent aid distribution center established in Houma.
- Distribution center established in the upper Ninth Ward main at Mt. Carmel Baptist Church on Pauline St. Eventually transfers to the parking lot across from Mt. Carmel Baptist Church on Pauline Street. Mount Carmel becomes primary housing center volunteers and residents.

- House of Excellence opens on Franklin Ave. in the mid-city area with distribution center, career advice, First Aid station and computer lab for residents and volunteers.
- Established large scale volunteer house gutting program in the Seventh and Ninth Wards to aid residents and keep whole neighborhoods from being torn down by the state.
- Established the "Blue House" in Lower Ninth Ward; begin large-scale aid distribution at Deslonde and North Derbigny streets.

Direct Action

- Established self-defense patrols with local residents to defend against white vigilantes from Algiers Point militia and law enforcement.
- Copwatch group is formed to monitor and document heavy police activity and abuse.
- Violated military/police barricades to secretly deliver aid to "closed" Seventh and Ninth Wards.
- Begin pilot program distributing free home building supplies to local residents taking direct action to cut locks and "rehome" evicted families.
- Common Ground volunteers engage in civil disobedience and protests to stop housing evictions.

Health

- Trash cleanup.
- Mayday DC Collective arrives to set up First Aid station in Bijal Mosque in Algiers.
- Established second medical clinic and aid distribution in Algiers at St. Mary Baptist Church.
- First soil and water samples were taken by an environmental engineer and other volunteers throughout region to determine toxicity levels for safety of residents and volunteers.
- Pagan Cluster begins first experiments with bioremediation techniques to restore soil.
- Common Ground Health Clinic broadens its free medical services for a holistic approach including social work, massage, acupuncture, counseling, and herbal remedies.
- Experiments with first compost toilets for incoming Common Ground volunteers.
- Established garden clean up and planting project in Treme neighborhood.

Communications

- Independent media center established, including Internet, phone, and fax capabilities, as well as emergency two-way communications center with clinic and mobile units.
- CommongroundRelief.org, an open source website, goes live.
- Free Radio Algiers, our microradio station, goes on air, broadcasting in FM in a twelve-mile radius with public service information, updates and music.

Organizing

- Began support (food, shelter, legal) of influx of immigrants (who were mostly non-English speaking) living in a park lured to New Orleans for work by unscrupulous contractors.
- Co-organized march across Mississippi bridge into Gretna in commemoration of people being blocked from fleeing disaster by police.
- NOHEAT (New Orleans Housing Emergency Action Team) begins eviction defense efforts.
- Began our first large scale antiracist trainings for incoming volunteers with People's Institute For Survival, providing analysis, education and organizing through orientations, "Undoing Racism" trainings, caucuses and workshops.
- NOLAW (New Orleans Legal Action Workers) begin prisoner support and legal aid with our first legal aid office.
- Common Ground volunteers use direct-action tactics to block bulldozers from destroying empty houses in the Ninth Ward.

Outreach

- First relief volunteers arrive from Austin with large amount of aid supplies and communications equipment.
- First scouting missions into the bayous to assess damage and assist with search and rescue.
- Sent first responder emergency crew to Lake Charles communities after Hurricane Rita.
- Sent first delegations to flooded affected areas in Coastal parishes of Louisiana to offer aid after Rita: Vietnamese fishing villages, First Nation Communities.
- On behalf of Common Ground, Malik Rahim attends People's Hurricane Relief Fund conference in South Carolina and speaks at antiwar demo in D.C.
- The *Katrina Portraits* book project begins.

- Organized Roadtrip for Relief, modeled after the civil rights era freedom rides, to get young volunteers to the Gulf on a large scale. This brings 5,000 volunteers in a single week.
- First version of Common Ground Volunteer Handbook appears; gives short history, logistics and philosophy.

Other Groups

- Two Food Not Bombs (Hartford and Tucson) chapters arrive to serve food in the Seventh and Ninth Wards as well as in the coastal bayou areas where people were still left.
- Internationally recognized French aid organization Secours Populaire *Français* provides Common Ground medical and computer equipment after rejection by Red Cross.
- Pastors for Peace and Islamic Relief Charities provide material aid and water.
- Veterans For Peace establishes a base in Slidell; begins regular supply lines of material aid to Common Ground which boosts our relief efforts.
- Continued support for Mama D and the Soul Patrol in the Seventh Ward.
- Supported local resident in Algiers helping to shelter and feed hundreds of abandoned dogs.
- Malik and scott invited by governments of Venezuela (via Pastors for Peace) and France (via Secours Populaire) to speak.
- Aidsail consults with Common Ground to provide aid and incorporate as a nonprofit in Louisiana.
- Volunteer leaves to form Four Directions, focusing on First Nation communities with support from Common Ground.
- Common Ground's Lower Ninth Ward Women's Center opens on Louisa St. at a daycare center to provide safe shelter for women and children. Resident Donna Banks coordinates. It eventually becomes an autonomous project.

2006

This was a heady year; anarchist organizing in the Gulf Coast was strong. Nascent projects grew into full-fledged programs while new projects were initiated. During this year there were between two and five thousand volunteers resisting and building during any given week.

Material Aid

- Establish citywide tree clearing and removal services.

- Continue to provide referral services for hospitals, social services beyond our abilities, etc.
- Mobile distribution of food and aid continues of growing immigrant communities occupying parks and open spaces due to lack of housing.
- Gained management rights of the Woodland Apartments, a 361-unit apartment complex on thirteen acres in Algiers. Initiated affordable and sustainable community housing with support programs such as onsite medical aid access, before and after-school activities for youth and their families including: Tupac Amaru Shakur Children's Breakfast Program, a kids summer camp, and bimonthly Community Unity Day celebrations.
- Common Ground's Kids and Community Collective is established to offer free after school programs for underserved kids at numerous locations. It also gave free school supplies and backpack to kids. Over one thousand kits were given away.
- Common Ground establishes a tool lending library for residents who are working on their homes in three wards.

Direct Action
- Common Ground volunteers support parishioners by occupying the radical St. Augustine's Catholic Church founded in 1842 for a month to keep it from being torn down.
- Common Ground volunteers take direct action to defy police and the school board. They cut the locks, and with residents gut the moldy debris and reopen Martin Luther King, Jr. School, which becomes an exemplary school in New Orleans.
- Common Ground volunteers continue to engage in civil disobedience and protests to stop housing evictions.

Health
- Meg Perry Healthy Soil Project formed to test soils, and build up toxic soils in neighborhoods to support food security through community gardens.

Communications
- Common Ground appears in multiple media stories, gaining recognition as an organization.
- Expanded micro-radio communications, then turned them over to People's Hurricane Relief Fund for use in their communities.
- Common Ground's newspaper, *Breaking Ground*, is established and distributed by the thousands across the region.

Organizing
- Established volunteer housing and support at ArtEgg Warehouse in mid-city.
- Large scale volunteer housing is established at St. Mary's Catholic School on Congress St. in the Ninth Ward for spring break.
- Two thousand volunteers arrive weekly during spring breaks from colleges and high schools.
- Common Ground supports ongoing protests organized by People's Hurricane Relief Fund for the Right of Return, police accountability and stopping impending public housing demolitions.
- Created a Student Solidarity Network of thirty-five college groups who have mobilized volunteers and donations to support the people of New Orleans.

Other Groups
- Established RUBARB (Rusted Up Beyond All Recognition Bikes), a free bicycle repair shop and distribution center. Eventually it becomes an autonomous project.
- Social Change Caravan to New Orleans partners with Common Ground to provide bus transportation and accommodations at no cost to over a dozen Katrina survivors, to get back home to New Orleans from Seattle.

2007–2008
Over these years, Common Ground shifted from large-scale relief efforts like house gutting, bio-remediation, and aid distribution to its rebuilding efforts. Volunteer activities were scaled back. In 2007, we maintained steady flows of volunteers that averaged one thousand per week. In 2008, the average was closer to a hundred. Our four main areas of focus were: health, reconstruction, environment and advocacy. That year, Thom Pepper became executive director.

Health
- Common Ground volunteers and residents established our third permanent clinic, the Lower Ninth Ward Health Clinic on Claude Ave.
- Common Ground Latino Health Care Outreach Project is established through the clinics to support immigrant communities.

Reconstruction
- September 2007: Common Ground Relief shifts its focus from direct relief to rebuilding.

- Initiated a project called Rebuild Green that built a model home in the Lower Ninth Ward showcasing sustainable design and alternative energy sources.
- In 2008, the first house next to levee in the Lower Ninth was rebuilt. It is directly behind Common Ground's current house, which operates as its headquarters and offices.
- Common Ground initiates worker-training programs to build construction worker cooperatives.

Environment

- Common Ground organizes massive 2007 Spring Break Clean-Up in the Lower Ninth Ward; over 1,500 volunteers come from colleges and high schools.
- Initiated and supported wetlands restoration by providing public education materials and using volunteer labor to plant thousands of plants across the bayous along the coast.

Advocacy

- Initiated what is now called Project Hope in East St. Bernard Parish, a volunteer site and distribution center.
- Initiated and supported numerous community and tenant councils that were springing up with residents wanting to regain say in their futures.
- In 2008, Common Ground sends volunteers to the Gulf Coast to aid and assist those directly affected by Hurricane Gustav.

Other Groups

- Federation of Southern Cooperatives: Common Ground established mutual aid with farmers throughout the Gulf, sustaining existing cooperatives and learning how to replicate them in New Orleans.
- Common Ground partnered with the Make It Right Foundation to support the initiative to rebuild homes in the Lower Ninth that were sustainable, hurricane-proof, and affordable.

TODAY

The days of anarchy have passed, but Common Ground Relief continues to do deep work that impacts individuals and communities within New Orleans. Its motto remains "Solidarity Not Charity."

NOTES

1   The phrase "traditionally marginalized communities" and the other variations used in this book came to me from conversations about descriptions and traditional stereotypes of communities with Simon Sedillo and participants of the defunct Latino organization Youth Liberation Network, which existed in Tejas from the late 1990s until 2003.

2   "It is better to speak about Power, because there are places in which the action of the State is not perfectly definable as such and it makes more sense to speak of Power—in this case, the Power of a dominant class that spreads to other areas, culture for example." From "Interview with Subcomandante Marcos" by Infoshop Berkeley, May 11, 1994, http://www.spunk.org/texts/places/mexico/sp000654.txt.

3   Herman Wallace won his freedom after forty-six years in solitary confinement in Angola Prison. He died a free man two days after his release. I saw him freed and will always carry that. Albert Woodfox remains the person held longest in solitary confinement in modern U.S. history—forty-seven years at the time of this writing. He will be free.

4   Bernard Hibbitts, "Martial Law Declared in New Orleans as Levees Break, Waters Rise," *Jurist Legal News & Research Journal,* August 30, 2005, http://jurist.law.pitt.edu/paperchase/2005/08/breaking-news-martial-law-declared-in.php.

5   So far as I know, this story has never been reported. Years later, I wondered if he saw those atrocities or had heard about them. As time wore on I was to find out that there were many cases where people "heard" horrible things had happened, but had not witnessed them firsthand; then they turned out not to be true. Was this the case? It was a horrible, brief conversation between strangers I had to make critical decisions with. It played into some of my fears, my anger with the failures of the state, and the racism of the white rescuers. I believe it to be true, even if the details were distorted. The state probably did kill people that we will never ever know about.

6   Robert Lekachman, *Greed Is Not Enough: Reaganomics* (New York: Pantheon, 1982) (quoted in Bertram Gross, *Friendly Fascism: The New Face of Power in America* [Cambridge: South End Press, 1999], xiii).

7   With Erin Howley, Cesar Maxit, Cliff Pearson, Jill Natowitz, Mike Moren, and Kendall Clark.

8   Incidentally, the silly cult movie *The Anarchist Cookbook*, "about a group of people living in an anarchist commune in East Dallas," was inspired by our little organization and collective house. When filming began, they asked us to consult. We refused have anything to do with it because we could see it was going to be a caricature of what we were doing.

9   With Rod Coronado, Scott Parkin, Patrick L., Nicole C., and others.

10   There was much discussion about whether potential property destruction and confrontation was violent or not at Earth First! gatherings and in the pages of the *Earth First!* journal.

11 "'This Is Criminal': Malik Rahim Reports from New Orleans." *San Francisco Bay View*, September 1, 2005, http://sfbayview.com/2008/'this-is-criminal'/.

12 Robert Hillary King, *From the Bottom of the Heap* (Oakland: PM Press, 2012), 22.

13 What I believed then, I now know: the vigilantes and the police both killed and injured innocent people in the aftermath. A.C. Thompson, "Katrina's Hidden Race War," *The Nation,* December 17, 2008, http://www.thenation.com/article/katrinas-hidden-race-war; Trymaine Lee, "Rumor to Fact in Tales of Post-Katrina Violence," *New York Times*, August 26, 2010; United Press Int'l. "New Orleans Police Guilty in Beating Death" April 13, 2011; Jerry Seper "3 NOPD Convicted: Man Shot, Burned in Car," *Washington Times*, December 10, 2010.

14 Buenaventura Durruti was a central anarchist figure in Spain who organized many militant actions throughout his life. He headed the largest anarchist column during the Spanish Civil War.

15 See Lance Hill, *The Deacons for Defense* (Chapel Hill: University of North Carolina Press, 2006), 179–81; Orissa Arend, *Showdown in Desire* (Fayetteville: University of Arkansas Press, 2009), 120–23; and the John Brown Anti-Klan Committee's pamphlet *Take a Stand Against the Klan*. I am also relying on conversations with New Orleans community organizer Kalil Shayid and former Panther Marion Brown.

16 Including: Incite! Women of Color Against Violence, Nowe Miasto, the Iron Rail Bookstore, the Ashé Cultural Arts Center, Community Labor United, Critical Resistance, ACORN (Association of Community Organizations for Reform Now), Community Book Center, the Treme Center, Food Not Bombs, and many radical faith-based organizations.

17 Arend, *Showdown in Desire,* 120–23.

18 Author interview with Marion Brown for the film *Angola 3: Black Panthers and the Last Slave Plantation.*

19 Brice White, "The 30th Anniversary of the Desire Shoot-out," Interview with Malik Rahim on WTUL (91.5 FM) on March 13, 2000.

20 Author interview with Robert King in the film *Angola 3: Black Panthers and The Last Slave Plantation.*

21 See King, *From the Bottom of the Heap.*

22 Richard M. Walden "The Red Cross Money Pit," *Los Angeles Times*, September 25, 2005, http://articles.latimes.com/2005/sep/25/opinion/op-redcross25.

23 There are countless examples around the world of people who don't use the term "anarchism" while engaging in practices that I would describe as similar to anarchist ones. This includes the Zapatistas and APPO (Popular Assembly of the Peoples of Oaxaca) in Mexico, the Landless movements in Brazil, and the piqueteros in Argentina, countless indigenous cultures, and antiglobalization movements worldwide.

24 There have been many revisions of the Ten-Point Program. I am citing a later one that I find representative of the BPP's later political development.
     Ten-Point Program: What We Want, What We Believe
     1. We want freedom. We want power to determine the destiny of our Black and oppressed communities.
     2. We want full employment for our people
     3. We want an end to the robbery by the capitalist of our Black and oppressed communities.
     4. We want decent housing, fit for the shelter of human beings.
     5. We want education for our people that exposes the true nature of this decadent American society. We want education that teaches us our true history and our role in the present-day society.

6. We want completely free health care for all Black and oppressed people.

7. We want an immediate end to police brutality and murder of Black people, other people of color, all oppressed people inside the United States.

8. We want an immediate end to all wars of aggression.

9. We want freedom for all Black and poor oppressed people now held in U.S. federal, state, county, city and military prisons and jails. We want trials by a jury of peers for all persons charged with so-called crimes under the laws of this country.

10. We want land, bread, housing, education, clothing, justice, peace and people's community control of modern technology.

25 Huey Newton, *To Die for the People* (New York: Random House, 1972), 89; JoNina Abron's "Serving the People: The Survival Programs of the Black Panther Party," in *The Black Panther Party Reconsidered*, Charles E. Jones, ed. (Baltimore: Black Classic Press, 1998).

26 U.S. Department of Justice, FBI Report to Attorney General, July 15, 1969.

27 "Support in Algiers, New Orleans," September 10, 2005, which was widely distributed on forums and e-mails. See Appendix 1.

28 Francisco DiSantis, Danielle Handler, Skot Odierno, Natalina Ross, and Jackie Sumell were the first to arrive into the unknown from Austin.

29 This quote rephrases part of a conversation I had with Robert King later. I asked him to reiterate the content of the talk for me.

30 Even though we called ourselves the Common Ground Collective, when our website went live a few weeks later it was called Common Ground Relief. Both names were valid, but it created endless confusion, so we often just referred to ourselves as Common Ground.

31 Many of the VFP veterans, including Cindy Sheehan, had just come directly from Camp Casey in Crawford, Texas in a caravan to the Gulf.

32 Jacob Appelbaum (who I had worked with at the Ruckus Society and later WikiLeaks) and Joel Johnson with the support of the organization C.U. Wireless hacked our communications to connect us to the outside world using open source and low-tech computer technology.

33 Rene Feltz and Tish Stringer of Houston Indymedia organized the communications for evacuees at the Astrodome. The box was built by members of Austin Airwaves.

34 Some of the key organizers behind PHRF were: Curtis Muhammad, Shana Griffin, Malcolm Suber, Althea Francois, and Mayaba Liebenthal. They all had radical organizing histories in their hometown of New Orleans, which they brought to the organizing framework of PHRF. In 2006, after an internal split in the organization, Kali Akuno of the Malcolm X Grassroots Movement became the executive director of PHRF. Curtis Muhammad left to found POF (People's Organizing Fund). Both were critical grassroots organizations with different focuses. See Muhammad, "Legal Disclaimer," http://www.peoplesorganizing.org/disclaimer.html.

35 This document, first drawn up by the PHRF interim coordinating body in September 2005, evolved over the years. This is taken from the October 2005 version that was formally adopted in early 2006.

36 Through the Pastors for Peace, Malik and I also received an invitation from Hugo Chávez's government to visit Venezuela and share hurricane relief strategies. Although I disagreed with Chávez's government, I was proud to have been invited. Eventually we sent a delegation in early 2006. Years later, this fact would be used by extremist right-wing media and the FBI to try to discredit Common Ground's efforts with bogus allegations of colluding with terrorists.

37 Excerpt from transcript of a newscast interview with author on CNN. Aired September 20, 2005.

38   Cats were conspicuously absent. It was as if they had vanished in the flood. Months later, as the hordes of dogs receded, mothers, kittens, and stray toms returned.

39   James Chionsini, from the 2007 Common Ground Volunteer Handbook.

40   From transcript of presentation "Building Coalitions of People of Color," at University of California, San Diego, May 12, 1993, http://www.elkilombo.org/coalition-building-among-people-of-color/.

41   Naomi designed Common Ground's ubiquitous "power fist with a hammer" logo. She is a global justice organizer and spiritual activist from North Carolina.

42   Including Charles Verdin of the Pointe-au-Chien Tribe, Albert Naquin of the Jean Charles Band of Biloxi Chitimacha, Marlene Foret of the Grand Caillou/Dulac Band of the Biloxi Chitimacha, and Sharon LeBouef of the Bayou Lafourche Band of the Biloxi Chitimacha.

43   It was the second effort (the clinic being the first) that, although still intertwined with Common Ground, became an autonomous project in a network born out of Common Ground's initial impetus.

44   Patrick Reinsborough and Doyle Canning, *Re:Imagining Change: How to Use Story-Based Strategy to Win Campaigns, Build Movements, and Change the World* (Oakland: PM Press, 2010), 43–57.

45   Patrick Reinsborough "De-colonizing the Revolutionary Imagination: Values Crisis, the Politics of Reality and Why There's Going to Be a Common Sense Revolution in This Generation." *Journal of Aesthetics and Protest* 1, no. 2 (August 2003), http://smartmeme.drupalgardens.com/sites/smartmeme.drupalgardens.com/files/sM.DeColonizingImagination.pdf.
      http://www.journalofaestheticsandprotest.org/1/de_colonizing/index.html.

46   This changed in late 2006, when neighborhood survivor councils were formed and small assemblies were established in a few surviving neighborhoods. This led to more input and community control.

47   It had many similarities to the CNT/FAI (National Confederation of Labor/Iberian Anarchist Federation) run by mostly Spanish anarchists in the 1930's. The CNT/FAI was the largest coordinated network of anarchist trade unions, collectives, organizations, and communes throughout many regions of Spain. Projects worked collectively and autonomously under its banner.

48   Chris Crass, "But We Don't Have Leaders: Leadership Development and Anti-Authoritarian Organizing" (originally appeared in *Colours of Resistance* magazine in 2003). http://www.peopleofcolororganize.com/organizing/dont-leaders-leadership-development-antiauthoritarian-organizing/.

49   Removal was usually done by consensus of the coordinators. This could take lots of time, energy, and conversations. In rare cases we used varying levels of physical force to remove people who were dangerous to volunteers or the communities around us.

50   scott crow, "Anarchy and the Common Ground Collective." Infoshop.org, March 13, 2006, http://news.infoshop.org/article.php?story=20060313145800704.

51   Greenberg, Benjamin. "Obligatory Listening—Malik Rahim and Scott Crow Talk About Common Ground," http://minorjive.typepad.com/hungryblues/2005/10/obligatory_list.html.

52   We estimate that over five thousand people, mostly middle-class and college-age, attended these weekly trainings during 2005–2006.

53   She kept this up for years; Josh eventually graduated from high school.

54   Jessica Azulay "Abuse, Forced Labor Rampant in New Orleans Justice System," *New Standard*, October 12, 2005, http://www.infowars.com/articles/police_state/police_violence/abuse_forced_labor_rampant_in.html.

55   http://www.no-law.org/main.html.

56 Carolina was instrumental in a coalition that eventually brought immigrants' plight to the surface on May Day 2006 in a mass march through New Orleans. After this, public pressure mounted for accountability among the contractors. Common Ground health clinics also initiated a permanent health care program called the Latino Health Outreach Project that exists currently.

57 The Common Ground Collective raised over a million dollars over the next two years from individual donations.

58 Weeks later, one of the men even sought medical attention for his mother at our Teche Street clinic as if nothing had happened.

59 Months later, PHRF and the Common Ground Collective would work together to set up more tenant and neighborhood councils. Common Ground also supported PHRF's house gutting programs and campaigns to stop public housing demolition.

60 Our Austin delegation played a tournament with the Zapatistas in Chiapas, and has sent groups to the Anti-racist World Cup in Italy.

61 House gutting became a major volunteer program of the Common Ground Collective. Thousands of participants coming from around the country to "get dirty," gutting hundreds of houses to keep them from demolished or ruined, so they could be restored.

62 Lauren, Lisa, and Starhawk are some of the cofounders of this group. They have done workshops, trainings, and actions at numerous mass summits worldwide between 2000 and 2010.

63 As time passed, Common Ground's efforts also included organizing legal clinics for tenants. Through our coalition efforts, we worked to ensure that landlords did not evict tenants because they were not able to return. We also focused on supporting the fourteen thousand evacuated public housing residents in resisting the destruction of their homes with a combination of direct action and legal means.

64 The Roadtrip for Relief brought over two thousand people for a week. The efforts focused on the lower wards where we opened shelters and gutted buildings, among other projects. It became a successful strategy for students over each holiday break to come by the thousands to dedicate their energies in the Gulf.

65 At the same time, our emergency relief efforts were expanding. We were still providing thousands of pounds in basic aid, but basics like food, water, and emergency medical attention needs were not as critical as in previous weeks. Countless other groups had arrived or formed and were helping, such as the S.O.S. (Saving Ourselves) Coalition and Rainbow Family hippies in Mississippi who we worked with in mutual aid. There were also churches and other smaller relief groups that were springing up all over the region.

66 For the complete Brandon Darby ordeal, see Kristian Williams, "Witness to Betrayal: scott crow on the Exploits and Misadventures of FBI Informant Brandon Darby," *Toward Freedom*, December 2013, http://www.towardfreedom.com/29-archives/activism/3388-witness-to-betrayal-scott-crow-on-the-exploits-and-misadventures-of-fbi-informant-brandon-darby.

67 The APLC filed FBI FOIA's on about thirty activists, forty organizations and events in Austin going back to 2000. Ninety-five percent of the requests came back with little to no information.

68 The Holy Land Five were part of an international relief organization that provided health and educational aid to Palestine from international donors. I had worked with two of the peace activists, Mufid Abdulqader and Shukri Abu-Baker, on other humanitarian projects. After 9/11, we protected them and other local Muslims from retaliatory attacks at their community center. The HF5 are now serving longer

sentences than any white activist and are in extreme prison isolation. For more information, see http://freedomtogive.com/.

69   He had originally been convicted by an all-white jury in 1973, which was ruled unconstitutional. This was to be his first retrial since then. In 2014 he was exonerated and freed, only to die from cancer two days later.

70   Jessica Gordon Nembhard and Ajowa Nzinga Ifateyo, "African American Economic Solidarity," Grassroots Economic Organizing, http://www.geo.coop/archives/GEO71DS-AfricanAmericanEconomicSolidarity.htm.

71   Jessica Lustig, "Occupy Sandy's Street Medics Go Door-to-Door in Coney Island," *New York Magazine*, http://nymag.com/daily/intelligencer/2012/11/occupy-sandy-goes-door-to-door-in-coney-island.html.

72   Ibid.

ACKNOWLEDGMENTS

The words spilled within these pages could never have happened without much input and exchange of ideas from people across a spectrum of my life. Although I have written this, it is all just an interpretation built on historical foundations large and small. I want to thank deeply the many whose paths crossed with mine engaged in walking and asking all along the way.

Thanks to those who contributed in bringing both editions of this book to life

Romy Ruukel: For steering the 2nd edition through my messy revisions, insertions, and new essays and making them seamless. You are a poetic surgeon. It has been a pleasure to collaborate.

Alejandro de Acosta: Thank you sincerely for being a tremendous editor and confidant of the 1st ed. Your structuring and invaluable input helped in shaping vague thoughts into something that gave my words meaning I wanted them to have. Your input and craft was absolutely invaluable. You helped me grow as a writer and to reflect more deeply on what I wanted to say. I have learned a lot from it.

Andrea Gibbons: For steering the course of the first edition from its inception of early writings and fragments of my notebooks from New Orleans. Your belief in this provided the spark. Thanks for the encouragement and direction when I lost hope. Your advice and input has always been greatly valued. It took a while, but we got here.

James Clark: For your friendship, providing draft feedback and sharing your observations starting from when I first got back from New Orleans and all along the way. You helped me reach from some dark places to shape the ideas.

PM Press: Ramsey Kanaan for the friendship and collaboration I have deeply valued. Craig O'Hara, Gregory Nipper, Stephanie Pasvankias, Steven Stothard, and the rest of the PM crew: Thank you for the amazing author support. It has been a pleasure and a team effort.

John Yates: For the cover art and your history of provocative political images.

Shelley Fleming: For editing some of the early drafts of essays that became this book.

Special thanks

Emily Crow: My mom—your strength and sacrifices during the difficult and happy times of our lives will never be forgotten. Thanks for the solid foundations and the continued love. You are an inspiration!

Ann Harkness: My lifetime love and partner, who has given me tremendous support and collaboration in our lives that I will always be indebted to. I cannot thank you enough for all that I have learned from you. I love you dearly. You have been my muse. Let's continue to laugh out loud!

Milo Smith: My son, you have grown into a remarkable man, who I have learned a lot from as we have grown up together.

Dr. Helen Harkness: Thank you for all your support in helping me grow to take the chances I needed and learn about myself along the way. You have been a great mentor.

Robert H. King: Your friendship and presence has taken us down many roads together that will never be forgotten. Your freedom and continued voice for justice stands as a beacon of hope for others.

Malik Rahim: Your commitment to making the world a better place and willingness to fight for it against all odds have been inspiring. Thanks for taking a chance on a farfetched idea for liberation in New Orleans.

Dr. John P. Clark : For sharing your words, wisdom, heart, and background. You have helped me deepen my knowledge and practice of liberatory thought beyond political confines.

Sharon Johnson: Your quiet strength through the CGC's beginning and willingness to risk everything for ideals is admirable. Your hard work and commitment will always stay in my heart.

Albert Woodfox: You give me hope by your friendship and persistence to gain just freedom for yourself and others. It's imminent, my brother!

Scott Parkin: For sharing your understanding, support, and dialog over the years. Your friendship has been deeply valued. Your an inspiring organizer with a big heart.

Thanks and Acknowledgments

Ernesto Aguilar, Karla Aguilar, Premadasi Amada, Jen Angel, Angola 3 Support Committee, Ruben Arellano, Aragorn Bang!, Greg Berger, Cathie Berry-Green, Darwin Bond-Graham, Peter Boehmer, Bo Brown, Marion Brown, Bob Buzzanco, Nathan Buckley, Antonio Bueller, Chris Burns, John Bush and Cat Bleish, Brackin Camp, Liz Canfield, Ginger Cassidy, Ward Churchill, Kathleen Cleaver, Jake Conroy, Rod Coronado, Nikki Craft, John Charles Crow, Brad Crowder, Chris Dixon, Karly Dixon, Dotmatrix (Leona), Jack Downey, Roxanne Dunbar-Ortiz, Thorne Dreyer, Marina Drummer,

Lorenzo Komboa Ervin and JoNina Ervin, Jenny Esquivel, Simon Powell Evans, Renee Feltz, Lisa Fithian, Zakk Flash, Scott Fleming, Matt Gossage, David Graeber, David Graeve, Andrej Grubačić, Jane Harkness, Josh Harper, Scott Hendrie, Arwyn Hicks, Charles Hillman, Tim Holland (MC Sole), Erin Howley Lawrence Jarach, Hadi Jawad, Tracey Hayes, D'Ann Johnson, Randy Johnson, Kate Kibby, D. King, Sandra Kirkpatrick and Chris King, Dee Krastansky, Louisiana Kreutz, Gabriel Kuhn, Bonnie LeBaron, Chris Lefeve, Bob Libal, Kelly Locker, Antonio Long, Rockie Gonzalez and Tane Ward, Patrick Lyons, Joaquin Mariel, Abby Martin, Harley Martin, Wynne Martin, David Martinez, Michael May, Laurel McCardy, Denise McDermott, Daniel McGowan, Lara and Paul Messersmith-Glavin, Cesar Maxit Cindy Milstein, Jackson Mitchell, Justus Mobray, Nupur Modi, Colin Moynihan, Chuck Munson, Jill Natowitz, DJ Pangburn, Dr. David Pellow, Brent Perdue, Leslie James Pickering and Theresa Baker, Crystal Poole and Rob Adams, Will Potter, Sasha Porter, Sharon Presley, Marilee Ratliff, Gordon Roddick, Ben Rosenfeld, Deb Russell, Ernest Samudio, Petey Schnell, Simon Sedillio, Ryan Shapiro, Gail Shaw, Adam Sherburne, Marina Sitrin, Cory Skuldt, David Solnit, Rebecca Solnit, Sarah Cheatham Somera and Rob Somera, Ramsey Sprague, David Starfire, Dave and Josie Strano–Shapiro, Andy Stepanian, Maylee and Shawn Stevenson, Tish Stringer, Nick Tenaglia, Adam Thompson, Marcia Carter Tillison, Brian Traven, James Tuttle, Kevin Van Meter, the Ware family: Carol, Heather, and Owen, Randeep Walia, Diana Welch, Peter Werbe, Kristian Williams, Mariann Wizard, Johnny Wolf, Billy X, Doug Zachary, and the kids from our communities who are inheriting our futures and making their own. To all the schools, community spaces, and people who have hosted me over the years and all the indy journalist who I have had conversations with.

Common Ground Collective/Relief

Shakoor Aljuwani, Randall Amster, Jacob Applebaum, Naomi Archer, Jessica Azulay, Donna Banks, Gabe Barry, David Bedient and Hali Stone, Reginald Bell, Zoe Bender, Roger Benham, Patricia Berryhill, Blank, Darwin Bond-Graham, Nate "Iggy" Brimmer. Sarah Cameron, Eric Carter, Casey "LouLou," Clarence, Alice Craft-Kerney, Rain Crowe, Aislyn Colgan, Hattie Dague, Natasha Dedrick, Francsico DiSantis, Jimmy Dunson, Kerul Dyer, Kim Ellis, Josh Everett, Brian Frank, Greg Griffith, Aaron Guyton, Leenie Halbert, Danielle Handler, Doris Hicks, Sue Hilderbrandt, Liz Highlymen, Justin Hite, Annie Hostetter, Joel Johnson, Grace Keller, Michael Kozart, Sakura Kone, Cj Lince, Jamie "Bork" Loughner, Bay Love, Lori Mac, Erroll Maitland, Kobe Maitland, Emeline Mead, Scott Mechanic, Mikkel, Kiyoko

McCrae, Noah Morris, The Mroczek brothers (Dana, Coley, and Damen), Jess Niederer, Tyler Norman, Skot O, Mo O'Brien, Peter O'Connell, Dixie Pauline, Stevie Peace, Thom Pepper, Emily Posner, Casey Pritchett, Jeremy Prickett, Bill Quigley, Carolina Reyes, Soleil Rodriguez, Lauren "Juniper" Ross, Sasha Reid Ross, Natalina Ross, Flux Rostrum, Todd Sanchioni, Pauly Sarkozy, Suncere Shakur, Starhawk, Michelle Shin, Sonia Silbert, Jenka Soderberg, Emily Tilton, Isabelle Troadec, Topher, Josh Tree Tucker, Crystal Uchino, Usnia, Carl Webb, Scott Weinstein, Victoria Welle, Emily Westerlin, Sean White, Daniel Williams, Yvonne Wise, Mavis Yorks, Baruch Zeichner. This list is far from complete. If your name was mistakenly omitted, please forgive me. I have much love and respect for everyone's commitments, but time and an overloaded memory have obscured important details.

And to *all* the more than thirty-six thousand volunteers who had the courage to fight for New Orleans and the Gulf Coast with the Common Ground Collective in the struggle for justice and greater futures for everyone!

Other Organizations and CGC Collaborators

Aidsail (Christine Murto, and Dr. Jefferson Sai), Kali Akuno, BARHC Bay Area Radical Health Collective, Rev. Bart, Bill (Pastors for Peace), Rev. Brown, Catalyst Project (Ingrid Chapman, Claire Bayard, and Chris Crass), Critical Resistance (NO and National), Federation of Southern Cooperatives, Food Not Bombs, Four Directions Network, Dr. Paul Gainais, Holy Cross Neighborhood Association, Walidah Imarisha, INCITE! Women of Color Against Violence, Rasmus Holm, Infoshop.org, Iron Rail, Mayaba Liebenthal, Lower 9th Ward Center for Sustainable Engagement and Development, Make it Right, Anne Moore, Michael Moore, Curtis Muhammad, Oxygen Collective, Pastors for Peace, Kate Paxton, People's Institute for Survival (Kimberly Richards, Ron Chisom, and Diane Dunn), People's Hurricane Relief and Oversight Committee, Rev. Powell, Kalil Shayid, Secours Populaire de France, Cindy Sheehan, Tajiri (Truth Universal), Veterans For Peace: (Margaret Hayes, Dennis Kyne, Polly Lynn, Gordon Soderberg, and the countless other veterans who gave so much critical support through the VFP), Women's Health & Justice Initiative, Women with a Vision.

And all of the people who decided to act in supporting communities. I am awed by the commitments, labor, and belief in making just worlds for everyone that were exhibited by the thousands of people critical to these worthy endeavors.

Some Inspirations and Shout-outs (look them up!)

Carol Adams, Aid & Abet Booking, all political prisoners and prisoners of conscience, AK Press, American Indian Movement, Anarchist Black Cross, Anarchist News, Angola 3, Animal Liberation Front, anarchist soccer, Anonymous, Ashanti Alston, Austin Common Ground, Bill Ayers, Black Mask/UATWMF, Black Panther Party, bolo bolo, Brave New Books, Breaking the Set, Brown Berets, Burning Books (Buffalo), Cabaret Voltaire, Camp Casey, C4SS, Century Modern, Stuart Christie, community gardens, Consolidated, COBRA (Central Oklahoma Black and Red Alliance), CrimethInc., Dead Prez, *Democracy Now!*, Dirty South Earth First!, Earth First!, Earth Liberation Front, Ecology Action, EZLN (Zapatista National Liberation Army), *Fifth Estate* magazine, Flores Magón brothers, Flying Brick (RVA), Food Not Bombs, free schools, Franz Fanon, Freedom Archives, Godspeed You! Black Emperor, Greenpeace, Daniel Guérin, Fannie Lou Hamer, Jeremy Hammond, Noelle Hanrahan, Icarus Project, Industrial Workers of the World, Indymedia, Infoshop.org, Inside Books Project, insurrection, George Jackson Brigades, Geronimo ji Jaga, Marty Kheel, Yuri Kochiyama, Dr. Len Krimmerman, Dr. Terry Kupers, Little Black Cart, Chelsea Manning, Marie Mason, Harvey Milk, Cindy Milstein, Ministry, Monkeywrench Books (Austin), Kiilu Nyasha, Occupy movements (to all the encampments!), Occupy Sandy, OpOk, Lucy and Albert Parsons, Peaceful Streets Project, People's Lunch Counter (Dallas), Public Enemy, The Ragblog (Austin), Lauren Regan and the Civil Liberties Defense Center, Boots Riley, Rising Tide North America, Penelope Rosemont, David Rovics, Ruckus Society, Sacramento Prisoner Support, Ron Sakolsky, SHAC campaign, Skinny Puppy, Edward Snowden, Spanish anarchists, Linda Stout, surregionalism, TALON Conspiracy, Test Dept., Treasure City Thrift (past and present), UPROAR (Dallas), utopia, Weather Underground, WikiLeaks, Wooden Shoe (Philly), Ross Winn, Young Patriots.

Remembrances

Gene Akins (1937–2010): Anarchist and community organizer with a big heart, who loved the people.

Pam Dashiell (1948–2009): Lower Ninth Ward resident and dedicated organizer.

Althea Francois (1949–2009): Former Panther and cofounder of PHRF.

Helen Hill (1970–2007): Longtime New Orleans committed activist and artist.

Geronimo ji Jaga (1947–2011): Former Panther and political prisoner who taught me about resistance and love.

Meg Perry (1979–2005): A shining volunteer at Common Ground who died serving the people.

Anita Roddick (1942–2007): A supporter of justice and love throughout her life.

raul salinas (1934–2008): A poet, warrior, and inspiration.

Hali Stone (1972–2014): Common Ground volunteer and friend. Your smile, big heart, and energy will always burn in our hearts.

Bandele Tyehimba (1953–2012): Brother in struggle, leader of your community, and my friend.

Herman Wallace (1941–2013): Former Panther and Angola 3 member who fought for justice behind prison walls in solitary confinement. I miss you greatly.

FURTHER READING

This is a selection of writings and films that have informed and inspired me, or in which I have participated. Many titles have come out in multiple editions over the years. In some cases, I have made reference to the latest version available.

Anarchism

Ackelsberg, Martha. *Free Women of Spain: Anarchism and the Struggle for Women's Emancipation*. Oakland: AK Press, 2005.

Acosta, Alejandro de, ed. *Individualist Anarchism writings by Emile Armand*. Austin: Pallaksch Press, 2012.

Avrich, Paul. *Anarchist Voices: An Oral History of Anarchism in America*. Princeton, NJ: Princeton University Press, 1995.

Bookchin, Murray. *The Spanish Anarchists: The Heroic Years 1868–1936*. New York: Harper & Row, 1978.

Brigati, A.J. *The Voltairine de Cleyre Reader*. Oakland: AK Press, 2004.

Christie, Stuart, and Meltzer, Albert. *The Floodgates of Anarchy* Oakland: PM Press, 2011

Clark, John P. *The Impossible Community: Realizing Communitarian Anarchism*. New York: Bloomsbury, 2013.

Cornell, Andrew. *Oppose and Propose!* Baltimore: AK Press, 2011.

Crass, Chris. "'But We Don't Have Leaders': Leadership Development and Anti-Authoritarian Organizing." In *Towards Collective Liberation: Anti-racist Organizing, Feminist Praxis, and Movement Building Strategy*, 165–70. Oakland, PM Press, 2013.

CrimethInc. *Fighting for Our Lives*. September 2002. http://www.crimethinc.com/tools/ffol.html.

Dolgoff, Sam. *The Anarchist Collectives: Workers' Self-Management in the Spanish Revolution, 1936–39*. New York: Free Life Editions, 1974.

Ervin, Lorenzo Komboa. *Anarchism and the Black Revolution*. Philadelphia: Monkeywrench Press, 1994.

Gelderloos, Peter. *Anarchy Works*. Berkeley: Ardent Press, 2010.

Guérin, Daniel. *Anarchism*. New York: Monthly Press Review, 1970.

Hahne, Ron, and Ben Morea. *Black Mask & Up Against the Wall Motherfucker*. Oakland: PM Press, 2011.

Malatesta, Errico. *The Anarchist Revolution: Polemical Articles 1924–31.* London: Freedom Press, 1995.

Milstein, Cindy. *Anarchism and Its Aspirations.* Oakland: AK Press, 2010.

P.M. *Bolo'Bolo.* 30th anniversary edition. Brooklyn: Autonomedia/Ardent, 2011.

Rosemont, Penelope. *Dreams and Everyday Life.* Chicago: Charles H. Kerr, 2008.

Shwarz, Sagris, and Void Network, eds. *We Are an Image From the Future: The Greek Revolt of December 2008.* Oakland: AK Press, 2010.

Sitrin, Marina. *Horizontalism: Voices of Popular Power in Argentina.* Oakland: AK Press, 2006.

Solnit, David, ed. *Globalize Liberation: How to Uproot the System and Build a Better World.* San Francisco: City Lights, 2004.

Ward, Colin. *Anarchy in Action.* London: Freedom Press, 1996.

Black Panther Party

Arend, Orissa. *Showdown in Desire: The Black Panthers Take a Stand in New Orleans.* Fayetteville: University of Arkansas Press, 2009.

Hayes, Worth K. "No Service Too Small: The Political Significance of the Survival Programs of the New Orleans Black Panther Party." *Xulanexus* 3 (2004).

Jones, Charles E., ed. *The Black Panther Party (Reconsidered).* Baltimore: Black Classic Press, 1998.

King, Robert Hillary. *From the Bottom of the Heap: The Autobiography of Black Panther Robert Hillary King.* Oakland: PM Press, 2012.

Newton, Huey P. *To Die for the People.* San Francisco: City Lights Books, 2009.

Shakur, Assata. *Assata: An Autobiography.* Westport, Conn.: Lawrence Hill & Co., 2001.

Common Ground Collective/Relief

Anti-Racist Working Group of Common Ground. "Striving for Solidarity: Lessons in Anti-Racism Organizing." Summer 2007. http://katrinareader.org/striving-solidarity-lessons-anti-racism-organizing.

Chapman, Ingrid. "Hearts on Fire: The Struggle for Justice in New Orleans," ZNet, September 2007. http://tinyurl.com/3duvje4.

Ilel, Neille. "A Healthy Dose of Anarchy." *Reason*, December 2006. http://reason.com/archives/2006/12/11/a-healthy-dose-of-anarchy.

Imarisha, Walidah. "From the Ground Up: Race and the Left Response to Katrina." *Left Turn, January 2006.* http://www.walidah.com/node/103.

McClure, Molly. "Solidarity Not Charity: Racism in Katrina Relief Work." November 2005. http://news.infoshop.org/article. php?story=20060319185418325.

"Ms. Foundation for Women: Katrina Women's Response Fund Grantees Speak Out Donna Banks." https://www.commondreams.org/ news2006/0830–01.htm.

Nembhard, Jessica Gordon and Ajowa Nzinga Ifateyo. "African American Economic Solidarity." GEO Newsletter. #71, 2006. http://www.geo. coop/archives/GEO71DS-AfricanAmericanEconomicSolidarity.htm.

Rahim, Malik. Interview on *Democracy Now!* "New Orleans Hit by Another Hurricane of Racism, Greed and Corruption." August 30, 2007. http://www.democracynow.org/2007/8/30/new_orleans_hit_ by_another_hurricane.

Steinberg, Michael. "Malik Speaks, Part 1." January 13, 2008. http:// neworleans.indymedia.org/news/2008/01/11936.php.

Zapatismo and Zapatistas

Carr, Barry, "From the Mountains of the Southeast: A Review of Recent Writings on the Zapatistas of Chiapas." *Journal of Iberian and Latin American Studies* 3, no. 2 (December 1997): 109–23.

Cleaver, Harry. "Nature, Neoliberalism and Sustainable Development: Between Charybdis & Scylla?" April, 1997. http://libcom.org/ library/nature-neoliberalism-sustainable-development-cleaver.

Elorriaga, Javier. "An Analysis of Evolving Zapatismo." *In Motion*, January 1997. http://www.inmotionmagazine.com/chiapas1.html.

Khasnabish, Alex. "Globalizing Hope: The Resonance of Zapatismo and the Political Imagination(s) of Transnational Activism." 2004. http://tinyurl.com/m6l8dqs.

Marcos (Subcomandante), and Juana Ponce de Leon, eds. *Our Word Is Our Weapon: Selected Writings*. New York: Seven Stories Press, 2001.

Podur, Justin. "From Aguascalientes to Caracoles." September 2003. http://podur.org/node/980.

Zapatistas. "To the Solidarity Groups Meeting in Brescia. The Flowers, Like Hope, Are Harvested." In *Ya Basta! Ten Years of the Zapatista Uprising,* edited by Subcomandante Marcos and Žiga Vodovnik. Oakland: AK Press, 2004, 200–201.

Other Readings

Churchill, Ward, and Jim Vander Wall. *Agents of Repression.* Cambridge: South End Press, 2002.

DeFronzo, James. *Revolutions and Revolutionary Movements.* Boulder: Westview Press, 1996.

Flaherty, Jordan. *Floodlines: Community and Resistance from Katrina to the Jena 6.* Chicago: Haymarket Press, 2009.

Glick, Brian. *War at Home: Covert Action Against U.S. Activists and What We Can Do about It.* Cambridge: South End Press, 1999.

Herman, Edward, and Noam Chomsky. *Manufacturing Consent: The Political Economy of the Mass Media.* New York: Pantheon Books, 1988.

Hill, Lance. *The Deacons For Defense: Armed Resistance and the Civil Rights Movement.* Chapel Hill: University of North Carolina Press, 2004.

Potter, Will. *Green Is the New Red: An Insider's Account of a Social Movement Under Siege.* San Francisco: City Lights Publisher, 2011.

Solnit, Rebecca. *A Paradise Built in Hell: The Extraordinary Communities that Arise in Disasters.* New York: Viking, 2009.

South End Press Collective, eds. *What Lies Beneath: Katrina, Race, and the State of the Nation.* Cambridge: South End Press, 2007.

Taibo II, Paco Ignacio. *'68.* New York: Seven Stories Press, 2004.

Williams, Kristian, Lara Messersmith-Glavin, and William Munger, eds. *Life During Wartime: Resisting Counterinsurgency.* Oakland: AK Press, 2013

Films

crow, scott, and Ann Harkness. *Angola 3: Black Panthers and the Louisiana State Penitentiary.* PM Press, 2008.

Flux Rostrum/Common Ground Collective. *Solidarity Not Charity.* http://tinyurl.com/kamxlmt.

Holm, Rasmus. *Welcome to New Orleans.* Fridthjof Film, 2006. https://www.youtube.com/watch?v=V__lSdR1KZg.

Imarisha, Walidah. *Finding Common Ground.* Third World Newsreel, 2006.

Galloway, Katie, and Kelly Duane De la Vega *Better This World.* PBS, 2012.

Meltzer, Jamie. *Informant* Music Box films, 2013.

Warison, Dar Robard, and Declan Ryan. *Hellp.* Integrity Pictures, 2006 http://www.imdb.com/title/tt0768196/?ref_=ttfc_fc_tt.

Websites

CG Stories: A resource and archive on the history and stories of the Common Ground Collective. http://cgstories.org/

Katrina Reader: A resource documents about social justice efforts after Hurricane Katrina. http://katrinareader.org/

ABOUT THE AUTHORS

scott crow (b. February 18, 1967) is an international speaker and author. He grew up in a working class family and since has engaged his varied life as a co-op business co-owner, political organizer, educator and strategist, filmmaker, dad and underground musician. For over two decades he has participated in or co-founded several organizations and cooperative businesses focusing on diverse socio-political issues in the quixotic quest for collective liberation rooted in the ideas that many call anarchy. Beginning in the late 90s, he was targeted by the FBI as a domestic terrorist threat for his political activities and put under investigation for almost a decade.

His first book, *Black Flags and Windmills: Hope, Anarchy, and the Common Ground Collective*, has been critically lauded. His writings have appeared in *Grabbing Back: Essays against the Global Land Grab* (AK Press) and *What Lies Beneath: Katrina, Race and the State of the Nation* (South End Press) as well as in radical publications including *Fifth Estate*, Infoshop.org, *Earth First! Journal*, and Anarchistnews.org. He's the author of the forthcoming books *Towards a Politics of Possibilities* and the anthology *Setting Sights: Perspectives on Armed Self-Defense.*

He has appeared in international media including the *New York Times*, *Democracy Now*, CNN, NPR, RT News, *Mother Jones*, *Rolling Stone*, *Der Spiegel*, and *Vice*, and in the documentary films *Informant* (Music Box), *Better This World* (PBS), and *Welcome to New Orleans* (Fridthjof Films). With his partner, he made the documentary film *Angola 3: Black Panthers and the Last Slave Plantation* (PM Press).

The *New York Times* characterized him as an "anarchist, veteran organizer and an aficionado of civil disobedience" and NPR's *This American Life* called him "a living legend among anarchists." He is often found speaking at college campuses and community spaces internationally. For more information visit http://www.scottcrow.org and http://www.emergencyhearts.com.

Kathleen Neal Cleaver has been involved in the human rights movement most of her life. In 1967, while a staff member of the Student Nonviolent Coordinating Committee (SNCC), she moved to California and joined the Black Panther Party for Self-Defense. She and her husband, Eldridge Cleaver, founded the International Section of the Black Panther Party in Algiers, Algeria, and worked there until 1973.

Cleaver graduated from Yale Law School in 1988 and practiced law in New York before joining the faculty at Emory Law School. She has worked to free imprisoned political activists, including Geronimo ji Jaga, Mumia Abu-Jamal, and Marilyn Buck. She coedited (with George Katsiaficas) the collection *Liberation, Imagination, and the Black Panther Party* (2001) and edited the posthumously published *Target Zero: A Life in Writing* (2006) by Eldridge Cleaver. She is the author of the memoir *Memories of Love and War*.

John P. Clark lives in New Orleans, where his family has been for twelve generations. He teaches philosophy and environmental studies at Loyola University and works with community education groups. He has long been active in the green movement, an international movement for ecology, peace, social justice, and grassroots democracy. His books include *Max Stirner's Egoism*; *The Philosophical Anarchism of William Godwin*; *The Anarchist Moment*; *Anarchy, Geography, Modernity: Selected Writings of Elisée Reclus*; and *The Impossible Community: Realizing Communitarian Anarchism*. His alter ego Max Cafard wrote *The Surregionalist Manifesto and Other Writings*, *FLOOD BOOK*, and *Surregional Explorations*. He writes the column "Imagined Ecologies," for the journal *Capitalism Nature Socialism*, and edits the cyber-journal *Psychic Swamp: The Surregional Review*. An archive of over two hundred of his articles and papers can be found at http://loyno.academia.edu/JohnClark and http://www.johnpclark.info/, http://www.maxcafard.info/ and http://www.psychicswamp.info/. He is a member of the Education Workers Union of the IWW.

ABOUT PM PRESS

PM Press was founded at the end of 2007 by a small collection of folks with decades of publishing, media, and organizing experience. PM Press co-conspirators have published and distributed hundreds of books, pamphlets, CDs, and DVDs. Members of PM have founded enduring book fairs, spearheaded victorious tenant organizing campaigns, and worked closely with bookstores, academic conferences, and even rock bands to deliver political and challenging ideas to all walks of life. We're old enough to know what we're doing and young enough to know what's at stake.

We seek to create radical and stimulating fiction and non-fiction books, pamphlets, T-shirts, visual and audio materials to entertain, educate and inspire you. We aim to distribute these through every available channel with every available technology—whether that means you are seeing anarchist classics at our bookfair stalls; reading our latest vegan cookbook at the café; downloading geeky fiction e-books; or digging new music and timely videos from our website.

PM Press is always on the lookout for talented and skilled volunteers, artists, activists and writers to work with. If you have a great idea for a project or can contribute in some way, please get in touch.

PM Press
PO Box 23912
Oakland, CA 94623
www.pmpress.org

FRIENDS OF PM PRESS

These are indisputably momentous times—the financial system is melting down globally and the Empire is stumbling. Now more than ever there is a vital need for radical ideas.

In the six years since its founding—and on a mere shoestring—PM Press has risen to the formidable challenge of publishing and distributing knowledge and entertainment for the struggles ahead. With over 250 releases to date, we have published an impressive and stimulating array of literature, art, music, politics, and culture. Using every available medium, we've succeeded in connecting those hungry for ideas and information to those putting them into practice.

Friends of PM allows you to directly help impact, amplify, and revitalize the discourse and actions of radical writers, filmmakers, and artists. It provides us with a stable foundation from which we can build upon our early successes and provides a much-needed subsidy for the materials that can't necessarily pay their own way. You can help make that happen—and receive every new title automatically delivered to your door once a month—by joining as a Friend of PM Press. And, we'll throw in a free T-shirt when you sign up.

Here are your options:

- **$30 a month** Get all books and pamphlets plus 50% discount on all webstore purchases

- **$40 a month** Get all PM Press releases (including CDs and DVDs) plus 50% discount on all webstore purchases

- **$100 a month** Superstar—Everything plus PM merchandise, free downloads, and 50% discount on all webstore purchases

For those who can't afford $30 or more a month, we're introducing **Sustainer Rates** at $15, $10 and $5. Sustainers get a free PM Press T-shirt and a 50% discount on all purchases from our website.

Your Visa or Mastercard will be billed once a month, until you tell us to stop. Or until our efforts succeed in bringing the revolution around. Or the financial meltdown of Capital makes plastic redundant. Whichever comes first.

The Angola 3: Black Panthers and the Last Slave Plantation

Directed by Jimmy O'Halligan.
Produced by scott crow and Ann Harkness.
Narrated by Mumia Abu-Jamal

ISBN: 978-1-60486-020-7
$19.95   DVD (NTSC) 109 minutes

The Angola 3: Black Panthers and the Last Slave Plantation
tells the gripping story of Robert King, Herman Wallace
and Albert Woodfox, men who have endured solitary confinement longer than
any known living prisoner in the United States. Politicized through contact with
the Black Panther Party while inside Louisiana's prisons, they formed one of the
only prison Panther chapters in history and worked to organize other prisoners
into a movement for the right to live like human beings. This feature length movie
explores their extraordinary struggle for justice while incarcerated in Angola, a
former slave plantation where institutionalized rape and murder made it known as
one of the most brutal and racist prisons in the United States. The analysis of the
Angola 3's political work, and the criminal cases used to isolate and silence them,
occurs within the context of the widespread COINTELPRO being carried out in the
1960s and 70s by the FBI and state law enforcement against militant voices for
change.

In a partial victory, the courts exonerated Robert King of the original charges
and released him in 2001; he continues the fight for the freedom of his two
brothers. The ongoing campaign, which includes a civil case soon to come before
the Supreme Court, is supported by people and organizations such as Amnesty
International, the A.C.L.U., Harry Belafonte, Ben Cohen and Jerry Greenfield of Ben
and Jerry's Ice Cream, Ramsey Clark, Sen. John Conyers, Sister Helen Prejean, (the
late) Anita Roddick, Bishop Desmond Tutu and the ANC. Herman Wallace and
Albert Woodfox have now endured as political prisoners in solitary confinement for
over thirty-five years.

Narrated by Mumia Abu-Jamal, *The Angola 3* features interviews with former
Panthers, political prisoners and revolutionaries, including the Angola 3
themselves, and Bo Brown, Geronimo (ji Jaga) Pratt, Malik Rahim, Yuri Kochiyama,
David Hilliard, Rod Coronado, Noelle Hanrahan, Kiilu Nyasha, Marion Brown, Luis
Talamantez, Gail Shaw and many others. Portions of the proceeds go to support the
Angola 3. Features the music of Truth Universal written by Tajiri Kamau.

Extras include: "Angola 3" music video for a song written and produced by Dave
Stewart (of the Eurythmics) in support of the A3 featuring Saul Williams, Nadirah
X, Asdru Sierra, Dana Glover, Tina Schlieske and Derrick Ashong. Directed by
Robin Davey. Plus a trailer for the film which features outtakes not in the feature.

From the Bottom of the Heap: The Autobiography of Black Panther Robert Hillary King

with an introduction by Terry Kupers

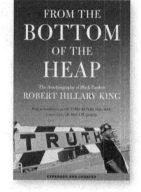

ISBN: 978-1-60486-575-2
$17.95   272 pages

In 1970, a jury convicted Robert Hillary King of a crime he did not commit and sentenced him to 35 years in prison. He became a member of the Black Panther Party while in Angola State Penitentiary, successfully organizing prisoners to improve conditions. In return, prison authorities beat him, starved him, and gave him life without parole after framing him for a second crime. He was thrown into solitary confinement, where he remained in a six by nine foot cell for 29 years as one of the Angola 3. In 2001, the state grudgingly acknowledged his innocence and set him free. This is his story.

It begins at the beginning: born black, born poor, born in Louisiana in 1942, King journeyed to Chicago as a hobo at the age of 15. He married and had a child, and briefly pursued a semi-pro boxing career to help provide for his family. Just a teenager when he entered the Louisiana penal system for the first time, King tells of his attempts to break out of this system, and his persistent pursuit of justice where there is none.

Yet this remains a story of inspiration and courage, and the triumph of the human spirit. The conditions in Angola almost defy description, yet King never gave up his humanity, or the work towards justice for all prisoners that he continues to do today. *From the Bottom of the Heap*, so simply and humbly told, strips bare the economic and social injustices inherent in our society, while continuing to be a powerful literary testimony to our own strength and capacity to overcome.

"For a person to go through 29 years in one of the most brutal prisons in America and still maintain his sanity and humanity, that's what makes people want to listen to Robert."
—Malik Rahim, cofounder of Common Ground Collective

"Friendships are forged in strange places. My friendship with Robert King and the other two Angola 3 men Herman Wallace and Albert Woodfox is based on respect. These men, as Robert reveals in this stunning account of his life, have fought tirelessly to redress injustice, not only for themselves, but for others. This is a battle Robert is determined to win and we are determined to help him."
—Gordon Roddick, activist and cofounder of the Body Shop

Black Mask & Up Against the Wall Motherf**ker: The Incomplete Works of Ron Hahne, Ben Morea, and the Black Mask Group

Ben Morea and Ron Hahne

ISBN: 978-1-60486-021-4
$15.95   176 pages

Founded in New York City in the mid-1960s by self-educated ghetto kid and painter Ben Morea, the Black Mask group melded the ideas and inspiration of Dada and the Surrealists, with the anarchism of the Durruti Column from the Spanish Revolution. With a theory and practice that had much in common with their contemporaries the San Francisco Diggers, Dutch Provos, and the French Situationists—who famously excommunicated 3 of the 4 members of the British section of the Situationist International for associating too closely with Black Mask—the group intervened spectacularly in the art, politics and culture of their times. From shutting down the Museum of Modern Art to protesting Wall Street's bankrolling of war, from battling with Maoists at SDS conferences to defending the Valerie Solanas shooting of Andy Warhol, Black Mask successfully straddled the counterculture and politics of the 60s, and remained the Joker in the pack of both sides of "The Movement."

By 1968 Black Mask dissolved into "The Family" (popularly known as Up Against The Wall Motherf**ker—the name to which they signed their first leaflet), which combined the confrontational theater and tactics of Black Mask with a much more aggressively "street" approach in dealing with the police, and authorities. Dubbed a "street gang with analysis" they were reputedly the only white grouping taken seriously by the Black Panther Party, and influenced everyone from the Weathermen to the "hippy" communal movements.

This volume collects the complete ten issues of the paper *Black Mask* (produced from 1966–1967 by Ben Morea and Ron Hahne), together with a generous collection of the leaflets, articles, and flyers generated by Black Mask, and UATW/MF, the UATW/MF Magazine, and both the Free Press and Rolling Stone reports on UATW/MF. A lengthy interview with founder Ben Morea provides context and color to this fascinating documentary legacy of NYC's now legendary provocateurs.

Creating a Movement with Teeth: A Documentary History of the George Jackson Brigade

Edited by Daniel Burton-Rose
with a preface by Ward Churchill

ISBN: 978-1-60486-223-2
$24.95   320 pages

Bursting into existence in the Pacific Northwest in 1975, the George Jackson Brigade claimed 14 pipe bombings against corporate and state targets, as many bank robberies, and the daring rescue of a jailed member. Combining veterans of the prisoners', women's, gay, and black liberation movements, this organization was also ideologically diverse, consisting of both communists and anarchists. Concomitant with the Brigade's extensive armed work were prolific public communications. In more than a dozen communiqués and a substantial political statement, they sought to explain their intentions to the public while defying the law enforcement agencies that pursued them.

Collected in one volume for the first time, *Creating a Movement with Teeth* makes available this body of propaganda and mediations on praxis. In addition, the collection assembles corporate media profiles of the organization's members and alternative press articles in which partisans thrash out the heated debates sparked in the progressive community by the eruption of an armed group in their midst. *Creating a Movement with Teeth* illuminates a forgotten chapter of the radical social movements of the 1970s in which diverse interests combined forces in a potent rejection of business as usual in the United States.

"Creating a Movement with Teeth *is an important contribution to the growing body of literature on armed struggle in the 1970s. It gets us closer to knowing not only how pervasive militant challenges to the system were, but also the issues and contexts that shaped such strategies. Through documents by and about the George Jackson Brigade, as well as the introduction by Daniel Burton-Rose, this book sheds light on events that have until now been far too obscured."*
—Dan Berger, author of *Outlaws of America: The Weather Underground and the Politics of Solidarity*; editor of *The Hidden 1970s: Histories of Radicalism*.

"*The popular image of the 70s urban guerrilla, even on the left, is that of the student radical or New Left youth activist kicking it up a couple of notches. Daniel Burton-Rose's documentary history of the George Jackson Brigade is an important corrective in this regard. The Brigade, rooted in prison work, white and black, straights, bisexuals and dykes, was as rich a mixture of the elements making up the left as one could perhaps hope for. We all have much to learn form the Brigade's rich and unique history.*"
—André Moncourt, coeditor of *The Red Army Faction: A Documentary History*.